The Cat Men of Gotham

The Cat Men *of* Gotham

TALES OF FELINE FRIENDSHIPS IN OLD NEW YORK

℘— Peggy Gavan —℘

RUTGERS UNIVERSITY PRESS

New Brunswick, Camden, and Newark, New Jersey, and London

Library of Congress Cataloging-in-Publication Data
Names: Gavan, Peggy, author.
Title: The cat men of Gotham : tales of feline friendships in old New York /
Peggy Gavan.
Description: New Brunswick : Rutgers University Press, 2019. | Includes index.
Identifiers: LCCN 2018033646 | ISBN 9781978800229 (cloth)
Subjects: LCSH: Cat rescue—New York (State)—New York—History. |
Animal welfare—New York (State)—New York—History. |
Cats—New York (State)—New York—History.
Classification: LCC HV4766.N49 G38 2019 | DDC 636.8/083209227471—dc23
LC record available at https://lccn.loc.gov/2018033646

A British Cataloging-in-Publication record for this book
is available from the British Library.

∞ The paper used in this publication meets the requirements
of the American National Standard for Information Sciences—
Permanence of Paper for Printed Library Materials, ANSI Z39.48-1992.

www.rutgersuniversitypress.org

Manufactured in the United States of America

To Mom—Thank you for being my biggest fan and for encouraging me to follow my dreams.

CONTENTS

The Cat Men of Gotham

Introduction

During the nineteenth and early twentieth centuries, feline adventures ranging from the dramatic to the absurd were as popular in newspapers as they are on the internet today. Many reporters attributed anthropomorphic traits to the cats, which is reflected in some of the direct quotes I have selected for the stories in the following nine cat-lives chapters. Although most of the news articles were intended to make readers chuckle, horrific tales of cruelty were also reported in detail. Not only were stray cats sent to the gas chambers by the thousands every year and disposed of in street gutters, but they also faced danger in the form of callous children, misguided citizens, and heartless entrepreneurs on a daily basis. Even the city's street commissioners made light of the wretched situation with a tongue-in-cheek article in the *New York Daily Graphic* titled "Hints for Spring Gardening," which suggested that "old boots, hats, crockery, tin cans, ashes, dead cats, and potato parings should be sown broadcast in many streets, which are now in splendid order for planting." I share the following true accounts from newspaper archives not to shock or dishearten my readers but to provide a social and historical backdrop against which to better appreciate the simple acts of kindness and compassion that a few special men bestowed on the felines featured in this compilation of cat tales of Old New York.

$\cdot_\bullet^\bullet$

In 1890, five women in Manhattan's Washington Heights neighborhood formed the Society to Befriend Domestic Animals (SBDA). The mission of the SBDA was to provide food and shelter for homeless and maltreated animals and to "secure painless death for animals rendered decrepit by accident or incurable ailment." In addition to caring for numerous cats and a few dogs in the home for wayward animals on West 185th Street, they organized a band of female volunteers who fed about two thousand stray cats a week. Unfortunately, several of these Florence Nightingales for felines became Jack the Rippers. Instead of feeding the cats, they lured them with catnip and killed them with chloroform. In this manner, the women killed about fifty cats a night. Eventually, the ladies of the "Midnight Band of Mercy" were arrested and prosecuted by the American Society for the Prevention of Cruelty to Animals (usually referred to as the SPCA by the New York press), but not before they had killed more than three thousand cats.

In 1894, the SPCA agreed to take over the care and control of New York City's cats and dogs. To empower the SPCA with this authority, the New York State Legislature passed a law titled An Act for the Better Protection of Lost and Strayed Animals, and for Securing the Rights of the Owners Thereof. According to the law, any cat or dog found within the city limits without a collar bearing its name and owner's address could be seized and "destroyed or otherwise disposed of" if not redeemed within forty-eight hours. Shelter officials insisted that the doomed animals were treated kindly before they were humanely destroyed and therefore had a "happy 48 hours" if they had never known happiness before. The fee for redeeming a cat or dog was three dollars, which was a steep price that many New Yorkers were unable to pay. Consequently, countless loved pets were seized and destroyed.

Although the primary intention of the law was to abolish the use of dog catchers—who were often crooked and cruel and took pet dogs by force or theft—it was also enacted to help control the city's feline population. In summarizing the law, the *New York Times* said, "Every cat without a collar will be regarded as a tramp, and, although the cat catchers will not chase collarless tramp caterwaulers over back fences, they will find other means of getting them into their toils. The worthless animals will be put to death in as humane a manner as possible. Gas will be used to destroy them." When asked how the agents would catch collarless cats, John P. Haines, president of the city's SPCA, replied, "To catch these cats we shall rely upon the co-operation of our good citizens. For example, if a housewife knows of a homeless cat she can easily get it to come to her house or rooms by putting milk or other food in its way, and then catch it and put it into a basket. Then she can send us a postal card, and one of our men will be sent for the cat." By the end of 1899, 164,626 dogs and 315,645 cats had reportedly met their demise courtesy of the SPCA.

In the late nineteenth century, the furs of skunks, dogs, and cats were popular because they were durable and fairly inexpensive. One *New York Times* reporter noted that with cat skins selling for up to two dollars, "trappers and hunters might find profitable employment in the city back yards as well as the northern wilds." Brooklyn resident Herman Fritsch was just one of several New Yorkers who tried to take advantage of this employment opportunity. In 1895, he paid boys to collect stray cats, which he then killed by hanging inside his house. He'd skin the cats and bring the carcasses to saloon keepers and housewives in Williamsburg (who thought they were buying rabbit meat). Fritsch was able to get away with this atrocity for a few months until a large orange tabby broke free from the noose. The cat caused a commotion, which prompted neighbors to call the police. By the time the officers arrived, Fritsch had already recaptured and killed the cat. Fritsch said he didn't know it was illegal to kill cats in order to make a living. He was arrested and held on $200 bail pending charges from the SPCA. Oh, the irony!

During the summer of 1916, a polio epidemic caused widespread panic throughout the city. Movie theaters and libraries were closed, meetings and public gatherings were canceled, and children were kept from parks, pools, and beaches. Many people, wrongly convinced that cats and dogs were responsible for spreading the disease, released their pets to the streets. SPCA Superintendent Thomas F. Freel tried to convince the public that pets did not spread infantile paralysis, but his words fell on deaf ears. By the end of July, more than eight thousand dogs and seventy-two thousand cats had been disposed of in the society's gas chambers. Freel told the *New York Times*, "Since the beginning of the alarm over infantile paralysis, we have been receiving on an average of 800 requests a day for our men to call for unwanted domestic pets, mostly cats, in spite of the statement issued by Health Commissioner Emerson that cats do not carry the germs of the disease." Freel theorized that more cats were rounded up because many domestic cats had already been turned loose prior to the epidemic. "When people have to economize," he explained, "the first thing they decide to do without is the cat and out she goes."

One year later, Dr. Miner C. Hill, president of the Bowling Green Neighborhood Association (BGNA), organized an annual cat roundup to control the neighborhood's feral cat population. To encourage participation, the association paid five cents or provided tickets to a cat party for every cat delivered to the BGNA playground on Washington Street. The cats were placed in crates and handed over to the SPCA to finish the job. Over almost ten years, the Bowling Green cat massacre resulted in the murder of thousands of cats and kittens at the hands of the SPCA and poor children who would do anything for a shiny nickel. The BGNA later claimed that the roundup was done "for humanitarian reasons" because the cats were sick and starving. Unfortunately, many healthy pet cats were also captured during this annual open season on felines.

For most of the Dickensian cats of Old New York featured in this book, their turn of good fortune was simply a matter of being in the right place—or sometimes the wrong place—at the right time. But whether they were rescued from near death, protected from a harmful situation, or adopted off the streets to serve as mouser, mascot, money maker, or muse, they all owed their lives (or is that nine lives?) to the hero cat men of Gotham who came to their rescue and welcomed them with open arms and hearts. I must warn you now, not every cat in the following accounts had an easy life. Still, one cannot but admire the profound effect that many of these felines had on the brawny men who came to adore them and value them as much more than expert rodent exterminators or good-luck charms.

1

Seafaring Cats

The special relationship between sailors and cats dates back thousands of years. According to the United States Naval Institute, although ship cats were primarily responsible for killing the rats that gnawed at the ship's ropes and provisions, it was also common for crews to adopt or "liberate" cats from foreign lands. These cats served as souvenirs as well as surrogates for the pets the sailors had left back home. They also provided companionship and a sense of security for men who were often away from loved ones for long periods of time.

Many sailors believed that a cat's behavior could also help predict the weather. For example, if the ship's cat licked its fur against the grain, a hailstorm was looming. When a cat sneezed, rain was coming. If the feline was frisky, the sailors could expect high winds. Some superstitious sailors even believed cats could effect stormy weather with magic powers stored in their tails.

Feline mascots were also in high demand because sailors believed cats brought good luck to a ship. A ship that set sail without a cat would be plagued by bad luck. And heaven forbid a cat mascot fall overboard. Sailors thought this was a bad omen that would cause the ship to sink in a terrible storm. Even if the ship were to survive,

Crewmen of the USS *Olympia* on deck with their two ship cats in 1898. Note the one sailor playing with a cat using a mirror and sunlight. (Photograph by George Grantham [NH 43211], courtesy of the Naval History & Heritage Command)

a ship that lost its feline mascot to the sea would be cursed with years of bad luck.

In the 1800s and 1900s, cats of all nations gathered on the piers in Manhattan and Brooklyn. Feline colonies were especially prolific during wartime, when almost every ship had at least one cat. Although some of the cats were born on the piers, many were refugees that had traveled to New York on the various steamships taking part in the war efforts. Most of these cats, like Tom of the USS *Maine*, were old salts that spent their entire life at sea. Others, like Minnie of the Brooklyn Navy Yard, were landlubbers that preferred to stay behind on the docks to do their mouse-catching duties.

Today, most modern commercial and naval vessels no longer permit cats (the Russian navy sea kittens are one exception). However, recent news articles about sailors jumping into the seas to rescue drowning kittens and online videos of brawny recreational boaters bonding with their feline companions prove that the special bond between cat and sailor still thrives.

1893

The Brave and Brawny Cats of the Brooklyn Navy Yard

In the late nineteenth century, the Brooklyn Navy Yard was overrun with rats. The voracious rodents gnawed at every dock, causing extensive damage. The losses in rigging, spare sails, and other wares were also great. Officials tried traps and poisons, but the rats simply made a sport of it and got fat on the poisoned food. The United States Navy recruited some dogs to help with the cause, but the canines were no match for the clever rats (the dogs would bolt out of the yard in terror whenever they encountered the bold rodents). Unfortunately, there were very few mousers available during this time. To be sure, plenty of kittens had been born at the yard over the years, but most cats and kittens were quickly scooped up by sailors who wanted a good-luck mascot. The few cats left behind helped as best they could, but the rodent population was too much for only a few felines to handle.

The situation changed in 1893, when a few neighboring landlubber cats entered the Brooklyn Navy Yard to do some exploring. Upon discovering the large rodent population, these cats decided to hide from the sailors and stay in place rather than go out to sea. The new terra-firma cats went into high gear, and within a few years, the rodent population was under control.

In November 1900, President William McKinley appointed forty-two-year-old Francis Tiffany Bowles to the position of Rear Admiral, Chief Constructor of the Navy. By this time, there were more cats than rodents at the Brooklyn Navy Yard. However, the young officer told his men that they were not to hurt or interfere with any of the cats that prowled in the yard. Rear Admiral Bowles understood how valuable the felines were to the shipyard. They did not cost the government a penny, and in fact they saved the United States thousands of dollars a year by keeping the rats and mice away from the storage sheds and shops. Not only did the men abide by the officer's orders, but many were more than willing to share scraps of food with the mousers at lunch time. When the bells tolled at noon, the cats would come running to their respective dining stations.

Two of the veteran cats who arrived at the yard in 1893 were Tom and Minnie. These two black cats did their policing in the electrical building, where large quantities of oiled silk and other insulating materials were stored. The rats were quite attracted to these materials and had often gnawed on them before the dynamic feline duo came to town. Tom was a large cat, while Minnie, the smallest working cat in the yard, was not much bigger than a kitten. Despite her size, Minnie was the best ratter in yard. One workman told a *New York Times* reporter that she was probably the best ratter in the world. Minnie had full run of the machine rooms, and she knew how to protect every wheel and strap. She'd dodge among the whirling belts and wheels in hot pursuit and tackle rats as big as herself. She could jump up to eight feet; once she jumped down a flight of stairs to land on a rat's back. As one workman noted, "She deserves a gold medal for preserving the property of the United States government."

Jerry, the oldest cat in the yard, arrived soon after Tom and Minnie in 1893. His feline partner was George Dewey, who came to the yards in 1897. The two were responsible for patrolling the rigging loft in Building 8 on Chauncey Avenue. This loft had at one time been infested with rats and mice that did tremendous damage to the rigging. George and Jerry worked alongside the master sailmaker William L. Cowan, a veteran of the navy who had served with the Paraguay Expedition of 1858 and the Potomac Squadron during the Civil War. Cowan took charge of the sailmaking department at the Brooklyn Navy Yard in 1889, just after Commodore George Dewey ordered that every ship repaired at Brooklyn also have its sails made at the yard. According to Cowan, once George and Jerry went on the job, the loft was free of rodents, and he no longer had to worry about them running over his feet or trying to run up his pants. "You have no idea of the change that has taken place there," Cowan told the reporter. "The mice used to be awful. They were so bold and fearless that they would come scampering over our hands while we were working at the rigging here."

Jerry was the most unusual of the landlubber cats in the yard, as he was the only one to have gone to sea and come back. According to Cowan, Jerry took two trips on American ships and one voyage on the *Monongahela* with the Asiatic Squadron. Jerry also had a habit of taking long trips away from the shipyard about once a month, leaving George alone to handle the rodents in the rigging loft. No matter how long Jerry stayed away though, he would always return and work overtime when the mice started to show up again. One time, Jerry was taken against his will by one of the workmen who wanted to domesticate him. Jerry was not about to be a house cat, so he escaped and returned to the yard the next day. Some of the workers believed that he must have followed the sound of the lunch bell tolling at noon.

J. A. Cook, a workman in the ship carpenters' department, also had a cat, whom he named Joan of Arc. According to Cook, Joan of Arc was a Republican feline from Omaha; however, he noted, she could "smell a rat just as quick as if she were a Democrat." The workmen in this shop said they could set their watches by Joan, because she showed up every day at 11:55 a.m. to get some scraps of food and milk before any other cats arrived when the lunch bell rang.

Another Brooklyn Navy Yard cat was Jennie, a tortoiseshell feline employed in Building 20, the iron-plating shop. Here, she worked with her owner, Bob Duke, in the construction and repairs department. She was the expert ratter in residence, and it was her job to teach all her kittens the skills they needed to get their mouse. According to Duke, Jennie had kittens about every three months, and most of them were taken all over the world by the sailors who adopted them as ship mascots. Before the kittens headed to sea, though, Jennie would give each one lessons in rodent catching. She would do this by depositing a dead mouse on the floor and then carrying one of the kittens to the dead rodent. She'd then get into a crouching position at some distance from the mouse, pounce on it with a sudden spring, and growl fiercely. After repeating these steps several times, she would step aside and let the kitten mimic her actions.

During the war years, many of the shipyard cats headed out to sea as mascots of the warships, which helped keep the land-based population in check. But ten years after World War II ended, the cat colonies started getting out of hand, forcing the navy to set traps and override the old rules established by Rear Admiral Bowles in 1900. The cats had a hero in Bill Wade, a grizzled, tattooed old sailor and journeyman who thought cats were the greatest sailors in the world. Wade would go around springing the traps to help save all the cats that he cared for and loved. Twice he was suspended for disabling the cat traps. He must have done a good job saving them though: by the time he retired in 1965, there were about fifteen hundred cats on the property.

In June 1966, one week after the government officially closed the Brooklyn Navy Yard, Wade reached out to Judith Scofield, who had founded the Save a Cat League in 1957. The two met with Rear Admiral William Francis Petrovic, several enlisted men, representatives from the city health department, and representatives from the Brooklyn branch of the ASPCA to discuss the fate of the abandoned cats. The Save a Cat League was given three months to find homes for any cats the navy could safely trap. Just a few hours before the meeting, however, three men reportedly came to the yard and stole many of the cats. Scofield and Wade were furious. "What happened to those cats who were taken away just hours before we came and who were those men?" Scofield asked. "Are those cats covered by the agreement the navy made with us?" According to Scofield, many people had expressed a desire to have a shipyard cat, and her organization would have found good homes for all of them had they not been stolen.

Today, many descendants of the twentieth-century Brooklyn Navy Yard mousers that dodged capture are still roaming the property and living in feral cat colonies. As more neighborhoods throughout Brooklyn and the other boroughs are gentrified, cat activists must continuously address the city's serious feral cat problem by setting up food stations, building shelters, and implementing Trap-Neuter-Return to humanely control and reduce the cat population.

The New York Naval Shipyard, more popularly known as the Brooklyn Navy Yard, is located on the Wallabout Bay, a knee-shaped bend in the East River. The bay takes its name from a group of French-speaking Walloons from Belgium who settled on the Brooklyn waterfront in the mid-seventeenth century. One of the first settlers to the area was Joris Jansen Rapalje, a tavern keeper who purchased about 335 acres of land in June 1637 and established a farm near what was then called Waal-Bogt Bay (bay of the foreigners). Over the years, Wallabout Village grew into a small farming and milling community of about a dozen interrelated families living along the shore of the bay, just north of present-day Flushing Avenue.

In 1791, the shipbuilder John Jackson and his brothers Samuel and Treadwell acquired from the Commissioners of Forfeiture a one-hundred-acre crescent-shaped tract adjacent to the bay. The Jackson brothers built a small shipyard on an existing dock and about ten houses for their workers. Ten years later, in 1801, they sold their shipyard to the United States government for $40,000. President John Adams's administration authorized the establishment of a naval shipyard in Brooklyn in 1801, and in 1806 the property became an active United States Navy shipyard.

In 1966, Secretary of Defense Robert McNamara closed the Brooklyn Navy Yard and ninety other military bases and installations. At the time of its closing, the yard comprised more than two hundred acres and employed more than nine thousand workers. New York City reopened the yard as an industrial park in 1969, and today the yard is managed by the Brooklyn Navy Yard Development Corporation.

DID YOU KNOW?

Following the Battle of Long Island in 1776, thousands of Continental Army soldiers were taken prisoner and transferred to British ships anchored in Wallabout Bay. Overcome by disease, fires, flogging, and squalid conditions, about 11,500 soldiers died on the overcrowded prison ships. Many of the dead were thrown overboard or buried in mass graves in the mud flats along the bay. Others were hastily buried in a sandy hill adjacent to today's Flushing Avenue. During the years that the Jackson brothers owned the Wallabout Bay property, many bones of the dead Continental soldiers were exposed as the tide eroded the beach. Other graves were uncovered during grading for the navy yard. In 1808, the remains were placed in thirteen coffins, representing the thirteen original colonies. The coffins were reportedly placed in a vault on John Jackson's farm outside the navy shipyard wall, at the corner of Jackson Street (now Hudson Avenue) and York Street. In 1873, the remains were moved to a large brick vault in Brooklyn's Fort Greene Park. The renowned New York City architectural firm of McKim, Mead & White designed a monument for the vault in 1905, which was dedicated as the Prison Ship Martyrs Monument on November 14, 1908.

1898

Tom, the Old Navy Cat Who Survived the USS *Maine* Explosion

During the 1800s and early 1900s, the Brooklyn Navy Yard served as a pseudo receiving and distributing station for the animal mascots of US warships. Some of these animals were Brooklyn natives that were born at the navy yard, while others were visitors that stopped by during their many years at sea.

In the late 1800s, an Italian American sailor named Cosmero Aquatero was working as a barber on the USS *Vermont*, which was then serving as a store and receiving ship at the Brooklyn Navy Yard. During his years stationed in Brooklyn, Aquatero had kept a journal of the births and major events in the lives of these animal mascots. In March 1898, a reporter from the *New York World* interviewed Aquatero about some of the famous ship mascots. One of the mascots that was well documented in Aquatero's book was Tom, the mascot of the battleship USS *Maine*. As one of only about ninety crew members to survive a massive explosion on board the *Maine* in the Havana Harbor in 1898, Tom's life was quite remarkable.

According to Aquatero's records and a statement made by a marine orderly following the explosion, Tom was born on the USS *Monitor* at the Brooklyn Navy Yard in 1885. (An article in the *St. Paul Globe* says Tom was born on a farm in Pennsylvania, but I prefer to trust the servicemen.) Tom reportedly began his navy career on board the USS *Minnesota*. When an officer from that ship was transferred to the *Maine*, he brought Tom with him. A gray and black tabby, Tom was very respected by the sailors. There wasn't a sailor throughout the world who hadn't made his acquaintance with Tom over the years, and each mariner who sailed with Tom placed his greatest confidence in the cat. By 1898, when this story takes place, thirteen-year-old Tom was the oldest active cat in the United States Navy.

The USS *Maine* and her sister ship, the USS *Texas*, were the first modern warships built in the United States. Both ships were built in response to the United States' increasing concern over the growing naval power of several South American nations. The Navy Advisory Board was especially troubled by Brazil, which had commissioned several battleships from Europe, most notably the *Riacheulo* in 1883. Congress authorized the construction of the *Maine* in 1886, and two years later its keel was laid down at the Brooklyn Navy Yard. The 6,682-ton, steel twin-screw battleship was launched from the yard on November 18, 1889. Due to some equipment setbacks, however, the *Maine* was not commissioned until September 17, 1895, under the command of Captain Arent S. Crowninshield. The ship spent most of its active career with the North Atlantic Squadron, operating from Norfolk, Virginia, along the East Coast and the Caribbean. On April 10, 1897, Captain Charles Dwight Sigsbee relieved Captain Crowninshield as commander of the *Maine*.

In January 1898, the *Maine* was deployed to Havana, Cuba, to protect US interests during the Cuban War of Independence. Three weeks later, on February 15, a massive explosion ripped through the forward section of the ship at about 9:40 p.m. Most of the *Maine*'s crew were sleeping or resting in their hammocks in the front of the ship when the explosion occurred. The officers were in their staterooms or smoking quarters, which were in the rear of the ship. When the explosion occurred, Captain Sigsbee was in his stateroom with his pet pug, Peggie, who was sleeping at his side. At the exact moment of the explosion, the captain was placing a letter in an envelope. As the captain reported in the *Century Magazine*, there was a trembling and lurching motion of the vessel, and all the electric lights went out. Then there was intense blackness and smoke.

Somehow, Peggie the pug managed to find her way to the poop deck, which was the highest intact part of the ship above water. Trembling with fright, she reportedly stood at the place she was taught to go to when the lifeboats were lowered. She waited there with the captain and Executive Officer Richard Wainwright as crews from nearby ships, including the *Alfonso XII* and the *City of Washington*, manned lifeboats to rescue the surviving crewmen. After all the survivors were rescued, Captain Sigsbee and Executive Officer Wainwright stayed on deck for as long as they could before they reluctantly abandoned the *Maine*, which continued to burn and explode throughout the night. Sigsbee boarded the *City of Washington*, where he reported the happenings by message to the secretary of the navy as follows: "Maine blown up in Havana Harbor at 9:40 tonight and destroyed. Many wounded and doubtless more killed or drowned. Wounded and others on board Spanish Man-of-War and Ward Line Streamer. Send Light House Tender from Key West for crew and a few pieces of equipment above water. No one has clothing other than that upon him. Public opinion should be suspended until further notice."

When the explosion took place, Tom was sleeping three decks below the upper deck. The force was so great that he was fired through the three steel decks. The sailors never saw Tom blow to the ship's surface and thus assumed he had perished. However, the next morning Executive Officer Wainwright discovered Tom, who was crying pitifully while crouched on a part of the wreck that was still above water. The officer manned a lifeboat to rescue Tom and took him to the USS *Fern*, where the cat was treated for minor injuries, including burns on his paw. In an article for *St. Nicholas*, an illustrated magazine for children, the captain's wife, Eliza Lockwood Sigsbee, wrote, "Tom was wounded in one foot, and was doubtless feeling very blue indeed, with his favorite sleeping-place destroyed, no friendly hands to minister to his wants, and nothing but ruin and water on every side! How glad he must have been to hear a voice that he knew, and to be taken on board the USS *Fern* in Havana harbor!"

USS *Maine* berth deck cooks with ship cat Tommy in 1896. (Library of Congress, Prints & Photographs Division, Detroit Publishing Company Collection, LC-DIG-det-4a14827)

A few days after the explosion, Tom posed for pictures on a wicker armchair that had been salvaged from the *Maine*. (According to Mrs. Sigsbee, the photo session was going very well until Bruiser, the *Fern*'s large dog, came near and caused a ruckus.) Tom was then rewarded with the softest bed on the ship. Some reports say the old navy cat finished out his service with the *Fern*, while others suggest Executive Officer Wainwright adopted the cat as his own.

At the time of the disaster, there were approximately 26 officers, 290 sailors, and 39 marines onboard the *Maine*. Of these, 2 officers and 251 men were killed immediately by the explosion. Although 102 men were saved, 7 sailors later succumbed to their injuries. Two other cats, including one that had joined the ship in Cuba only a few days before the explosion, were also killed in the blast.

Suspicion immediately fell upon the Spanish, and the American public responded in outrage. Many took on the rallying cry "Remember the *Maine*! To hell with Spain!" Bold headlines in William Randolph Hearst's *New York Journal* and Joseph Pulitzer's

New York World also helped to stoke the flames of anti-Spanish sentiment. A month later, on March 21, 1898, the United States Naval Court of Inquiry declared that a naval mine caused the explosion, but it did not directly place the blame on Spain. Don Enrique Dupuy de Lôme, the former Spanish ambassador to the United States, declared that there was no chance of Spanish involvement and that the explosion had been an accident. Subsequent diplomatic failures to resolve the issue, combined with ongoing losses to US military investment and public resentment over Spain's suppression of the Cuban rebellion, led to the start of the Spanish-American War in April 1898.

The one-sided war didn't last long. On December 10, 1898, the Treaty of Paris was signed between the United States and Spain, officially ending the war while guaranteeing Cuba's independence and forcing Spain to cede Guam, the Philippines, and Puerto Rico to the United States. In 1974, a team of naval investigators led by Admiral Hyman G. Rickover concluded that the *Maine* explosion was probably caused by a fire in the coal bunker that ignited its ammunition stocks and not by a Spanish mine or act of sabotage.

1917–1922

Woo-Ki, Tai-Wan, and the Refugee Pirate Cats of Chelsea Piers

During World War I, hundreds of cats from all over the world were left stranded at the Chelsea Piers when their respective troopships and freighters left the Hudson River harbor without them. Even several years after the war ended, these refugee mascots continued to prowl the piers at night in search of food and shelter. The news media called them the Chelsea Pirate Cats.

On January 21, 1917, a *New York Times* reporter stopped by Pier 58 to interview the veteran night watchman Sam Smithers about a reported clowder of cats that had taken over Chelsea Piers. The cats prowled in large bands and lived on bones, dried prunes, and raw rubber (according to the sailors, the latter enabled the cats to spring from pier to pier in search of prey). Their piercing howls of protest and baleful looks kept many a watchman awake at night. The watchmen also had to keep the peace between the refugees and the current mascots: any time one of the marooned felines stole onto a cat-occupied freighter, the fur would fly.

According to Smithers, the leader of the pack in 1917 was a large, rough-looking cat with reddish fur and large yellow eyes with red pupils that glared like port lights at sea. The tomcat was called Tai-Wan, because he had apparently arrived in New York by way of the *Jumpsejee Jeegeeboy* from the Yangtze River in China.

"Look at them waiting to see where I hide my bit of supper so that one of them can pinch it when my back is turned," Smithers said while about twenty cats sat watching his every move. The watchman told the reporter that he had saved Tai-Wan's life by using a pole when the feline fell into the water while getting off his ship. "Since then he haunts me at night, and if I have to drop off to have a snooze in the corner, he sticks his claws into my legs or rubs his wiry whiskers against my face."

Following World War I, there were very few ships at port, especially during the Christmas season. When the few remaining crews went ashore to spend the holidays, the pirate cats that lived in the sheds along the river were hard-pressed to find a meal. In December 1922, Woo ki, a one-eyed Chinese feline from Fuzhou, was reportedly the leader of the pirate cat pack. He had stowed away on the freighter *Wei-hai-Wan* and arrived in New York a few weeks before Christmas. As chief pirate, it was Woo-Ki's job to lead the stranded stowaway cats toward the guards on duty and encourage them to steal the men's dinners.

On Christmas Eve that year, Woo-ki and his band of refugee cats zeroed in on poor Smithers. (Smithers told a news reporter that he had to carry his dinner around all day to keep it away from the hungry felines.) Apparently, the band of pirate cats realized that a large Christmas feast was being prepared on the White Star Line's RMS *Olympic*, and they had no intention of being left out of the celebration. They apparently also knew a sucker when they saw one.

That Christmas, the *Olympic* was the only US ship docked at the Chelsea Piers whose crew did not go ashore to celebrate. The ship had just returned to New York a few days earlier from Southampton and Cherbourg; its masts were covered with ice, and some glass ports had been broken by the heavy seas it had encountered. On Christmas morning, though, its saloons were decorated with holly and evergreens in preparation for a holiday feast of turkey, plum pudding, and mince pie. The festivities began at 9:30 a.m. with fifteen athletic competitions on the pier for the crew, including sack races, an egg-and-spoon race, and a tug-of-war between married and single men (the married men reportedly always won). At 1:00 p.m., the men enjoyed their Christmas dinner, which was accompanied by beer for the crew and red and white wine for the officers and engineers. What these men probably didn't realize, however, was that they were not the first ones to dine on the ship that day. According to Smithers, the cats' constant howling and begging had whittled down his defenses, and by Christmas morning the felines had prevailed. I can't quite imagine how he was able to do this— and it's comical if you try to picture this scenario—but at 8:00 a.m., Smithers mustered up the four-legged pack and took them aboard the *Olympic*. Once on the ship, the crafty kitties were invited to partake in their very own feast fit for pirate kings.

Two days following the Christmas dinner, the crew of the *Olympic* performed its annual Christmas concert in the White Star Line's waiting room at Pier 61. I'd like to believe that many pirate cats were in attendance, adding a few tenor meows to the chorus.

DID YOU KNOW?

Everyone knows that curiosity kills the cat, despite its nine lives. For the seafaring cats of the World War II era, it was curiosity and a wartime ban on ship whistles that left them stranded on the Chelsea Piers ship terminal.

During the Second World War, New York Harbor was the busiest port in the world, with 39 active shipyards and 750 of 1,800 existing docks, piers, and wharves classified as active. According to the New-York Historical Society, at the height of the war, a ship left the harbor every fifteen minutes. The Chelsea Piers served as a major embarkation point for troop carriers that took US servicemen overseas. Many of these troop carriers, or troopships, were originally passenger liners that had been turned over to the armed forces for the war efforts. Prior to the war, the passenger ships' horns would blast three times before embarkation: thirty minutes before the gangplank was lowered, fifteen minutes later, and then five minutes before the lines were cast off. These three long blasts would give all the passenger ships' mascot cats that were perhaps checking out the restaurants on Eleventh Avenue enough time to return to the pier and embark via the lower gangplank. During the war, however, the horn blasts were banned, probably so city residents would not confuse them with air-raid sirens. Without the warning blasts, many felines missed their passage and were left to roam the piers in large bands of refugee pirate cats until they could find a new cat-less ship to welcome them.

1929

Olaf, the Viking Cat Rescued at Sea En Route to Brooklyn

A mascot there was who almost wasn't; but he has the life he almost hasn't. And the fact is this: Though he's somewhat wizened, though he almost isn't—he is.
—Angus MacGregor, *Hartford Courant*, October 12, 1930

According to an old maritime superstition, if a ship's cat was lost at sea, a member of the crew would follow the cat to Davy Jones's Locker shortly thereafter. Even worse, a lost mascot on a maiden voyage spelled constant bad luck for the ship for the next seven years. That is why when Olaf fell overboard on the *Sud Americano*'s maiden voyage from Kiel, Germany, to Pier 44 in Brooklyn, the captain and crew did not hesitate to attempt a daring rescue.

Olaf was described in the newspapers as a blond Viking cat with "tramp traits." The tabby attached himself to the South American liner *Sud Americano* just before the twin-screw steamer was scheduled to go in service as an express passenger and freight liner out of Brooklyn to Rio de Janeiro, Montevideo, and Buenos Aires. Refusing to be left behind on the ship's maiden voyage to New York, Olaf reportedly eliminated his competition—a ship parrot named

Juan—and signed on as the new official ship mascot. For the next few days, Olaf inspected all the saloons and staterooms, introduced himself to the men in the engine room, and basically expressed his appreciation of the new role in general.

On the morning of July 2, 1929, when the ship was about eight hundred miles east of New York, Olaf was swept overboard by a heavy swell while sunning himself on the foredeck. According to several reports, the lookout in the crow's nest saw Olaf get carried out to sea and immediately cried out, "Cat overboard!" Captain Bjor Boettger asked if it was the ship's cat and ordered an immediate rescue when he heard that it was Olaf. First, he telegraphed to the engine room to *stop* and *slow astern*. Then he instructed Chief Officer S. Anderson and six oarsmen to man the aft lifeboat. The men, including Fourth Mate Hjalmar Larson, lowered the lifeboat in record time. Working in unison, they pulled at the oars hard against the heavy seas, turning the boat toward the small, dark object bobbing up and down in the waves. Despite the swells, Olaf swam courageously for about fifteen minutes as one would expect any seafaring cat to do, until one of the sailors scooped him up by the end of an oar. Upon returning the waterlogged Olaf to the ship, two "hefty Norwegian sailors," under the direction of Officer Anderson, started pumping air into Olaf's lungs, following instructions for humans in the ship's first-aid manual. After resuscitating the cat, the sailors wrapped Olaf in a blanket and brought him to the engine room to get dry. Later that night, the crew threw a large party on the ship to celebrate the heroic rescue.

A few days later, the *Sud Americano* steamed up to Pier 44 at the foot of Conover Street in Brooklyn, with Olaf reportedly standing in the bow and purring, his head and tail held up high. When Manuel Diaz of Garcia and Diaz—the New York agents for the South American Line—heard about the rescue, he said the Spanish Humane Society would undoubtedly award medals to the sailors who rescued Olaf. Many New York and Associated Press reporters came to interview Olaf, take his picture, and offer praise for him and his fellow officers. A recount of the events in California's *Oakland Tribune* concluded, "We shall have to thank Olaf for new proof that men are interested in things which are not sensational and sordid. The sailors who went to the rescue and the captain who turned the ship back are surely other fellows worth knowing. Most of us would like to sail with that bunch."

Two months after Olaf's rescue, the crew of the *Sud Americano* took part in New York City's third annual international lifeboat race on the Hudson River. The race was sponsored by the Neptune Association, an organization of shipmasters and dock officers who recognized the need for better lifeboat skills for rescue and emergency work at sea. On September 2, 1929, spectators lined up from Eighty-Sixth Street to 126th Street to watch the crews from various passenger ships compete in the two-mile race. According to reports, the Garcia and Diaz lifeboat crew from the *Sud Americano* pulled to victory against seven competitors, outdistancing their rivals by two boat lengths with a winning time of seventeen minutes and eleven seconds.

On September 6, William H. Todd of the Todd Shipyards Corporation presented the Todd lifeboat racing trophy to the crew at a luncheon aboard their ship at Pier 44. Captain C. A. McAllister, president of the American Bureau of Shipping, suggested that the crew may have won because they were all under age thirty and "were Norsemen whose ancestors were rowing boats while some of ours were shooting bows and arrows." Other news articles reported that the crew cheated by spreading grease on the bottom of the lifeboat. But perhaps the crew of the *Sud Americano* won simply because they had recently perfected their skills when rescuing Olaf.

About a year after the rescue, a reporter from the *Hartford Courant* asked Captain Boettger why he thought his ship was having such good luck with the weather and the crew. The captain reached under the mess table and picked up Olaf for the reporter to see. "Olaf is the plan this ship sails under," he said. "We saved Olaf's life, and he's bringing us good luck in exchange."

1933

Tommy Mulligan, the Norton's Point Lighthouse Cat of Coney Island

Tommy Mulligan was a British boxer best known in the New York metropolitan area for being knocked out in 1927 by world middleweight champion Mickey Walker of Elizabeth, New Jersey. Tommy Mulligan was also the name of a tough seafaring cat who was knocked off a ship destined for bad luck as it passed by Brooklyn's Coney Island in 1933.

According to news reports, Herbert Greenwood, the resident keeper of the Sea Gate Lighthouse (also known as Norton's Point Lighthouse) on the western point of Coney Island, found the half-drowned cat on the beach. He dried him off with towels and fed him a saucer of warm milk. As the old saying goes, the best way to a man's heart is through his stomach. The same applies to cats. Warm and dry, with a belly full of milk, Tommy knew he had found his forever land-based home. The handsome cat adopted fifty-year-old Herbert and his wife, Agnes, and settled in for good at the lighthouse. He spent his remaining eight lives sunning himself in the lighthouse in the summer months and keeping warm by the stove in the dwelling house in winter months.

When Tommy Mulligan washed ashore at Norton's Point, Herbert Greenwood had been living at the lighthouse for fifteen years. Greenwood was the fourth head keeper of the lighthouse, following Thomas Higginbotham (1890–1910), Ernest J. Larsson (1910), and Gilbert L. Rulon (1910–1918).

Born in Rhode Island on May 6, 1882, Greenwood grew up in New London, Connecticut, and joined the United States Coast Guard in 1900. He married Agnes Snow in 1910 and took over the Coney Island lighthouse in 1918. For twenty-seven years, Herbert tended to his lighthouse duties, climbing the eighty-seven steps to fill the oil lamp and clean the giant reflectors every day (and then, when the lamp was replaced by a five-hundred-watt bulb in 1936, cleaning the six revolving lenses and oiling the mechanism

Tommy Mulligan looks out the window of the Norton's Point Lighthouse on Coney Island in 1936. (Brooklyn Eagle Photographs, Brooklyn Public Library, Brooklyn Collection)

that turned the lenses on a regular basis). He took his job seriously, knowing that the lighthouse helped mariners get their bearings when approaching Norton's Point.

Although Herbert and Agnes led a secluded life at the lighthouse, they still got their mail delivered twice a day (back then the postman always rang twice) and had easy access to three major rapid-transit lines. After Herbert retired in 1944, they moved to New Haven, Connecticut, where Herbert died in July 1975. Adrian Boisvert took over as keeper until 1960, which is when Frank Schubert, the last keeper of the lighthouse, moved in with his family. When Schubert passed away in 2003, he was recognized as the last civilian lighthouse keeper in the United States.

❦❦

Up until the mid-1800s, Coney Island was described as "a barren and repulsive waste of sand." Save for the Coney Island House on the eastern end of the island (a seaside resort constructed in 1829 by the Coney Island Bridge and Road Company to generate toll revenue on the shell road that crossed the creek separating Coney Island from the mainland) and the Van Sicklen and Voorhies farmhouses at the center of the island (near today's Neptune Avenue and West Fifth Street in West Brighton), the majority of the island was barren and seldom visited by anyone other than fishermen and clam diggers.

Tourist development in the western part of the island began in the summer of 1845. That's when Alonzo Reed, the proprietor of the Fort Hamilton House, an elegant summer retreat at the foot of Fort Hamilton in Brooklyn, and Captain Thomas Bielby, the proprietor of the Coney Island and Fort Hamilton Ferry Company, opened a dance pavilion on what was then called Coney Island Point or The Point. Reed and Bielby's Coney Island Pavilion was simply a circular wooden dance platform perched on a tall sand dune and topped with a tent of sails. The men built the pavilion to attract families and day-trippers who wanted to get away from Manhattan for a few hours to have a picnic, dance a few waltzes in the sea breeze, eat clam chowder, and enjoy the fresh air. Bath houses were later added for those who wanted to swim, and sportsmen were encouraged to bring their guns if they wanted to hunt for sand birds. A long, wide plank connected the pavilion to a small pier about a quarter mile to the west in Gravesend Bay. The pier accommodated a sidewheeler steamboat ferry operated by Reed and Bielby, who charged twelve and a half cents each way for the hour-long ride to and from Fort Hamilton.

Unfortunately, the daily ferry service primarily attracted gamblers, ruffians, and prostitutes, giving The Point a bad reputation that lasted for decades. The seedy environment was a major deterrent to people seeking a more genteel getaway filled with sun, fresh air, and sand.

The Point's reputation as a den of gambling and prostitution was exacerbated in the 1860s, when Mike "Thunderbolt" Norton, a New York City alderman (1864) and state senator (1867), decided to get into the seaside-resort business. Norton had a reputation as a crooked politician with strong ties to Tammany Hall, the powerful political machine that controlled New York City's Democratic Party from 1821 to 1872 and from 1905 to 1932. He was in tight with Tammany's William Marcy "Boss" Tweed. He was also a member of the Tweed Ring, which reportedly extorted millions of dollars from the public treasury in the 1860s and early 1870s.

Norton and his partner, James Murray, reportedly used some of the Tammany extortion loot to buy the lease on the Coney Island Point and erect a resort near today's West Thirty-Third Street. The two-story frame resort, called the Point Comfort House, featured several furnished rooms for sleeping and a few bathing houses (this resort was later owned by John B. McPherson). The men also refurbished the old Coney Island Pavilion and bath houses. The new pavilion, which they called Norton & Murray's Pavilion, comprised three buildings, the largest containing about seven hundred bath houses. The center building was the pavilion proper, which contained a bar and restaurant. The third building was a small shanty bearing the sign "Concy Island Stock Exchange," which had an office of the Western Union Telegraph Company and tables for picnics. In 1874, the *Atlantic Monthly* described Norton & Murray's Pavilion as "a large, windy frame building that has weathered the storms of the coast for many a year." The article continued, "Every pore in its planks, every joint, every crack, is thoroughly saturated with sand. Sand, instead of pepper, appears to have been used in the compilation of its clam chowders and oyster stews; and it is here, of all places, that the sandwich appears to be most truthfully denoted by its time-honored name."

Norton was indicted in 1872 on charges of conspiracy to defraud the city and was arrested with Boss Tweed and other members of the extortion ring in 1873. After Norton jumped bail and skipped town (he reportedly fled to Canada), the Tammany fugitive returned to the court and turned state's evidence against the Tweed Ring in 1874. Although the western end of Coney Island was eventually redeveloped as a respectable residential community called Sea Gate in the 1890s, current maps still list the most western tip of the island as Norton's Point, and the lighthouse is still often referred to as the Norton Point Lighthouse.

In February 1889, J. O. Coleman, commissioner of street cleaning, sent a letter to all New York and Brooklyn representatives in Congress asking them to pass House Bill 11527 of 1888 "to establish lights on the western end of Coney Island." In the letter, Coleman talked about all the boats that navigated the narrow channel around the western point, including the excursion steamers and the garbage tug boats. He said his department had been maintaining a temporary light on the point for some time, but it was just a makeshift device. Congress eventually approved $25,000 to build two range lights at Norton's Point. However, when the Lighthouse Board tried to buy the necessary land, the owners asked for twice the estimated value of their property. No problem: the city simply condemned the property and obtained the land for $3,500.

Work on the tower, front beacon, fog bell tower, and two-story dwelling house began in March 1890. The $18,000 project was completed just four months later. The lighthouse, designed by Major David Porter Heap of the United States Lighthouse Service, featured a square skeleton tower with eighty-seven steps to the eight-sided lantern room. Thomas Higginbotham, the first lighthouse keeper, lit the beacon for the first time on August 1, 1890. The light, a fourth-order Fresnel lens powered by kerosene, flashed red every ten seconds and could be seen by sailors up to fourteen miles from shore.

DID YOU KNOW?

For many years before the permanent lighthouse was constructed, James J. Sangunitto was the keeper of a makeshift light at Norton's Point. Sangunitto was born in Genoa, Italy, in 1838. He arrived in the United States as an infant and moved to Coney Island with his father when he was nineteen. He married Sarah Mann and had six children: James, Albert, Mabel, Leon, Robert, and Richard. As keeper of the Norton's Point light, it was Sangunitto's responsibility to set up two oil lamps on poles every night. On several occasions, he and his wife helped survivors of vessels that had foundered on the Coney Island shores. In addition to their oil lamp duties, the family was also involved in the tintype portrait business. (Sarah reportedly introduced tintype studios to Coney Island and Brighton Beach, having purchased the photographic invention from a Frenchman.)

The Street Cleaning Department eventually installed a more permanent light on Norton's Point to protect its garbage tug boats, but Sangunitto's actions reportedly helped prevent many wrecks. After the new lighthouse was completed, Sangunitto worked there as a watchman. Before he died in 1936 at his home at 2817 West First Street, the ninety-eight-year-old lighthouse veteran was Coney Island's oldest resident.

2

Police Cats

The Municipal Police Act of 1844, which divided New York City into police precincts according to ward boundaries, and the Metropolitan Police Act, which followed in 1857, required that each precinct have a station house. Typically, the station houses featured offices for captains and sergeants on the first floor and sleeping accommodations on the upper floors for the patrolmen. Each station also had a small cell block (usually in the basement) and lodging rooms for the homeless. (Police Commissioner Theodore Roosevelt removed the requirement for housing the homeless in 1896.)

At first, most station houses occupied leased buildings, including former residential buildings adapted for police use. In 1862, the city appointed Nathaniel D. Bush, a detective sergeant in the department, to be the city's chief architect in charge of designing new station houses. Over the next twenty-three years, from an office at police headquarters at 300 Mulberry Street, Bush constructed, reconstructed, or repaired more than twenty police structures. These buildings were architecturally stunning, but they were not mouse-proof. Fortunately, almost every police station had at least one cat on the job.

According to the *New York Times*, there were then more than one hundred cats on active duty with the police department in 1915. These special felines were distributed among the station houses, court houses, and prisons throughout the city's five boroughs, where they were assigned specific police duties—most notably arresting mice and rats. Police cats had a special kinship with their human partners: like the policemen they worked with, they loved to collar the big rats.

Many cats on the job in Old New York were domesticated house pets that were donated to their stations by the policemen who worked there. Others were alley cats that had strayed into the stations purely by chance. Some cats lucked out with a cushy assignment at police headquarters, while others had more dangerous posts at the city prisons. But it was probably the flatfoot felines assigned to rural precincts that earned the most merit awards. As was noted in the *New York Times*, were it not for the presence of police cats in rural neighborhoods, these station houses would have been overrun by vermin from the neighboring stables and piggeries. Brawny policemen in undeveloped neighborhoods who faced all kinds of danger in vacant lots and wooded fields did not hesitate to admit that it would be quite unsettling to be awakened at night by rats running across the floor of the station dormitory. It was thus no doubt reassuring for them to fall asleep knowing their trusted feline backups were keeping watch and covering them.

The police and prison cats of New York City often made the headlines of the national newspapers, especially when they were instrumental in a great mouse caper. These old articles provide evidence that many of these felines were very much respected and adored by police officers and prison wardens, who loved nothing more than an opportunity to brag about the antics of their cat to any news reporter who would listen to their story.

1893

The Tombs' Feline Warden That Befriended Prisoners on Murderers' Row

Old Nig, my friend, comes every day—
A silent friend and leal;
No confidence does he betray,
He is as true as steel.
When I have shrunk from baser man,
And would my woe impart;
I've turned to Nig for no more than
a sympathetic heart.

> —Carlyle Wentworth Harris, Murderers' Row,
> the Tombs, New York City, 1893

On March 23, 1891, Carlyle Wentworth Harris, a twenty-two-year-old medical student at the New York College of Physicians and Surgeons, was arrested for the murder of his young bride, Helen Neilson Potts. District Attorney Charles E. Simms Jr. charged him with first-degree murder for poisoning Potts with an overdose of morphine in the form of sleeping pills.

Potts was an eighteen-year-old student at the Comstock School, an elite finishing school for girls at 32 West Fortieth Street, when she secretly married Harris in February 1890. She died just before dawn on January 31, 1891. When Harris was first told that his wife was dead, he reportedly cried out, "My God, what can they do to me?" Asked why "they" would do anything to him, Harris explained that he had written a prescription for his young bride even though he was not yet a licensed physician.

Following a trial in January 1892, the jury found Harris guilty of murder in the first degree. Despite his defense attorney's request for an appeal, Harris was sentenced to death. He spent ten of his last months of life in a cell on Murderers' Row at New York City's Halls of Justice and House of Detention—better known as the Tombs.

The Helen Potts murder was one of the most notorious crimes of the nineteenth century. It was loaded with scandal and had everything the public could want in a headline news story: sex, murder, drugs, and a well-to-do young couple. First, there was the secret marriage ceremony under alias names that neither family knew about until Harris's botched abortion on Potts forced them to reveal the marriage. Then there was the medical class in which Harris learned all about the effects of morphine. And finally, there was the fact that Harris had admitted to a friend that he would often lace a girl's ginger ale with whisky to break down her inhibitions and had even gone as far as marrying some girls by using a different name just to sleep with them.

In the months and days leading to and following Harris's trial and execution, the New York press could not get enough of him and his scandalous lifestyle. But it wasn't until almost ten years later that a very innocent aspect of the case was revealed: the friendship between Harris and Old Nig, the prison police cat who visited him every day on Murderers' Row. In 1901, the *Syracuse Evening Telegram* reported that Harris had written a short poem about Old Nig, the large black cat who had worked for more than eighteen years in New York City's largest prison.

According to the *Evening Telegram* and the *New York Times*, Old Nig arrived at the Tombs in 1883, when the Tombs prison keeper Connelly brought the young kitten into the damp and gloomy old building to help control the mice and rat population. His arrival came during the regime of Warden James Finn, Deputy Warden Mark Finley, and Night Deputy Warden Orr. Over the next eighteen years, the cat served under eight administrations and reported to numerous wardens, including Tammany Warden Thomas P. "Fatty" Walsh, Charles Osborne, John J. Fallon, and John E. Van de Carr. According to the *New York Sun*, during Warden Fallon's tenure, an order was given to shoot all the prison cats in the Tombs; only Old Nig was spared this merciless death. Through skill and years of experience, the veteran mouser kept the prison almost free of rats and mice.

Every attendant, helper, and prisoner in the Tombs reportedly had a personal acquaintance with the cat during his long tenure.

Constructed of gray Maine granite over a period of five years from 1835 to 1840, the Tombs prison was 253 feet long by 200 feet deep, taking up the entire block bounded by Centre, Elm, Franklin, and Leonard Streets. (Library of Congress, Prints & Photographs Division, LC-USZ62-63343)

All of these men, including the prisoners, expressed much regret when Old Nig died in the arms of keeper Connelly on May 31, 1901. The day after Old Nig's passing, the newspapers reported that his skin would be stuffed and his lifeless form would be placed in the warden's office.

Completed in 1838 on the site of a former spring-fed freshwater lake called Collect Pond, the Tombs had already been sinking for almost forty-five years when Old Nig first arrived. With a festering stench and perpetual dampness, the prison was hell on earth for the hundreds of inmates crowded into the 173 cells. An article published in the *New York Herald* described the continuous dreariness brought on by the overflowing cells: "[The prisoners are] here entombed to fester and offend until the moral atmosphere of the entire vicinage is impregnated with their odious exhalations, and the very soil seems to send forth in foul luxuriance the noxious shoots of crime and hardy guilt."

Long ago, the sixty-foot-deep Collect Pond (the center and deepest point was near the intersection of Leonard and Centre Streets) was a favorite place for picnics, fishing, boating, ice skating, and laundering. Contrary to popular legend, the pond was never a direct water source for residents; however, the subterranean springs leading from the pond fed two other water supply systems for the colonial city. The Tea Water Pump, located just southeast of the pond near Park Row between present-day Baxter and Mulberry Streets, provided water during the eighteenth century. And in 1799, Aaron Burr's Manhattan Company sunk wells south of the pond, which provided water until the Croton Aqueduct was completed in 1842.

Over the years, the operators of nearby tanneries, slaughterhouses, and other businesses contaminated the pond by dumping garbage into it. In 1785, the *New York Journal* reported that "suds and filth are emptied into the pond, besides dead dogs, cats, thrown in daily, and no doubt, many buckets [of bodily waste] from that quarter of town." A plan to clean the Collect Pond and create a ship harbor with a channel to the Hudson River was rejected, as was an earlier plan to turn it into a recreational park. At the start of the nineteenth century, the city approved a landfill project designed to give work to the poor. The pond was condemned, partially drained, and filled in using land from several hills, including Mount Pleasant and Bayard Mount near the intersection of Baxter and Grand Streets. Despite great efforts, the spring-fed pond refused to disappear. Carters were paid to dump whatever they could find to bury the pond, so by 1808 the old Collect Pond was a pile of mud, rubbish, and dead animals. Soon after 1811, a new neighborhood of tenements auspiciously called Paradise Square had risen atop the old watery pile. It's a bit ironic that on the block bounded by Elm (present-day Lafayette Street), Centre, Leonard, and Franklin Streets, the city erected its Corporation Yards of the Department of Street Cleaning.

In a span of less than ten years, the ground began to subside, emitting rancid gases and sending more affluent families scurrying for higher ground. By the 1830s, the site was known as the Five Points district, the notorious, if not definitive, slum of Manhattan. Unfortunately, by this time, the Common Council had already chosen the site of the Corporation Yards for a new jail that would replace the colonial-era Bridewell Prison in City Hall Park and other prisons that the British had erected before the American Revolution.

When excavation for the Tombs' foundation began in 1835, the builders knew they were in for a challenge. Quicksand and water rose and fell with the tides, threatening to literally bury the project. Engineers were called in to devise a system of pilings using large pine logs lashed together. As the *New York Times* reported many years later, the Tombs prison "was built upon a raft, inasmuch as the underlying foundation consisted of ranging planks imbedded or floated in the quicksand mud." Only months after the Tombs opened, the building began to sink, "warping the prison cells and causing cracks in the foundation" through which water trickled in and created pools on the stone flooring.

Not only was the prison damp and moldy, but the Egyptian Revival–style edifice designed by John Haviland was also dangerously overcrowded. Originally intended for about two hundred inmates, close to four hundred inmates were being housed by the time Old Nig was making the rounds. Although there were about six "comfortable cells" with a view of the street for richer men who could afford to live in style, most of the inmates were vagrants who were assigned to the small and damp cells with cement floors. Two prisoners sharing the single cot in each cell would sleep feet to head. If there were a third inmate, he would have to sleep on the cold stone floor. There was no exercise area, so prisoners were confined to their cramped cells for twenty-two hours a day and only let out to walk around the cast-iron walkway one hour in the morning and one hour in the afternoon. The male prison, where Old Nig spent his days, had a high ceiling and a dark and narrow hall with four tiers of cells. On the ground floor were cells for the mentally ill, and one floor above was Murderers' Row. The third tier was devoted to those who were charged with grand larceny and similar felonies, while the fourth tier was assigned to those who were charged with minor offenses.

On May 8, 1893, Carlyle Wentworth Harris died in the electric chair in the Death House at Sing Sing Correctional Facility in Ossining, New York. More than one thousand people watched as the black flag was raised to signal his death. Harris's mother, still convinced of her son's innocence, placed a column in the death notices section of several New York newspapers as follows: "Harris, Carlyle Wentworth, eldest son of Charles L. and Frances McCready Harris. Judicially murdered May 8, 1893." On his tombstone at the Albany Rural Cemetery, she had engraved, "Murdered by Twelve Men; If the Jury Had Only Known." She even expressed her anger on his coffin with this engraving: "Carlyle W. Harris. Aged 23 years, 7 Months and 15 Days. Murdered May 8, 1893. We would not if we had known—The Jury."

Two years after Harris's death, a New York City grand jury charged with investigating conditions at the prison declared that the Tombs was crowded and unhealthy and unfit to serve as a prison. After decades of planning, the prison was finally demolished and replaced with a new prison on the same site in 1902. Poor Old Nig died one year short of the grand opening of the new prison. Whether the cat's stuffed form survived the move to the new prison building in 1902 is not known.

In 1941, the city replaced the 1902 Tombs building with a twelve-story prison at 25 White Street. Although officially called the Manhattan House of Detention for Men—and at one time called the Bernard B. Kerick Complex—it is still referred to as the Tombs. In 1960, the property where the former Tombs stood was stabilized and placed under the jurisdiction of the city's Department of Parks and Recreation. While completing construction of the new Collect Pond Park in August 2012, workers stumbled upon a strange series of stone walls buried beneath the site. Archaeologists identified the stones as part of the foundation and perimeter wall of the second Tombs prison, built in 1902.

1904–1911

Pete and Bill, the Bronx Mousers on the Job in Morrisania

Although today we're more apt to associate the neighborhood of Morrisania as part of the South Bronx, only a century ago this southwestern section of the borough was still a sleepy little village surrounded by bucolic farms along the Mill Brook (Brook Avenue). The former Thirty-Sixth Precinct station house at the junction of Third and Washington Avenues was thus the perfect candidate for police cats in the early 1900s. A brief history of Morrisania will help set the stage for this tale of two rural mousers.

In July 1639, the Scandinavian sea captain Jonas Bronk (aka Bronck) sailed from Holland to New Amsterdam in the ship *Fire of Troy*. Upon arrival, he obtained from the Dutch West India Trading Company a land grant in what was then Westchester Township. The large tract comprised about five hundred acres south of today's 149th Street between the Great Kill—known as the Haarlem (Harlem) River—and the Aquahung River (now Bronx River). Bronck established his homestead, Emmaus, near present-day East 132nd Street and Lincoln Avenue. There he erected a stone house, several tobacco houses, a barn, and two barracks for his servants and farmhands.

Following Bronck's death in 1643, Dutch Governor William Kieft granted the land—called Bronck's Land or Bronksland—to Arendt Van Corlaer, the sheriff of Rensselaerswyck and the new husband of Bronck's widow, Teuntje (Antonia) Slagboom. The tract passed through the hands of several Dutch traders until about 1668, which is when a royal patent for Bronck's Land was issued to Samuel Edsor Edsall, an English settler and *bever* maker, or hatter, by trade. On June 4, 1668, Edsall conveyed the land to Colonel Lewis Morris and his brother Captain Richard Morris, a Barbadian merchant who had established himself in New York as an importer of sugar and flour. When Richard Morris died in 1672, his brother moved from the West Indies to claim the property and care for Richard's young son, also named Lewis. On March 25, 1676, Colonel Morris obtained from Governor Edmund Andros a patent to Bronck's Land and other adjacent lands—a total of about 1,920 acres bounded by the Bronx Kill at present-day East 132nd Street, West 170th Street, the Harlem River, and Intervale Avenue. Colonel Morris renamed the land Morrisania and constructed a manor house near the intersection of East 132nd Street and Cypress Avenue, in present-day Port Morris. The colonel and his workforce of paid laborers and slaves operated a gristmill and sawmill on the property. He exported corn, wheat, barley, oats, lumber, and a variety of livestock to the West Indies. The Morris family, which included Lewis Morris (a signatory of the Declaration of Independence) and Gouverneur Morris (author of the Preamble to the United States Constitution), continued to own and develop the land through the mid-nineteenth century. Gouverneur Morris sold the farm in 1848 to be subdivided into building lots, forming what would become the incorporated Village of Morrisania in 1864.

In 1869, Morrisania Supervisor William Cauldwell commissioned the construction of a two-story stone and brick structure designed by the local architects John Rogers and Edward H. Browne. This building, on lot no. 1 of the Village of Morrisania, served as the town's first meeting hall until 1874. That year, Morrisania and the neighboring towns of West Farms and Kingsbridge were annexed to New York City as the Twenty-Third and Twenty-Fourth Wards. The town hall building was adapted for use as a police station for what was then the Thirty-Third Precinct.

Morrisania was a large precinct patrolled by mounted policemen, so a wooden stable was erected for the horses of the mounted unit. Later, a dormitory annex was built for the patrolmen. The building was wired to receive special signals from telegraph boxes placed at the Harlem Bridge, near 175th Street on Eastern Boulevard (today's Bruckner Expressway), and near George P. Arcularius's Jerome Park Hotel at the intersection of Central Avenue (now Jerome Avenue) and Gerard Avenue.

The grounds on the triangular lot at the intersection of Washington and Third Avenues were reportedly quite lovely and featured a flower garden and pastures for the horses. Schoolchildren often stopped by to watch or feed the horses; a favorite was Shiner, a cherry bay horse who had been purchased for the precinct in 1883 at the old Bull's Head Horse Exchange on Twenty-Fourth Street in Manhattan.

As time went by and Morrisania became more populated, the old town hall building was no longer suitable for a police station. As Police Captain Theron R. Bennett reportedly noted, "The accommodations are wretched, but the place is comfortable." Twenty years later, in May 1904, workers began demolishing the building in preparation for a modern new station at 830 Washington Avenue. During construction, the precinct was temporarily housed in an abandoned tool factory that the city owned on Brook Avenue near the site of today's O'Neill Triangle.

Today this neo-Renaissance police station is home to the Forty-Second Precinct, which serves an area of about one square mile in the Morrisania section of the Bronx. The reader may recall the landmark station house from the movie *Fort Apache, the Bronx*— the building was used in exterior shots during the making of the 1981 movie starring Paul Newman.

In June 1904, when the Morrisania policemen were in their temporary quarters in the old tool factory, Bill was the precinct's mouser of record under the command of Sergeant William E. Egan. Bill may have been a good hunter, but he was also fond of human food and was prone to stealing Sergeant Egan's meals. The sergeant had never charged the cat with a crime, but on the night of June 29, when the loot was a porterhouse steak, the officer finally decided enough was enough.

According to Sergeant Egan, every day his son Albert brought his evening meal to the police station. On the night in question, Albert brought his father a large porterhouse steak. The sergeant was looking forward to dinner; but just as he was about dig in, another policeman appeared with a prisoner, and he was called to assist. As he walked from his desk, he heard the dish fall to the floor. Then he saw his feline namesake carry away his prized steak. Sergeant Egan told the *New York Times* that he was arresting the cat and charging him with larceny and that Bill would be arraigned later that day by Captain Patrick Byrne. I have a feeling the charges were dropped.

In 1911, the men of the Thirty-Sixth Precinct had been in their new station house for six years. The population was booming at this point, and one by one the old farms and vacant lots were disappearing as new housing was constructed to meet the heavy demand. It was during this era that a handsome white cat named Pete ruled the roost as the chief mouser of Morrisania.

Pete moseyed into the station house sometime around January 1910, when he was just a dirty white kitten. He immediately took a liking to Lieutenant Peter Brady, whose lap was just right for a catnap. Pete was the pride of the precinct, and the affection that he bestowed on Lieutenant Brady was fully returned. Every night the lieutenant would bring bits of food from the table to Pete, and he'd always make sure the cat had a fresh bowl of milk. Like many cats, Pete was stubborn, and he had strong likes and dislikes. His favorite resting place was on top of the station-house desk, but only if he liked the lieutenant on duty (and vice versa). When a lieutenant whom Pete disliked was on duty, he'd seek out a far corner of the station or make mischief. One time a lieutenant who didn't like Pete went to the back room for a few minutes, leaving Pete in charge of the station. Pete obviously did not like this man either, which he demonstrated by spilling a bottle of ink all over the police blotter.

One of Pete's favorite lieutenants was Charles Price, who, along with Lieutenant Brady, had joint custody of him. But Pete was most loyal to Lieutenant Brady, the man who had given him a job and a nice warm lap. So, when Lieutenant Brady was transferred to the Queensboro Bridge Squad (Bridge Precinct D) in July 1911, Pete began to sulk and lose his appetite. Lieutenant Price was eventually able to win him over with food and other treats, and all was well again for a while. But soon thereafter, Lieutenant Price was transferred to the Fourth Inspection District. Pete became disconsolate again, this time going on a complete hunger strike. For days, he refused to come out of his hiding spot among the prison cells in the basement. The policemen tried coaxing him with cream, milk, and fish, all to no avail. When they finally captured the stubborn police cat, the men decided to remand him to the Queensboro Bridge Squad at 245 East Sixtieth Street so he could be reunited with his namesake.

The Bridge Squad was a much-smaller precinct of only forty-nine officers, several of whom patrolled the streets on bicycles. The station house, a small, three-story brownstone with basement that Lillie McGovern rented to the city for $1,200 a year, was not as lavish as the one in Morrisania, but I'm sure it provided plenty of mouse-catching opportunities. In any event, the reunion was short lived: Bridge Precinct D was abolished and merged with the Thirty-First Precinct in 1912. By 1915, according to an article in the *New York Times*, Pete was back at the Morrisania police station and doing quite well with his new favorite policeman, Lieutenant Frank O'Rourke.

DID YOU KNOW?

In 1816, James Morris, the son of Lewis Morris, built an estate on the site bounded by present-day Findlay Avenue, East 167th Street, Teller Avenue, and East 168th Street. This estate, later called the William H. Morris Mansion (William was one of James's twelve children), had a curious feature: the only stairway to the upper floors was hidden away inside a tiny room behind a small door leading off the grand hallway. Apparently, members of the Morris family were as afraid of discovering rats in their bedrooms at night as were the police officers of rural districts. According to Randall Comfort, who wrote about the mansion in *Valentine's Manual of Old New York* in 1923, "The owner evidently took no chances with possible nocturnal visitors of the early days."

1909

Claude, the Police Cat of East Harlem Who Did Justice to a Red Fox

If you've read Edith Wharton's *The Age of Innocence*, you may recall her describing "the one-story saloons, the wooden greenhouses in ragged gardens, the rocks from which goats surveyed the scene" near Mrs. Manson Mingott's white marble row house on Fifth Avenue. Although the novel is fiction, much of the story is based on Wharton's own life and experiences in Old New York. Mrs. Mingott's house is based on the real home on the northeast corner of Fifty-Seventh Street and Fifth Avenue where Wharton's great-aunt Mary Mason Jones lived in the late 1800s. The wooden structures, rocks, and goats were also very real in the nineteenth century.

Walking through the streets of Manhattan today, one may find it hard to believe that the northern section of the island was once sparsely developed, save for some rickety shantytowns where squatters of mostly Irish or Italian descent lived among the communal goats and chickens. To be sure, there were a few luxury apartment buildings and tenements here and there—the circa 1884 Dakota at Seventy-Second Street among the most notable—but they were few and far between. During the 1800s, the Upper West Side from about Fifty-Ninth Street to Harlem was known as Goatville (or sometimes Goat Town). Before the extension of the Eighth Avenue elevated railroad prompted new housing construction above Central Park, there were hundreds, if not thousands, of goats in Goatville. There were also many goats roaming free on the Upper East Side, especially before some well-to-do residents of Yorkville and East Harlem formed the Anti-Goat Club to expel the goats in 1884. By 1909, when this story takes place, most of the goats were gone; however, as old pictures show, East Harlem was still rural. Therefore, Policeman Randolph Miksobsky of the Thirty-Ninth Precinct should not have been too surprised when he came across what he thought was a real red fox on Fifth Avenue and 108th Street during his nightly patrol.

According to the story reported in the *New York Times*, when Policeman Miksobsky first saw the fox on the curb from a distance, he thought it was still alive. He crept upon "the dangerous beast," pulled out his gun, and shot a hole in the poor critter. After realizing he had been fooled by a good taxidermist, he picked up the stuffed fox and brought it back to the station house on East 104th Street.

Claude, a mottled-brown police cat who shared mousing duties with another station cat, named Pete, took immediate interest in the fox. For the next two days, he investigated the stuffed fox from a distance while plotting to capture it. He'd casually walk by Sergeant Lasky's desk over and over, "looking piercingly at the red fox on the floor" until he was satisfied that his enemy had been lulled into submission. He finally lunged at the fox, grabbed it by the neck, and leapt up to the sergeant's desk with his prize. He then shook the red fox several times and tipped over two bottles of red ink, which reddened the fox even more. Trailing the ink-red fox behind him, Claude took his prisoner to the captain's room, where Acting Captain Connors was taking a bath. Hearing the commotion and seeing red all over the room, he called for the reserves, who caught Claude and the red fox within a few minutes.

The Thirty-Ninth Precinct of East Harlem was established in 1863 as the Twenty-Third Precinct. The precinct shared a station house constructed in 1874 at 432–434 East Eighty-Eighth Street with the former First Mounted Squad. The station was then under the command of Captain John Sanders, a military veteran who had been awarded for jumping in the water and saving seven persons from drowning, including two little girls who had fallen into the East River. During these early days, the Twenty-Third Precinct's jurisdiction was bounded by East Seventy-Ninth and East 110th Streets, from Fifth Avenue to the East River.

Although construction was starting to pick up in the late 1800s, much of the land in this part of Manhattan was still undeveloped. As Augustine E. Costello noted in *Our Police Protectors* in 1885,

This is a precinct that is being built up, and there is yet unbuilt territory on which to erect homes for thousands. . . . This district has an Italian colony, of which it is not very proud, House of the Good Shepherd, a shanty district, the repair shops of the Third Avenue Elevated Railroad, a neat little park opposite the Blackwell's Island lighthouse, and some elegant villas nearby, the Astoria Ferry, the boat ferry to Blackwell's Island, and some mansions of stately magnificence on Fifth Avenue, opposite [Central Park]. There are also the Harlem Flats, with the Harlem Gas Works, and the stables of the Second Avenue Railroad Company.

The precinct was renumbered the Twenty-Seventh in 1887, but that designation didn't last long. As East Harlem continued to develop, a new precinct and a new station house a little farther north were needed. In 1890, the New York Police Department's annual report noted that negotiations had begun to secure two vacant lots at 177–179 East 104th Street for a station house to accommodate a new precinct comprising portions of the Twenty-Seventh and Twenty-Ninth Precincts. (The adjacent lot at no. 175 was occupied by Engine Company No. 53 of the city's fire department.) The police architect Nathaniel D. Bush filed an application in April 1892 for a five-story station house with a two-story brick prison and lodging house at the rear of the property. Construction began in May 1892, and what the *New York Times* called "the best [station house] in the city" was completed in June 1893. Captain Josiah A. Westervelt of the City Hall Precinct was placed in charge of the new Twenty-Eighth Precinct. Its jurisdiction extended from East Ninety-Sixth to East 116th Streets, between Fifth Avenue and the East River, and included Ward's Island.

Following consolidation in May 1898, all the police precincts in the city were renumbered. The Twenty-Eighth became the Twenty-Ninth until 1908, when it was renumbered the Thirty-Ninth. It was renumbered again as the Thirteenth Precinct in 1924 and then went back full circle to the Twenty-Third Precinct in 1929. The station house served the precinct until a new facility opened in 1974 at 164 East 102nd Street. Hope Community Hall, a nonprofit housing organization, moved into the old police station on East 104th Street. The organization purchased the building in 1981 and occupied it until 1994, when it relocated across the street. In 1999, the former station house was designated a New York City landmark.

DID YOU KNOW?

Prior to the 1800s, the two lots on which the police station at 177–179 East 104th Street was erected in 1893 were under water. More specifically, they were under a broad outlet for a brook that had its source in the high grounds of what is now Central Park. This body of water was part of a large parcel of land owned by Johannes Benson, the first grantee of record whose deed from Jan Loussen Bogert goes back to 1706. Benson's land, which extended from about present-day East Ninety-Fourth Street to East 108th Street between the East River and Fifth Avenue, was composed of drowned lands (salt marshes and intersecting creeks) to the east of Third Avenue and more fertile plains to the west. In later years, the property was conveyed to Benjamin Benson and his wife, Susannah, who in turn conveyed the deed to their son Samson in August 1791. When Samson Benson passed in 1821, the land was conveyed to his daughter, Margaret, the wife of Andrew McGown. In 1834 and 1835, Margaret conveyed part of her land to her son Samson Benson McGown and part of the land to Edward Sanford, a prominent member of the New York Bar. Thirty-five years before the vacant lots on East 104th Street were purchased for the men and cats of the East Harlem police precinct, Sanford and almost 225 other passengers aboard the SS *Arctic* perished when the Collins Line paddle steamer sunk on September 27, 1854, while on passage from Liverpool to New York.

1911

Buster and Topsy, the Rival Feline Mascots of the Lower East Side

In 1909, a block of old frame tenements and stables at the junction of Delancey and Clinton Streets was demolished to make way for a large concrete-block police station designed by the city architect Edward Pearce Casey. Shortly thereafter, the policemen attached to the old Delancey Street police station moved into their new home on Clinton Street. Two years later, the city shut down the nearby Eldridge Street police station. The men of that precinct moved into the Clinton Street station house on December 6, 1911.

The grandiose, five-story building at 118–120 Clinton Street, with nine dormitories for 250 men, was more than adequate to accommodate everyone—everyone, that is, except for Buster and Topsy, the two rival police cat mascots. Although the 6 lieutenants, 12 sergeants, and 178 patrolmen merged peacefully under the command of Captain Henry W. Burfeind, the feline mascots refused to do the same. What a surprise.

Buster, a small, black-and-white, male cat, had been on the job with the Thirteenth Precinct on Delancey Street when he and his fellow officers moved into Clinton Street in 1909. Topsy was a large, white, female cat who had been attached to the former Tenth Precinct on Eldridge Street. When the two precincts merged and Topsy moved into her new digs on Clinton Street, little Buster got the short end of the stick.

During the cats' first month together in the Clinton Street station house, Buster was often bullied by his much-larger female rival. According to the *New York Times*, Buster spent most of his time on the streets living the life of a peddler, while Topsy "grew bigger and fatter and more police-like than ever on the choice fare of the police station whose chief catship she had successfully usurped." During this time, Buster was relegated to an outdoor windowsill, while Topsy occupied a throne on the lieutenant's desk.

On New Year's Day 1912, some of the policemen found poor Buster mewing miserably in some mud on Clinton Street. They brought him back to the station house, where they tenderly petted him and washed him with what the press called "well-intentioned but almost fatal vigor." When he was dry, they hung a small placard on him that read, "A Happy New Year to All!" The men then led the small cat into the main assembly room, where he was treated to a large bowl of milk. Buster was in the middle of this meal when Topsy woke from her nap on Lieutenant Jones's desk. She jumped off the desk, spilling a bottle of ink all over the lieutenant in the process. (Ink bottles spilled quite often in the presence of police cats.)

I don't know what the two cat mascots said to each other, but I do know that Buster returned to the outdoor windowsill covered in scratches. Later that night, when the men couldn't find him, a special alarm went out to search for a small, black-and-white cat last seen moping on Clinton Street and wearing a sign on his back. By midnight, when he hadn't been located, the policemen started to spread rumors that Buster had killed himself.

Buster apparently returned at some point that morning. According to the *New York Herald*, the policemen began to take sides in favor of one police cat or the other. Unfortunately for the male cat, Topsy's side was strong enough to keep poor Buster outside. From that point on, whenever two officers met on post, the first question asked was, "Are you a Topsy man or a Buster man?"

Prior to moving to the station house on Clinton Street, Buster had lived with his police protectors in a circa 1803 station house at 178 Delancey Street, on the northwest corner of Attorney Street. Although this station had been reconstructed numerous times, it was then considered one of the oldest police stations—if not the oldest—in New York City. According to official records, the station was housed in a one-story building at the rear of a lot on the corner of Delancey and Attorney Streets (the city purchased this lot from John R. Linngsten in 1814 for $1,000). In early years, 178 Delancey Street served as a public meeting place for nearby residents. Later on, the building was home to Clinton Engine No. 41 (more familiarly known as Old Stag), Hose Cart No. 5, and Hook and Ladder No. 5 of the city's volunteer fire department. Sometime around 1826, a relief watch house for the city's Second Watch District was erected in the rear of the firehouse (the main watch house was at the Essex Market). The men assigned to this watch house were responsible for protecting the streets at night and, more specifically, looking out for fires in the neighborhood.

In 1831, the city's new Fire and Building Department called for a new two-story brick building on the corner of Delancey and Attorney Streets to better accommodate the volunteer engine and ladder companies. The plan was to house the fire apparatus on the first floor and to rent the second floor. (According to city records, the second floor was at one time occupied by Public Primary School No. 7.) The building featured a cupola, from which two men could watch for fires at night and give the alarm by ringing a bell and hanging a pole out the window. The pole had a lantern on the end, which the men would point in the direction of the fire.

In 1844, the Board of Alderman adopted an ordinance establishing a Municipal Police, which replaced the old night-watch system with a day and night police force. The Municipal Police was divided into seventeen wards, each comprising a patrol district and a district headquarters. The policemen of the Thirteenth Ward moved into the small building at 178 Delancey Street in 1846, sharing their headquarters with the volunteer engine and ladder companies.

In 1894, the Board of Police Commissioners called the Delancey Street station "a primitive and unimproved building" that was not only unsuited for the growing requirements of the precinct but "also dangerous to the health of the officers stationed there on account of its bad sanitary condition." Even though the building was now three floors, there was not enough room to properly accommodate all the men, and the underground prison cells had been cited for code violations by the Board of Health. Despite ongoing bad reports, the building continued to serve as a police station for almost fifteen more years before the new Clinton Street fortress was ready for Buster and his police buddies.

Soon after the police moved out of Delancey Street, the New Bridge Theatre, a moving-picture theater owned by Max Rothbart, moved into the old station. (This theater made the headlines in 1912 when it advertised a movie showing actual scenes from the murder of the notorious gambler Herman Rosenthal.) In 1917, the city sold the building and other property to the Salem Land Company in exchange for a large plot of land that the company owned near the Francis B. Riggs Estate on Inwood Hill, on the northeastern tip of Manhattan. The Salem Land Company in turn sold the old building to Jacob Branfman, who operated a kosher-meat company and delicatessen (Jacob Branfman Company Wurst Factory). Sometime before 1942—the year Jacob Yeager purchased the building for $10,500—the top two floors were removed.

Recently, all that was left of the vacant commercial building were graffiti-covered walls.

❧❧

The station house at 105–107 Eldridge Street, where Topsy spent most of her life as a police cat, was located on a double-wide lot that the city had purchased on July 3, 1867, from Herman F. Bauer and his wife, Bertha, for $24,500. The four-story building and two-story prison were designed by the police department architect Nathaniel D. Bush. Prior to moving into this building in 1868, the policemen of the old Tenth Ward—later the Tenth Precinct—were originally housed in the old Essex Market. This market dates back to 1818, which is when the city's Board of Alderman voted to build a marketplace, forty by twenty feet, at the center of Grand Street between Ludlow and Essex Streets. The market, one of thirteen such New York City marketplaces constructed in the early nineteenth century, was named for Essex Street, which was laid out in 1765 along the east side of the Great Square, also known as Delancey's Square. This grand public square was located near the center of James Delancey's large farm and bounded by present-day Eldridge, Essex, Hester, and Broome Streets.

To address numerous complaints about the narrowness of the streets surrounding the 1818 market, the city purchased seven lots north of Grand Street owned by Nicolas Governeur and erected a new one-story market on this site in 1823. There were then fourteen butcher stands in the center of the building, with fish and vegetable stands on each end. In October 1836, this market was ordered to be taken down to make way for a much-larger complex. The new building featured an expanded market with forty-four butcher stands on the ground floor, a large room for public use on the second floor, and living quarters for the clerk of the market and for the men of the aforementioned Second District Watch. In 1846, the policemen of the Tenth Ward (also called the J District) moved into the public space on the second floor (the police entrance was on Ludlow Street).

Seven years later, in the spring of 1852, the city replaced the old market with a large, three-story brick building that cost $50,000.

The second and third floors of this new Essex Market were occupied by the Tenth Ward police station house, police court, justice court, Superintendent of Streets and Lamps, and drill rooms for the military. The Eastern Dispensary—a medical care center for indigents—also occupied two rooms on the second floor. The market proper featured sixty-three market stands (twenty-four butcher, twenty vegetable and poultry, eight butter and cheese, six fish, two smoked meats, two coffee and cakes, and one tripe).

In 1868, the policemen of the Tenth Precinct finally distanced themselves from the butcher and vegetable stands when they moved into their new station house at 105–107 Eldridge Street. The old market building remained occupied for many years after the police moved out. In the 1890s, it housed a market and school on the first floor, public meeting rooms and two long and narrow school rooms for seventy-eight pupils on the second floor, and the Volunteer Firemen's Association on the third floor. In the cellar were basket stores, book stores, a furniture store, and other shops. A resolution was passed in June 1895 to close the old market and allow the Board of Education to take over the building for a school, even though it had poor ventilation and unsanitary facilities. As the *New York Journal* reported in September 1896, "Where now some veterans of the volunteer fire department meet once a month, and where rats, human and otherwise, hold carnival in the interval, at least 4,000 children will be taught. The Commissioners of the Sinking Fund have come to the aid of the Board of Education in its struggle with the great problem of finding school room for the horde excluded, and has turned over this property."

In 1912, the city leased the Eldridge Street police station to Moritz Tolk, a saloon owner. The following year, the noted architect Louis A. Sheinart converted the upper floors into lofts. In 1917, Francis B. Riggs, the Paris agent for New York financier and real estate developer Robert Walton Goelet, traded a large tract of land in Inwood Heights for the old police station and several other downtown municipal properties that were of equal value to his land uptown. Over the past one hundred years, the old police station on Eldridge Street has been occupied by a saloon, a silk shop, a dress company, a Chinese restaurant, and a bar.

DID YOU KNOW?

Shortly after Andrew H. Green founded the American Scenic and Historic Preservation Society in 1895, he suggested the establishment of a public park at the northern end of Manhattan. His dream came true in 1917, when the New York City Department of Parks took over the 20,649 acres of land it had acquired in Inwood Heights in exchange for the old Delancey Street police station, Eldridge Street police station, and other unused municipal properties. This land comprised 336 city lots acquired from Francis B. Riggs and 64 city lots acquired from the Salem Land Company. The city demolished all the country homes, philanthropic institutions, and other buildings on the site and landscaped the property for public use. Inwood Hill Park officially opened on May 8, 1926. Today, the park contains the largest remaining natural forest and salt marsh in Manhattan and is the city's second-largest public park.

1915

Sir Tom, the Rural Police Cat of Washington Heights

In 1915, give or take a year, a young woman from one of the fashionable new apartment buildings in the Washington Heights neighborhood of Manhattan brought a speckled hen to the police station at West 177th Street and Haven Avenue. The hen was set loose among the three dozen or so other hens that lived in a large field behind the former Robert C. Rathbone mansion, which now served as a police station. The hen spent the rest of her years living in rural luxury along the Hudson River with the policemen of the brand-new Forty-Second Precinct.

Lady Alice, as the men called the hen, loved spending time with the policemen. In fact, she preferred being with them than with her fellow hens. She loved sitting on the men's shoulders and eating out of their hands. Lady Alice also enjoyed the company of Sir Tom, the police station's resident rat catcher. The two animals would drink out of the same water bowl and play together in the kitchen garden behind the station, where the men had planted vegetables to conserve food during the war years. (Lady Alice reportedly never nibbled on the vegetables, preferring instead to dig for worms.) On cold nights, the police cat and hen would cuddle together in front of the station's wood-burning stove.

For Lady Alice, Sir Tom, and the men of the Forty-Second Precinct, life was good in the old Rathbone mansion. According to articles in several New York newspapers, the large, rambling frame structure on the banks of the Hudson River was surrounded by tall fruit and shade trees. The old-fashioned kitchen garden had box hedges around the beds, and the grounds featured beautiful lawns. The view from the house and wooded property, which was bounded by Haven Avenue, Fort Washington Avenue, West 176th Street, and West 177th Street, "was a very fine one, and extended for miles up and down the Hudson River." The five-acre parcel also featured large sheds and stables that had once accommodated up to one hundred horses when the mansion served as the clubhouse for the Suburban Riding and Driving Club.

The history of the Forty-Second Precinct begins in June 1912, when Police Commissioner Rhinelander Waldo created two additional police precincts to serve the people of the rapidly developing northern tip of Manhattan along the shores of the Hudson and Harlem Rivers. The new Thirty-Seventh Precinct, stationed at 407 Lenox Avenue, was bounded by West 110th and 145th Streets. The new Forty-Second Precinct was bounded by West 165th Street, the Harlem River, Dyckman Street, and the Hudson River. It also included the Harlem River Speedway, a two-mile path between West 155th and Dyckman Streets used for horse-drawn carriages and early motor cars. For the Forty-Second Precinct, the city leased from Rose C. Newman a new two-story brick store with cellar and loft at 1389 St. Nicholas Avenue near 179th Street. The plan was to use this building as a temporary police station until a permanent building was constructed. Unfortunately, the building was stuffy and hot, which made it difficult for the men on duty to get a good night's sleep.

In the summer of 1913, newly elected Commissioner Arthur Woods promised the policemen better quarters. After a short search, he selected the old Rathbone mansion, which was then known as the Arrowhead Inn. The owner of the property was Benjamin Altman, of B. Altman and Company department-store fame. Although Altman had originally intended to improve his real estate holdings and sell the land to developers, he changed his plans and leased the building to the city for use as a temporary police station. On July 31, 1913, the 196 patrolmen and 25 mounted patrolmen of the Forty-Second Precinct moved into the rambling, three-story frame home. For the next ten years (so much for temporary), the men lived in rural luxury in what became known as the best station house in New York City.

The new police station had a large dormitory with about thirty beds for the police reserves on the ground floor in what had once been the inn's dining room and another dormitory for the men on duty on the second floor. Every day, the men awoke to the sounds of chirping birds. They spent their leisure time swimming, fishing, boating, gardening, playing handball and tennis, watching cows graze in an adjoining field, and playing with Lady Alice and Sir Tom. Lieutenant Robert Quinn was the poultry man put in charge of the thirty-seven police hens. Policeman William Hemmer was in charge of the gardens, in which the men planted beans, beets, onions, celery, tomatoes, and all kinds of flowers. (Every married man went home several times a week with all the vegetables he could carry, and every week a fresh bouquet of flowers appeared on the lieutenant's desk.) Some of the men, like Sergeant John McCullum, were members of the Metropolitan Boat Club. They practiced their skills by rowing canoes across the Hudson River to New Jersey. (The *New York Sun* once reported that the men of the Forty-Second Precinct had "greatly reduced their girth" after living at their new location for about a year.) Most of the men also got to socialize with Diamond Jim Brady, W. C. Fields, and many other famous people who were good friends with Ben Riley, the proprietor of the new Arrowhead Inn adjacent to the station.

❧❧

The Forty-Second Precinct station occupied the former home of Robert Chesebrough Rathbone, a Civil War veteran, volunteer firefighter, and insurance broker. Sometime around 1889, Rathbone had purchased the house and property on what was then called Depot Lane (or Depot Road), a tree-lined country road that winded down from the foot of West 177th Street to the Fort Washington Depot of the Hudson River Railroad. I'm not sure whether Rathbone ever lived in the house—according to the 1900 census, his son and business partner, R. Bleecker Rathbone, resided on Depot Lane—but I do know that in 1897 the property was leased by the Suburban Riding and Driving Club, a popular organization for horsemen established in May 1894. The riding club added a new wing to the home that featured open glass sides, which, along with a spacious piazza and open fireplace, made the room quite inviting for visitors who stopped by on sunny winter days after a sleigh ride. The club also reportedly featured a café and main dining hall finished in rich red and a ladies' parlor with velvet carpeting, green walls, and big easy chairs and divans.

In 1904, Rathbone sold all his property along Depot Lane to Roxton Realty. The real estate syndicate planned to develop the 105 lots, but for unknown reasons the plans fell through. By 1908, development in Washington Heights was in full swing. All the streets were opened, sewers were installed, and the large rock formations that were once the most prominent feature on Manhattan's upper west side had been removed to make way for apartment buildings. Despite all the surrounding development, the area around the old Depot Lane remained bucolic. That year, Benjamin (Ben) Crawford Riley, an innkeeper from Saratoga, New York, leased the former Rathbone property and opened a roadhouse inn for high-society horsemen, called the Arrowhead Inn. For the next five years, the Arrowhead Inn drew large crowds of sporting men who came to feast on Riley's specialty, frogs' legs (in later years, Riley would boast that he had served more than four million frogs' legs at his establishment). Riley's famous four-in-hand road races, which he started in the fall of 1908 to complement the National Horse Show at Madison Square Garden, also drew large crowds. Participants would race from the hitching post at the inn to the Garden, where

Ben Riley's new Arrowhead Inn fronted Haven Avenue just north of West 177th Street. The police station was across the street on the south side of West 177th Street. (Seymour B. Durst Old York Library Collection, Avery Architectural & Fine Arts Library, Columbia University)

the horses would be judged in the ring. The winners received a $500 cup called the Arrowhead Inn Challenge Trophy. The first year, entrants included Alfred G. Vanderbilt, Paul A. Lorz, C. W. Watson, J. Campbell Thompson, George W. Watson, Morris E. Howlett, and Morgan P. Leiby. Howlett's Fort Washington Road Coach won in forty-two minutes, beating Vanderbilt's Brighton to London Coach by eight minutes.

When Riley's lease on the Rathbone house expired in May 1913, he decided to build a new inn one block north on Haven Avenue, on a two-acre plot occupied by the estate of W. H. Summerville, for about $160,000. Riley added a bungalow-style hotel to the site, and he remodeled the existing house to feature sunken gardens and a restaurant that could seat about a thousand people. Two months after Riley moved out, the men of the Forty-Second Precinct took possession of the Rathbone mansion.

❧ ❧

On the morning of January 15, 1916, Ben Riley noticed flames coming from the second story of the police station. He ran to the house and called out to Lieutenant Sauder, and then he sounded the fire alarm. The twenty men who had been gathered in the assembly room went into action. They first woke up the still-sleeping policemen in the smoke-filled dormitory on the second floor, and then they headed up to the top floor to awaken Captain Abram C. Hulse. A few other men released all the hens from their run, which adjoined the building. (The news reports do not make mention of Sir Tom, but hopefully someone also saved the station house cat.) While the men waited for the firemen to arrive, they set up a bucket brigade. In short time, the fire on the second floor—caused by a faulty chimney flue—was extinguished, and the building was saved. The men spent the next hour rounding up Lady Alice and her sister hens.

The old house continued to serve as a "temporary" police station for the next seven years. But by 1923, when many of the country mansions along Fort Washington Avenue had already been replaced by large apartment houses to meet the city's housing shortage, it was time for the proprietor of the Arrowhead Inn and the men of the Forty-Second Precinct to leave their rural home in Washington Heights.

In October 1923, Riley sold his block of land bordered by West 177th and 178th Streets, Haven Avenue, and Northern Avenue (now Cabrini Boulevard) and opened a new Arrowhead Inn at 246th Street and Riverdale Avenue (Henry Hudson Parkway). A few months later, in January 1924, the old Arrowhead Inn was demolished to make way for several six-story elevator apartment buildings, including those at 227 Haven Avenue (extant) and 851 West 177th Street. Most of these apartment buildings were later condemned by the city and demolished in order to make way for access ramps to the George Washington Bridge.

Today, what was once the site of the great lawns of Riley's second Arrowhead Inn is now occupied by the ramps and a small park. A looping road leading to West 178th Street is all that remains of this section of Haven Avenue, which once ran all the way to 181st Street.

And the old Forty-Second Precinct—now called the Thirty-Fourth Precinct—operates out of a modern station house at 4295 Broadway near West 183rd Street. Although no longer rural, the precinct has jurisdiction over five hundred acres of parkland, including Inwood Hill Park and Fort Tryon Park.

DID YOU KNOW?

In the late 1600s, the hilly region on the western side of Washington Heights was known as the common lands of Jochem Pieter's Hills. The land to the east, between present-day Broadway and the Harlem River, was called Jochem Pieter's Flats. Captain Jochem Pietersen Kuyter, a sea captain under the king of Denmark, came to America in 1639 with his friend Jonas Bronk and other pioneers. He obtained a grant of four hundred acres from Director General William Kieft and built a thatched-roof house somewhere near present-day 125th Street. He and his wife were killed by Native Americans in March 1654, in retaliation for a massacre at Corlear's Hook in February 1643, in which more than forty natives were killed.

In 1691, Joost van Oblienis, one of the earliest settlers in Nieuw Haarlem, was one of several men who were allotted a portion of Jochem Pieter's Hills. The Oblienis farm extended from about present-day 170th Street to 185th Street, from the Albany Post Road (Broadway) to the Hudson River. The Oblienis homestead was located near present West 176th Street, between Fort Washington Avenue and Broadway. (Archaeological remains of the old homestead were discovered when 176th Street was opened between Broadway and Fort Washington Avenue in the early 1900s.)

When Joost van Oblienis passed away in 1706, his son Hendrick acquired the farm. Hendrick sold the upper one hundred acres to the tobacco farmer Blazius Moore in 1769; he conveyed the lower tract to his son, also named Hendrick. The lower tract, bounded by present-day West 173rd and West 178th Streets, passed to Jacob Arden, a butcher, during the Revolution in 1775. About one hundred years later, this land was occupied by the house that would eventually become home to the men, hens, and cat of the Forty-Second Police Precinct in 1913.

1934

Arson and Homicide, the Flat-Footed Felines of Police Headquarters

From the day he was born, Homicide was destined to be a police cat. No one knows where he came from or if he ever attended the police academy, but the flat-footed feline knew exactly what it meant to be on the job in New York City.

Homicide sauntered into the New York City Police headquarters building at 240 Centre Street in January 1934. The large black cat with translucent green eyes and prominent whiskers couldn't have chosen a more magnificent place to work and live. The 1909 monumental Beaux-Arts-style building, which was constructed of limestone and granite and crowned with a gilt dome, had been designed "to impress both officer and prisoner . . . with the majesty of the law." The five-story structure featured a grandiose entrance hall; a basement shooting range and printing center; carpeted offices for the commissioner and officers on the second floor; a third- floor law library; a fourth-floor Police Academy equipped with a gymnasium ("where fat policemen [could] reduce their weight"), drill room, and running track under the roof dome; a fifth-floor Rouges Gallery, radio broadcasting station, and telephone exchange (formerly a telegraph bureau); and a rooftop wireless plant and observation deck.

Homicide's arrival at police headquarters was not welcomed by Arson, the black-and-orange-striped Tammany tiger who, up until that point, had been the top mouser cop. Arson was so upset by his replacement that he reportedly ran down the Centre Street steps just minutes after Homicide went on post and never came back. (The men said he was "'out among the goats' where bad policemen go," but that report was never confirmed.) For the one thousand or so men attached to police headquarters, Arson's departure was not a mournful event. Arson was more like a slipshod Keystone Cat who "walked like a detective of the old school" and was simply not cut out for the job. Although Arson loved his beat, he never made a collar. What he did make was a lot of noise—even when he walked on carpeted floors, the mice could hear him in time to scamper away to safety. "And that's why we called him Arson," Lieutenant James R. Smith told a reporter from the New York Times. "He was all burned up because he never caught a mouse."

Homicide, on the other hand, was very light on his feet. He was also a conscientious police cat who would start his patrol every day at 6:00 p.m. and cover every mouse hole from the prisoner cells in the basement to the squad rooms, bureaus, and other rooms on the upper floors. Unlike Arson, who simply passed up a room if he couldn't get in, Homicide would get up on his hind legs in front of every locked door and give his best police-whistle meow until Sergeant Joe Wrynne or Sergeant Tom Lake came to assist him. While he may not have attended police academy, he did have great respect for the Police Rules and Regulations book, which he used as his personal bed for cat naps.

On one particularly warm night in July 1934, Homicide ambled down to the cell blocks, where a few prisoners were catnapping in the heat. While an ordinary cat like Arson would have just gone through the motions of patrolling in the extensive heat, Homi, as the men called him, was all business. He quietly perched over a dangerous mouse hole, narrowed his eyes, and patiently waited for the perp to appear while "turning over in his mind his favorite passages from Police Regulations." When the opportunity came, he leaped at a large mouse and captured the convict in his jaws. As the prisoner struggled to escape, Homi ran up the stairs to the first floor, sprinted down the corridor, and jumped up onto Lieutenant Smith's desk. He dropped the exhausted prisoner on the desk blotter, saluted the lieutenant with a nod of his head, and ran back down to the basement to continue his watch. Highly pleased with the collar, Lieutenant Smith called all the police reporters to share the story. "[He] brings his prisoner right up to the desk, mind you, and has me book him. I've seen them come and go, in my time, but never before a cat that brings 'em back alive and books 'em. I'm recommending a citation for an extra ration of liver. Homicide's a first-grade cat, from now on."

❦

According to early records, the history of the New York City police headquarters goes back to 1884, which is when the first principal office of the city's Municipal Police was located in City Hall. There was also a branch office at the corner of Bowery Lane and Third Street, with office hours from 9:00 a.m. to sunset. In 1857, headquarters were established at 88 White Street; only six months later, the department moved to 413 Broome Street. In 1863, the year of the city's notorious Draft Riots, the department took possession of its new headquarters at 300 Mulberry Street, a four-story, ninety-foot-wide building constructed of white marble and pressed brick with white marble trimmings.

Right from the start, the location of the Mulberry Street headquarters was a strategic mistake. Sandwiched between tenement houses and isolated from major north-south and crosstown streets, it was in actual peril during the Draft Riots and had to be protected with a strong militia during the Orange Riots of 1871. Although plans for a new site were considered from time to time, the police and their four-legged friends had to make do on Mulberry Street for more than forty years until any proposals were seriously considered.

In September 1902, Police Commissioner John N. Partridge suggested moving police headquarters to the location of the Central Market, a large meat and produce market bounded by Seventh Avenue, West Forty-Seventh and Forty-Eighth Streets, and Broadway (now the site of the Renaissance New York Times Square Hotel). Another proposal suggested a site on Eighth Avenue between Fifty-Sixth and Fifty-Seventh Streets. The winning proposal came from Chief Engineer Eugene E. McLean of the Department of Finance, who submitted a report on the decrepit condition of the public markets in Manhattan. McLean believed all the city markets had outlived their usefulness and could be put to much better use. In his report, dated October 29, 1902, he recommended demolishing the Central, Clinton, Union, Tompkins, and Catharine markets. He suggested constructing the new police headquarters on the site of the old Centre Market, which was located on a large triangular lot on Centre Street between Broome and Grand Streets. He thought the Centre Market site would be ideal for police headquarters, as it was centrally located and fronted three major thoroughfares.

On April 24, 1903, the Board of Estimate approved a new police headquarters building and selected Francis L. V. Hoppin and Terence A. Koen of 244 Fifth Avenue as the architects. A year later, on June 27, 1904, the Board of Estimate approved the old Centre Market site. The official opening of the new building was delayed by construction of the Lexington Avenue subway, but at midnight on November 28, 1909, Police Commissioner William F. Baker finally announced that the new police headquarters was ready for business. His first act was to press a key that switched all the telegraph and telephone lines from the old building at 300 Mulberry Street into the telegraph bureau on the fifth floor of the new building on Centre Street. As soon as he pressed the key, a message was received from the steamship *Havana* advising that Dr. Frederick Cook, the arctic explorer, was not onboard.

By 1930, New York City Police Commissioner Grover Aloysius Whalen was already complaining about the twenty-year-old building, saying he wanted to replace it with a bigger place—perhaps a skyscraper, about twenty stories tall. It would be another forty-three years before he got his wish, and the new headquarters building was six stories short of his ideal. In 1973, the city's police department moved to One Police Plaza, a red-brick box on Park Row near City Hall and the Brooklyn Bridge. The glorious old headquarters building on Centre Street sat empty and devoid of humans and felines for years until 1983, when the city accepted the proposal of the developer Arthur Emil to turn it into luxury condominiums called the Police Building Apartments. Emil paid the city $4.2 million and spent another $20 million in renovations. Today the building has fifty-five high-end condos on six floors, including, in the central clock tower, a fifty-five-hundred-square-foot penthouse that was once owned by Calvin Klein and one of the most unique residences in New York City: a ten-room apartment in the former gymnasium, which at one point had an asking price of $31 million. Residents of 240 Centre Street have access to several luxury amenities, including a twenty-four-hour doorman, concierge, fitness center, and large private garden. Pets, including cats, are allowed.

DID YOU KNOW?

A century before the city's Centre Street police headquarters building was erected in 1909, the wedge-shaped plot bounded by Grand Street, Centre Market Place, Centre Street, and Broome Street was the site of the old Centre Market. The market's history dates back to 1812, when a proposition was made to establish a public market on a portion of the old Nicholas Bayard farm called Bayard's Mount, between Orange Street (now Centre Market Place), Rynders Street (now Centre Street), and Grand Street. The proposition took a back seat to the War of 1812, but in July 1817 the city purchased the lot from Morris Martin for $5,000. A market house, measuring eighty by twenty-five feet, was planned at an estimated cost of $1,000. The market opened in November 1817, and the fourteen butchers who had stands at the Collect Market (located between Broadway, Cortlandt Alley, and Walker Street) transferred to the new Centre Market.

Business was good in the beginning, and vendors like Thomas Mook—who sold the first beefsteak at the market to Daniel Spader of Mulberry Street—Thomas Varian, William Bowen, and sisters Aunt Katy Burr and Aunt Fanny Watson prospered with their meat, fish, floral, and produce stands. This simple market was replaced by a much-grander two-story brick Greek Revival building in 1838. The new market had stalls for vendors on the ground floor and a large drill room upstairs for the Seventh Regiment (until it relocated to the Central Park Arsenal in 1848) and, later, for the Sixth, Eighth, and Seventy-First Regiments. From 1846 until about 1857, several upper rooms were also occupied as a station house for the Fourteenth Police Ward.

3

Fire Cats

Many years ago, the Fire Department of the City of New York permitted firemen to keep one dog or one cat (not both) or singing birds in their firehouse (apparently there was no limit on the number of singing birds allowed). These animals, in addition to the horses that pulled the apparatus, provided companionship for the men, who were often required to stay at their firehouses for more than a week at a time with only a few hours off. As Alfred Michael Downes wrote in *Fire Fighters and Their Pets*, "A gentler phase of the fireman's life is shown in their devotion to their horses and pets. Dogs, cats, and even monkeys are adopted in the firehouses, and share the affections of the men with the horses."

I've never known a cat to be fond of smoke and fire, but Old New York had numerous feline fire-department mascots. According to a report in the *New York Press* in 1903, there were about 90 dogs and 120 cats among the two hundred fire companies in Manhattan and Brooklyn that year. Some stations had only one dog or one cat, but many broke the rules by having one or more of each. Sometimes the cats, dogs, and horses would fraternize as one happy family, but usually the firehouse dog and cat were sworn enemies, with the dog taking reign over the apparatus floor and the cat ruling over the living quarters upstairs. I'm not sure about the cats' relationships

Piccolo, the feline mascot of Hook and Ladder Company 326, Coney Island, 1949. (Brooklyn Eagle Photographs, Brooklyn Public Library, Brooklyn Collection)

with the singing birds, but I have a feeling that very few firehouse *aves* were fond of the firehouse felines.

The *Press* summed up the fire department cat as follows:

It is a curious feature of the fire department cats, and yet thoroughly characteristic of the animal, that they take no interest whatsoever in the active work of their company. The noise and activity that always follows the ringing of an alarm, the wild dash of the men for the sliding poles and the thundering rattle of the engine and tender as they leave the house have practically no effect on these cats. They learn to scuttle out of the way of the firemen, but beyond that they pay no attention to the commotion. And while the fire-engine dog is barking like mad and tearing around the opened doors of the house, his serene highness the cat has rolled himself up for another nap on one of the fireman's cots.

Most firehouse cats were alley cats that would have otherwise been ignored by the public, but a few aristocratic cats more suited to a velvet settee in a Fifth Avenue parlor also made themselves at home in the firehouse. In 1915, several pedigree fire cats made the headlines when the Empire Poultry Association's Palace Poultry Show introduced a new class for firehouse cats that promised to be "the greatest of the novelties of this section of the show." Ordinary fire cats also made the newspaper headlines, especially when firemen rescued their feline mascot at a large conflagration or taught their cat how to slide down the pole. Some cats, such as Smoke of the Lafayette Street firehouse, got more publicity than they welcomed, while others, like Chops and Peter of Engine Company No. 14, stayed under the radar until the distraught firemen reported their deaths to the press. And a few felines, such as Pete in Brooklyn and Tootsy in Manhattan, made the headlines by breaking the fire-cat mold and responding to fires with their fellow two-legged and four-legged firehouse friends.

1886

The Ten Lives of Hero, the Fire Cat of Engine Company No. 1 in Chelsea

In 1825, John Leake Norton distributed some handbills advertising a raffle for his land on the west side of Manhattan. His plan was to divide his portion of the Norton Farm, also called the Hermitage

Farm, into parcels of four to sixteen lots and sell them at a price starting at $600 for the smaller parcels. According to the *New York Times*, the drawing took place in the Shakespeare Tavern at Fulton and Nassau Streets. "Over mugs of ale, between smoke rings drawn from long pipes, adventurous citizens bought the Norton farm." That same year, Norton ceded to the City of New York all that land that would be required to open Thirty-Ninth through Forty-Eighth Streets on the west side. The city paid him $10 for this land.

The old Hermitage Farm had been in Norton's family since November 1757, which is when John Leake purchased a large farm that had once been part of a land grant bestowed by Governor Richard Nicolls to Johannes Van Brugh. Leake purchased the 150-acre farm from the estate of Joseph Murray, who had built a country home on the land that he called "The Hermitage." The farm was a diagonal tract bounded by Broadway and the Hudson River, from about Forty-Second to Forty-Eighth Streets. Much of the property west of Eleventh Avenue comprised sunken lands under the Hudson River and the Great Kill, a large stream that emptied into the Hudson at the foot of what is now Forty-Second Street. The Hermitage was right about where McCaffrey Playground is today, on West Forty-Third Street between Eighth and Ninth Avenues. When Leake died in 1792, he bequeathed the land and the Hermitage to his niece, Martha, the wife of Samuel Norton. Upon her death in 1797, the property passed to her son John Leake Norton (sons Samuel John Leake Norton and Robert Burridge Norton inherited adjoining farms).

In the years following the sale of the Norton Farm in 1825, residential development was brisk, particularly after the world's first street railway, the New-York and Harlem Rail Road, began running from Prince Street to the Harlem Bridge in 1832. Commercial development also picked up along the Hudson River after the sunken lands of the old Hermitage Farm and other properties along the Hudson River were filled in to expand Twelfth Avenue from Thirty-Sixth Street to 135th Street shortly after the railroad opened.

One of the larger commercial properties built during this time was the car stables of the Forty-Second Street and Grand Street Ferry Railroad, which were constructed on the old Norton land that had previously been under water, on the east side of Twelfth Avenue at the foot of Forty-Second and Forty-Third Streets. According to maps of that time, immediately to the south of the three-story brick car stables at 653–655 West Forty-Second Street was the large Consolidated Gas Company, and just to the north was the E. S. Higgins & Co. Carpet Factory. Numerous brick and brownstone tenements and frame buildings were also nearby.

The Forty-Second Street and Grand Street Ferry Railroad, also known as the Green Line (the president was John Green, and the cars' distinguishing light was green), was a horse-drawn streetcar line that zigzagged from the Weehawken Ferry (the West Shore ferry terminal) at the foot of Forty-Second Street to the Grand Street Ferry at the foot of Grand and Broome Streets on the East River. In 1866, approximately 565 horses were stabled in the Green Line car stables, in addition to fifty trolley cars and all the harnesses, bales of hay, and other equipment required to care for the horses.

At about 10:30 p.m. on June 12, 1886, the night watchman John Horner noticed smoke coming from the third-floor paint shop at the northeast corner of the car stables. He ran out and sounded the alarm, but by the time the fire engines arrived a few minutes later, the entire stable, covering eight lots on Forty-Second Street, eight lots on Forty-Third Street, and the entire riverfront, was engulfed in flames. At the time of the fire, most of the horses were in the building, including five that were upstairs in a special hospital for the horses. One sick horse was in slings awaiting treatment.

Under the direction of Superintendent John M. Calhoun, all the employees on site led the horses safely outside. Only the one horse in the slings perished in the flames (quite an amazing feat, considering that most car-stable fires of this period resulted in the deaths of hundreds of horses). The rescued horses were taken to Justice Murray's coach lot on Forty-Second Street between Tenth and Eleventh Avenues. After all the horses were out, the men focused on saving the trolley cars by pushing them out on the tracks along Forty-Second Street. All but four cars were saved, and almost all but forty harnesses were also saved.

While all this activity was going on, about a dozen or more cats that lived in the stables, including one especially brave tabby, were fighting for their lives as the building continued to burn all around them. Engine Company No. 1, which was stationed at 165 West Twenty-Ninth Street, was one of the many engine companies that responded to the conflagration. Many of the firemen from this company took it upon themselves to rescue the cats. The *New York Times* reported the following the day after the fire:

Rescued cats were a drug in the market at the Forty-second-street fire early yesterday morning. The car stables seemed alive with them when the fire was under control, and a half dozen firemen each got a cat. They were scorched, drenched, and thoroughly frightened animals when the firemen took them in charge. How they had managed to stay in the burning building for the two or three hours they must have been there before falling walls and floors sent them scurrying out of the doors into Forty-second-street without being burned to death is a mystery that even the firemen cannot solve.

Of all the cats saved by the firemen, there was one feline that evidently had at least ten lives. This kitty, later named Hero by the men of Engine Company No. 1, was rescued by John "Bucky" McCabe, the assistant chief of the department. According to the *Times*, the tabby had been seen lurking behind a chimney on top of the wall on Forty-Second Street just after the roof had collapsed. As the firemen approached her, she ran quickly along the wall toward the Hudson River, trying to limit the amount of time her paws had to land on the very hot bricks. At one point, she tried to jump from the wall to a telegraph pole, but instead she scurried along to a portion of the wall nearest the river, where the bricks were cooler. When the firemen found her again, they directed a stream of water against the wall below her to cool off the bricks. This only frightened her more, causing her to hide in a space in the wall.

The cat continued to hide for about an hour, until the firemen were forced to direct their hoses toward her once again to extinguish some flames in the area. Everyone had assumed that the poor cat had roasted to death, but when the water hit the wall, she jumped out of her hiding spot and tried to escape again. About five minutes later, "a forlorn-looking cat, with her hair well singed off," jumped from a window on Forty-Third Street. Assistant Chief McCabe caught her and, wrapping her up tenderly, turned her over to the care of one of the firemen from Engine Company No. 1. The men immediately brought the kitty to their engine house and treated her burned and blistered paws with liniment and tender care. According to news accounts, by the next day, Hero was recovering, and her paws "were resuming something like their normal condition."

Metropolitan Steam Engine Company No. 1, the city's first paid fire company, was organized on July 31, 1865. It was one of thirty-five steam engine companies organized that year under a state act titled An Act to Create a Metropolitan Fire District. This bill, passed into law on March 30, 1865, provided for the City of New York (at that time consisting only of Manhattan) and the Eastern and Western Districts of Brooklyn to be united to form the Metropolitan Fire District of the State of New York. The act also established a Board of Fire Commissioners (four citizens appointed by the governor) and required that the volunteer departments turn over all their property, apparatus, and firehouses to the new paid department. The company's first station house was at 4 Centre Street, on the northeast corner of City Hall Park, in the former headquarters of the Exempt Engine Company. (The Exempt Engine Company was organized on November 14, 1854, at the Gotham Saloon at 298 Bowery, headquarters for the Gotham Base Ball Club. It was a reserve corps that was composed exclusively of exempt members of New York's volunteer fire department.)

On February 17, 1873, Engine Company No. 1 was reorganized at 165 West Twenty-Ninth Street. The city had purchased this structure from Alexander McCutchen and his wife for $3,500 in 1862. The building had previously been occupied by Frederick William Nitschke's piano factory in the 1850s and later was the headquarters for the Fire Patrol No. 3 salvage squad, before Engine Company No. 1 took over. A new firehouse at this location, designed by the architect Napoleon LeBrun, was constructed in 1881; it was later renovated and still stands today (although it's now occupied by a commercial business). In 1946, Engine Company No. 1 moved to 142 West Thirty-First Street, where it currently shares quarters with Ladder Company 24. (Incidentally, Father Mychal Judge, the first officially recorded victim of the World Trade Center attack on September 11, 2001, was the chaplain for this firehouse.)

Hero's knight in shining armor was Assistant Chief McCabe, better known as Bucky. McCabe was a printer by trade who started his long career with the fire department as a runner with the volunteer fire department. He joined the city's new paid fire department in 1869 and was promoted to battalion chief in 1881 and to deputy chief in 1884. He retired due to health reasons in 1893 at the age of fifty-three.

On the morning of April 25, 1895, McCabe left his home at 78 West Washington Place, bought a revolver and a pack of cartridges, and walked over to the John E. Milholland Club at 111 Clinton Place (today's Eighth Street). McCabe was president of the political club, which had been founded in 1893 to fight the Platt Machine and Boss Thomas C. Platt, the reportedly corrupt leader of the Republican Party in New York State. After talking with some friends in the club for about an hour, he walked into the back room and shot himself in the head. According to news reports, McCabe had been privy to corrupt activity among some state senators and fire officers and chose to end his life rather than testify and implicate his close friends. As General Oscar H. Lagrange, president of the Board of Fire Commissioners, told the press during the hearings on April 28, "He had been intrusted by his associates, or some of them, with certain things that he could not tell. He expected to be called before this committee. He had Irish blood in his veins and could not be an informer, and he is dead."

Three months after McCabe's death, on July 16, 1895, a fire started in the cellar of the firehouse at 165 West Twenty-Ninth Street. Nearly all the members of the company were in the firehouse at the time. Although they were able to save the horses and the fire apparatus, a mother cat and two of her four little kittens perished in the fire. I can't say for sure that the mother cat was Hero, but one must note the irony.

Ten years later, on March 4, 1906, the rebuilt car barns at the foot of West Forty-Second Street were destroyed in another spectacular fire. This fire was even more devastating than the one twenty years earlier; one man was killed, and the fire forced the evacuation of hundreds of residents in nearby tenements and patrons at the adjacent Terminal Café (aka Annex Hotel). Once again, the car barns were rebuilt (this time sprinklers were installed), but sometime before 1941 the two-story brick building was demolished, leaving an empty twenty-seven-thousand-square-foot lot. When "the last of the car barns to fade from the New York scene" were taken down, the lot was leased by a syndicate that operated a large gas station on the site. The gas station was replaced by a twenty-story Sheraton Motor Inn, designed by Morris Lapidus, in 1960. Today, the site where a man named Norton sold his farm in 1825 and a tabby cat named Hero was rescued during a fire in 1886 is home to the Consulate General of the People's Republic of China in New York, which took over the Sheraton after it closed in the 1970s.

DID YOU KNOW?

The old Engine Company No. 1 firehouse on West Twenty-Ninth Street was constructed on what had once been the estate of James A. Stewart. Stewart was a wine merchant who had a country seat on Stewart Street, a diagonal street that intersected his property bounded by present-day Twenty-Ninth and Thirty-First Streets, the Bloomingdale Road (Broadway), and the Fitz Roy Road (near today's Eighth Avenue). In April 1809, Stewart advertised for sale or lease "a very convenient country seat" and a number of lots along Stewart Street. According to the ad in the *New York Evening Post*, the home was very roomy and featured four rooms on the first floor, fireplaces, a coach house, stable, about two acres of mowing ground or pasture, a garden with fruit trees, a good well, and "a cistern that never fails." The ad also boasted that Stewart Street would be "the handsomest road in the city," as it was fifty-eight feet wide and featured two rows of trees.

Sales of the lots, measuring twenty-five by one hundred feet, continued through 1810, which is when Stewart asked the Common Council to accept Stewart Street as a public road. But Street Commissioner Samuel Stillwell argued that the diagonal road could possibly interfere with the new grid plan then under consideration (the Commissioners' Plan of 1811). Stewart Street remained a staked road until most of the land was reorganized into conventional lots that conformed to the grid. Today, many of the buildings on West Thirtieth Street between Sixth Avenue and Broadway follow the original diagonal footprint of the old Stewart Street, which is clearly visible from satellite images. On the basis of aerial photos of the new thirty-eight-story Virgin Hotel, currently under construction at 1205–1225 Broadway, it appears that this building will also preserve the old diagonal footprint of Stewart Street.

1894

Ginger, the Shipbuilders' Fire Cat of the Lower East Side

In 1894, a stray orange tabby cat strolled into the firehouse of the Metropolitan Steam Engine Company No. 11 at 437 East Houston Street on the Lower East Side. This firehouse served the city's Fifth and Sixth Districts, which were then home to many eastern European Jewish, Irish, and Italian immigrants. Over the next few years, Ginger the fire cat mastered several tricks, courtesy of her trainers, the firemen William Lennon and Gus Shaw. Ginger could slide down the brass pole and "box" with her trainers while standing on her haunches. Although Ginger was smart enough to stay behind when the men went on fire calls, she did earn the title of firehouse mascot and capture the attention of a reporter who was writing about fire dogs for the *New York Times* in 1897.

Metropolitan Steam Engine Company No. 11, Ginger's adopted firehouse, has an interesting history with ties to New York City's early shipyard history. Prior to the Metropolitan Fire District Act of 1865, the engine company was a volunteer unit known as Live Oak Engine Company No. 44. This company was organized on August 2, 1824, in response to a great shipyard fire that took place a few months earlier, on March 14. The fire started about 5:00 a.m. in Noah Brown's steam sawmill at the foot of Stanton Street. The fire quickly spread, destroying the adjoining mill and large ship house of Brown & Bell. The flames then extended to the adjoining ship-yard of Isaac Webb & Co., where ship timber and a frame building were consumed. Engine Company No. 33, which was located at the north end of Cherry Street between Jackson and Corlears Streets (near present-day Corlears Hook Park), was cut off from the shore end of the shipyard by the sudden spread of the fire. Before the firemen could remove their engine from the scene, it caught fire and was destroyed. Several firemen were caught between the fire engine and the dock; four of them jumped into the East River and were rescued by boats from the shore.

This grand fire led to the formation of Live Oak Company No. 44 (aka Old Turk), which was organized by the master shipbuilders Isaac Webb (foreman), Jacob Bell, John Demon, Edward Merritt, and Foster Rhodes. The company ran independent of the city's volunteer fire department for a few years and operated out of a small frame house that the members built on Columbia Street near East Houston Street. The motto of Live Oak was "We Extinguish One Flame, and Cherish Another." During this time, the East River extended to the former Goerck Street (present-day Baruch Place), so the firemen of Live Oak were only a few blocks from the ship-yards of the Dry Dock district, which extended along the East River from Grand Street to Twelfth Street.

In 1828, Live Oak received the number 44 from the volunteer department. The city built a one-story brick firehouse with peaked roof on East Houston Street, about one hundred feet west of the former Lewis Street (near present-day Baruch Drive and Public School 188). On November 12, 1850, the city purchased a large lot on East Houston Street between Columbia and Cannon Streets for $3,200 from Jonathan Rider. Live Oak moved its firehouse to this location in 1851. The Metropolitan Steam Engine Company No. 11 of the paid department was organized twelve years later, in October 1865, with the following members: foreman Julian C. Harrison; assistant foreman John W. Miller: engineer Alfred Hoyt; driver W. H. Young; stoker J. Gorman; and privates J. A. Carroll, M. Knapp, G. J. Florence, H. McGinley, Q. Wyman, J. O'Neil, and B. C. Deane. Thirty years later, when Ginger the cat was making her home at the East Houston Street firehouse, Engine Company No. 11 had the following members: foreman Thomas R. Kane; assistant foreman Fred J. Rothenhausler; engineers James H. Frederick and Charles S. McArthur; firemen (first grade) Edward F. Haulton, Gustav Shaw, Henry Decker, William J. Lennon, James P. Judge, and Edward F. Birmingham; and firemen (second grade) Eugene Silverman and Henry Planson.

In August 1949, Mayor William O'Dwyer announced a new public housing development for the Lower East Side. The $31.4 million, twenty-eight-acre development, which was called the Baruch Houses in honor of Dr. Simon Baruch (an early advocate of public bathhouses), was a slum-clearance development project funded under the national Housing Act of 1949 signed by President Harry S. Truman. During the construction phase, six blocks of buildings between East Houston and Delancey Streets were razed, including those on Cannon, Goerck, and Mangin Streets. Most of these structures were old-law walk-up tenements with communal bathrooms and either no running water or cold water only. The firehouse of Engine Company No. 11, which had disbanded on October 15, 1957 (the company merged with Engine Company No. 91 at 242 East 111th Street), was also demolished to make room for the Baruch Houses. The new development, which was officially completed in August 1959, provided homes for 2,194 families in three- to six-room apartments with hot running water and rents averaging $9 per room or about $38.50 per month.

Today, under the New York City Housing Authority Pet Policy, residents of the Baruch Houses may own either one domesticated dog or one domesticated cat—weighing no more than 25 pounds—per apartment. There is nothing in the policy about singing birds.

1895

Tootsy, the Feline Firefighter of Engine Company No. 27

Tootsy was the beloved feline firefighter of Engine Company No. 27 on Franklin Street in Lower Manhattan. Born on the Fourth of July in 1895, Tootsy reportedly loved the smell of smoke as much as she treasured a fresh-caught mouse. She was a genuine fire cat who loved riding on the fire engine, conversing with the firemen, and sleeping in her favorite horse's harness. She was also quite beautiful and drew much praise from the public and the press when she appeared in the National Cat Show at Madison Square Garden. According to the *New York Press*, the firemen adored Tootsy so much that they would have rather parted with their shields than lose their "white-fleeced feline fire fighter."

Tootsy was born in the stall of Old Babe, a veteran fire horse who had joined the engine company twenty years earlier. Tootsy's mother cat was also a veteran of the firehouse; she joined the company in 1891 when she was a kitten. Tootsy was a bit shy of the horses, but she loved and trusted Babe, who had always been her mother's ally. Babe's bright harness caught the young Tootsy's fancy, and from the time she was six weeks old, it served as her "boudoir and reception room." Only when Babe had to don the harness to respond to a call would Tootsy retire to the desk of the house watchman.

As a kitten, Tootsy had a reckless, daredevil spirit. She would have responded to every alarm had the firemen allowed her to join them. Sliding down the brass pole from the third floor to the apparatus floor was second nature to her. Once she was on the apparatus floor, it took all the efforts of the firemen to keep her off the engines and tender before they swung out of quarters.

Tootsy's persistence paid off one cold winter evening in 1895. According to a news article, everyone in the company except Tootsy and the night watchman had been asleep upstairs when, a few minutes before midnight, the network of wires and bells broke the silence. "Tootsy saw Babe come galloping toward the harness, and the fierce light of a new resolve came into her eyes and she cleared away for action, and with one bound she landed safely on the pipe on the right-hand side of the engine. She lay close to the big boiler, so that the firemen could not see her."

As the engine dashed down Franklin Street and rattled over the paving stones, Tootsy held fast to the suction pipe. At one point, Captain Robert R. Farrell saw a man point excitedly in the direction of the driver. He leaned over and caught site of Tootsy, who had just been confronted by the engineer. The young cat then hopped playfully around the engine, "as though she were in quarters rather than traveling 20 miles an hour on a fire engine with a full head of steam on." Fearing that she would get lost at the fire, Captain Farrell grabbed the fire cat, opened his coat, and tucked her inside. At the fire scene, he handed Tootsy over to Fireman McCoy, who allowed her to stay on the engine as the men fought the blaze on West Broadway.

Although Tootsy tried to respond to other fires, her efforts were almost always thwarted by her mama cat, who would betray the kitten by meowing whenever she saw Tootsy on the engine's suction pipe. Despite her mother cat's efforts, Tootsy was determined to make one more fire run on the engine. Her chance came one snowy night when a second alarm came in for a fire on Broadway. (Engine Company No. 27 was a two-alarm station, which meant it only responded to the second call. Because the company was a two-alarm station, its horses had to remain hitched up long enough for the first officer arriving on the scene to sound a second alarm if needed.) As was reported in the *Press*, "Tootsy was dying to get into Broadway, where she could show herself to advantage. She had never been in Broadway, and then she knew that Commissioner Sheffield usually responded to second alarms and she resolved to see the young commissioner, or forfeit one of her nine feline lives in the attempt."

Two minutes after the first alarm was received, "the gong began its song of danger the second time." As the company moved out into the street, the firemen looked back and saw a white cat sound asleep in the station. Thinking it was Tootsy, and not her pregnant mama cat, the men decided it was safe to pull out of quarters. Tootsy saw her window of opportunity and leaped to the suction pipe as the engine started to move. The firemen didn't see the stowaway feline until they had reached Canal Street. Tootsy balanced herself on the pipe like a tightrope walker as the engine raced to the scene. There, she kept company with the engineer, meowed at the crowd, and kept a close watch on Commissioner James Rockwell Sheffield and Chief Hugh Bonner (they were both reportedly too busy to notice her green eyes riveted on them).

Back at headquarters, Tootsy got a reprimand from Captain Farrell. From that day on, she obeyed his orders and stayed at the firehouse with her mother to care for her younger siblings. To be sure, she still loved sliding down the brass pole, but she never rode to another fire. I don't know when she died, but if she passed before 1904, it must have been a sad day for the firemen. As one reporter noted in 1896, "When Tootsy dies there will be sorrow of the genuine kind in the engine house of No. 27."

If Tootsy did not die before 1904, she would have been the one to know great sorrow. On March 26, 1904, all of the men of Engine Company No. 27 were disabled and nine men were sent to the hospital in critical condition after falling unconscious during a fire at Charles Plunkett's broom factory at 205 Duane Street. According to a report of the incident in the *Evening World*, thirty-year-old fireman Thomas McGirr, who was not expected to survive, was at that time the only original member of the company, "all of his old comrades having met death in the past three years."

The Metropolitan Steam Engine Company No. 27 was organized on October 16, 1865. That year the company was manned by foreman Luke A. Murphy, assistant foreman David H. Beardsley, stoker James Davis, driver Charles Tucker, and firemen Edward Kelley, William Stoker, John Stanley, John Murphy, William Mason, Patrick Kennie, and Francis Walls.

Prior to transitioning to the paid fire department, the engine company was known as North River Engine Company No. 30 under the city's volunteer fire department. North River was organized on July 15, 1858, by B. F. Grant, William F. Searing, William McGrew, and other volunteers from the short-lived Eureka Hose Company No. 54. The company was originally headquartered at 153 Franklin Street, but in June 1861 the company moved into a three-story brick house at 173 Franklin Street, which the city had purchased from Andrew Clarke and his wife for $12,500.

The men continued to occupy the old North River firehouse at 173 Franklin Street until May 1881, which is when the city began accepting proposals to erect a new firehouse at the same location. The firemen relocated to 304 Washington Street, while Napoleon LeBrun & Son, the fire department's official architect, designed their new home. Napoleon Eugene Henry Charles LeBrun and his son Pierre followed their traditional firehouse layout, which included centered bay doors set within a cast-iron base and two upper floors faced in red brick and trimmed in terra-cotta and stone. The building was decommissioned as a firehouse when the engine company disbanded on November 22, 1975, and was reverted to a welding shop soon thereafter. However, some of features that date back to the days of Tootsy's sovereignty remain, including an embellished iron lintel over the apparatus entrance, several wood-sash windows, and a foliate frieze above the third-story windows.

1896

Peter and Chops, the Ebony and Ivory Fire Cats of the Flatiron District

On the night of an impromptu memorial service for Peter and Chops, the two fire cats attached to Engine Company No. 14 on East Eighteenth Street, the firemen shared their memories of the deceased felines with a reporter from the *New York Times*. According to the story, the following two blotter entries, recorded by Foreman Charles H. Shay, "were entered in sorrow, as they chronicled the end of two favorite Grimalkins."

July 22, 1896, 5:00 a.m.: Peter, cat, transferred to Bergh Society.

August 25, 1896, 11:25 a.m.: While responding to an alarm for Station 343, Chops, cat, jumped from seat of tender at Broadway and Eighteenth Street, and was killed by being run over and having neck broken.

Chops was one of several kittens whose mother cat had been rescued off the streets on the night of a large Democratic parade during the James Blaine and Grover Cleveland presidential campaign of 1884. He was a white cat with a few spots and a chopped-off tail that made him look like a Manx. Chops couldn't do many tricks, but he loved to eat. According to the firemen, Chops "was a Catholic cat and liked fish on Fridays." He also loved pie, which got him into trouble one time when he ate a custard pie belonging to Engineer Richard Gorman.

Chops was good chums with Peter, a jet-black cat who also had a stump tail. The two cats loved to perch on the desk blotter and rub themselves against the horses' legs while purring contentedly. But while Chops was a domestic cat who was content to stay at the firehouse all day, Peter was a more adventurous feline who excelled at catching rats in the cellars of nearby hotels and other establishments. Peter was also an expert acrobat who could slide from the second floor to the engine floor whenever the firemen tossed him onto the brass pole.

One of Peter's favorite places to visit was the renowned millinery firm of Aitken, Son & Co. on Eighteenth Street and Broadway. Here he could practice the sport of rat hunting and finesse his skills among the stacks of lacy bonnets and velvet hats. According to the firemen, Peter would wait until everyone had left the establishment at night, and then he'd cross the street, jump to a window, and enter through the open transom. Whenever he was successful, he'd bring the rat back to the firehouse, lay it on the floor, and meow "until someone appeared and expressed appreciation of its prowess and by a caress." Unfortunately, it was Peter's love of rats that cost him his life. Apparently, he devoured a poisoned rat and was in "death spasms" when he was admitted to the shelter operated by the Society for the Prevention of Cruelty to Animals, where he took his last breath.

Chops met his untimely death a month later while wearing his fire boots, so to speak. According to the men who loved him, Chops was sleeping on the company's tender when an alarm rang out for a fire at Third Avenue and Fourteenth Street. As the tender picked up speed at Broadway, Chops woke up to discover that he had been caught napping. Determined to return back to his post, the cat jumped from the tender. According to the men, "He turned a somersault as he fell, rebounded as he struck the pavement, shot under the tender, and a wheel ended his life."

During the memorial for the two cats, Fireman Joe De Size and Engineer A. W. Melvin were assigned to choose a burial spot (anywhere but the garbage dump on Barren Island) and to prepare a proper funeral so the men could pay their last respects. As the reporter concluded, the members of the company would no doubt be disconsolate until they got a new pet, and any stray kitten in the neighborhood would probably be snapped up and given a home at the firehouse. "It will certainly find there all the comforts of a good home as long as it lives."

Peter and Chops lived in New York City's Flatiron district, which is roughly bounded by Seventh and Park Avenues from Fourteenth to Thirtieth Streets. The neighborhood is named for the iconic Flatiron Building, constructed in 1902 on the wedge-shaped intersection of Fifth Avenue and Broadway. In the early nineteenth century, before there was a Flatiron Building, the district was mostly open pastures owned by farmers such as Casper Samlear, John Watts, John and Jacob Horn, and Isaac Varian. These farms may have existed for another decade or so, but the Commissioners' Plan of 1811 threw a wrench in the works when it divided the city into a rectangular grid pattern from Fourteenth Street northward.

Isaac Varian was a butcher by trade who resided on the Bowery Lane and conducted business at various locations throughout the city in the early 1700s, including the old Fly Market, Wall Street Market, and several places along the Bowery Lane. Varian and his wife, Elizabeth De Vouw Varian, had six children, all of whom were born in the city between 1732 and 1740. The Varian family accumulated a considerable amount of property along the old Bloomingdale Road (Broadway) in the mid-eighteenth century, including a large plot from Eighteenth to Twenty-First Streets that had once been part of a farm owned by Sir Peter Warren and a twenty-five-acre farm between Twenty-Sixth and Thirtieth Streets that had been part of the John Horn farm. (The Varian homestead stood on Twenty-Sixth Street just west of Broadway and was home to at least two generations of the family until it was demolished in 1850–1851 to make way for new townhouses.) During the nineteenth century, the many heirs to the Varian estate began selling off their allotted parcels to individual buyers and speculators. One of those parcels on Eighteenth Street was eventually conveyed to John L. Gross.

On December 30, 1861, Gross sold his house at 14 East Eighteenth Street to the city for $7,825. Two years later, the Metamora Hose Company No. 29 (organized in December 1854) relocated from Twenty-First Street and Broadway to its new firehouse on East Eighteenth Street. It occupied this building until October 6, 1865, when the Metropolitan Steam Engine Company No. 14 was formed under the new paid department to replace the old volunteer hose company. That year, the officers and men of the new steam engine company were foreman William H. Wilson, assistant foreman George B. Nicholson, stoker Charles F. Golden, driver John Berden, and firemen George W. Hall, Thomas Stephenson, Daniel J. Meyher, William P. Daniels, Thomas Gillett, Terence Brennen, and Charles E. Rhodes.

Two years before the passing of Chops and Peter, the fire department architect Napoleon LeBrun & Son was tasked with designing a new firehouse at 14 East Eighteenth Street. Featuring Corinthian columns on the third floor that support decorative arches over the windows and large terra-cotta medallions that pronounce the date of construction, the firehouse is what the *AIA Guide to New York City* describes as "a delicate Italian Renaissance town house for fire engines." The structure is still as beautiful today as it was during the days of Chops and Peter, although the active firehouse is no longer home to horses or ebony and ivory fire cats.

The Napoleon LeBrun & Son firehouse at 14 East Eighteenth Street is still home to Engine Company No. 14. (Photo by the author)

1913

Peter, the Pole-Sliding Fire Cat of Bushwick, Brooklyn

Sometime around 1905, a little orange tabby cat arrived at the new firehouse of Engine Company No. 152 in the Bushwick section of Brooklyn. No one knows how he arrived at 617 Central Avenue, but by 1913 he was a favorite mascot of the firefighters and a very popular cat in the neighborhood. During his years of active duty, Peter's greatest skill was sliding down the pole in the firehouse. According to firefighters who spoke to a reporter from the *Brooklyn Daily Eagle* in 1913, he could make the descent from the third-floor sitting room to the ground floor in three seconds. At the first sound of an alarm, Peter would dash to the pole and, with a flying leap, throw his paws about it and slide down. Then with one more leap, he'd land on the driver's seat of the company's 1907 Rech-Marbaker hose wagon. The firemen said he always seemed very proud to be the first member ready for action. Peter joined the men on every call and (although I find this hard to believe) would follow them up the ladder as far as possible, until the smoke and flames drove him back.

One day Peter took a bad fall from the ladder and had to go on sick leave. After that incident, he stopped going on calls. Although Peter would still slide down the pole and leap onto the driver's seat, he'd jump off the engine before it took off (after getting consent from Captain Henry B. Burtis). Engine Company No. 152 didn't switch from a horse-drawn wagon to its motorized American LaFrance pumper until May 26, 1919, so Peter was fortunate to be able to spend his retirement years resting with the horses. Even in his old age, he continued to perform his tricks for people who came to the firehouse to visit the legendary fire cat.

When Peter's engine company first went into service on April 1, 1897, it was called Engine 52 of the Brooklyn Fire Department. The company was led by foreman Edward Eichhorn and assistant foreman Louis Hauck. Less than a year later, on January 1, 1898, the boroughs of Brooklyn, Manhattan, Queens, the Bronx, and Richmond (Staten Island) were consolidated, creating the City of New York. At the time of its consolidation, the new city was the world's second largest, with a population of about 3.3 million (London was the largest city at this time). The Brooklyn engine company officially joined the New York City Fire Department (FDNY) on January 28, 1898, and about two years later was renumbered to Engine 152 to avoid confusion with Engine 52 in the Bronx. In 1913, twenty-six new companies were added in Brooklyn and Queens. At this time, engine companies in these two boroughs were given the prefix "2," so Engine 152 became Engine 252. One hundred years after it joined the FDNY, Engine 252 was reorganized as Squad 252 and assigned to the Special Operations Command Battalion, which comprises seven squad companies, five rescue companies, a hazardous materials unit, and three marine companies.

Peter's old firehouse, which still stands near the corner of Central Avenue and Decatur Street in Bushwick, was built on a former farm owned by William Van Voorhis (aka Van Voorhees) and, later, by August Ivins. The Van Voorhis farm was one of many relatively small plots in this section of Brooklyn owned by farming families including the Chaunceys, Coopers, Coverts, Moffats, and Schaefers; in fact, all the streets in this neighborhood were named for these farm owners (Decatur Street, opened around 1909, was previously called Van Voorhis Street).

On December 20, 1895, the New York City Fire Department purchased a standard lot for $2,400 from Mary L. Mintonge, the superintendent of a small school called the Women's Christian Temperance Union No. 5 at Hooper and Harrison Avenues. The three-story Flemish Revival firehouse of brick and Lake Superior red sandstone was designed by the Parfitt Brothers—Walter E., Henry D., and Albert E. The English immigrant brothers designed what the New York City Landmarks Preservation Commission called "one of the finest firehouses ever erected in Brooklyn," with a prominent scrolled front gable and stepped end gables that alluded to the seventeenth-century Dutch settlement of Bushwick. An atlas published by E. Belcher Hyde in 1916 shows that the brick firehouse was among the masonry minority, as most of the buildings in the neighborhood, including houses and stables, were of frame construction. The grand firehouse featured a room for the apparatus and horses on the ground floor, plus the foreman's office and a sleeping room for the foreman and his assistant; a sleeping room for the firefighters on the second floor; a sitting room on the third floor with a combination billiard/pool table; and a rooftop garden. In early days, the firemen could feel breezes coming from Jamaica Bay and the ocean beyond as they relaxed on the rooftop. In later years, their view was obstructed, but the men still enjoyed the garden on hot summer nights. Sometimes they even detected fires from atop the roof before the alarm was called in. Knowing cats as well as I do, I'm sure Peter also took many catnaps on the roof during his years with Engine 152.

DID YOU KNOW?

The earliest recorded history of the Brooklyn Fire Department goes back to April 7, 1772, when a meeting took place to choose six firemen in accordance with an act passed in 1768 "for the more effectual extinguishment of fires near the Ferry, in the township of Breuckelen, in Kings County." The men chosen were Joseph Sharpe, John Crawley, Matthew Gleaves, Joseph Pryor, John Middagh, and William Boerum. In 1785, another meeting of freeholders and residents took place at the house and inn of the widow Margaret Moser on the old Ferry Road (near today's Old Fulton Street). The men formed a volunteer fire department consisting of seven freeholders, who in turn voted to purchase a fire engine manufactured in New York City by Jacob Roome. This engine was one of the first fire engines, if not the very first, made in the United States (up to this time, England supplied all of America's fire engines). The first fire company established at this time was Washington Company No. 1, which was housed on Front Street near Fulton Street. An act passed on March 15, 1788, established a fire district for Breuckelen bounded approximately by the East River and present-day State Street, Boerum Place, Brooklyn Bridge Boulevard, and Front Street.

1924

Smoke, the Famous Lafayette Street Firehouse Cat Who Went on Strike

One upon a time, a fire cat named Smoke lived in a fairy-tale castle of a firehouse that was home to Engine Company No. 31, Water Tower No. 1, and the chief of the Second Battalion. Designed by Napoleon LeBrun & Sons, and completed in 1895 at a cost of $80,000, the French Renaissance firehouse at 87 Lafayette Street was what the department called "The Finest Firehouse in the World." To be sure, the grandiose structure had its share of critics—Montgomery Schuyler, writing about the "elaborate and pretentious" firehouse in *Architectural Record* in 1910, pondered, "But what has elegance to do with so grimly practical a business as putting out fires?"—but for many years the firehouse was a famous tourist attraction and a favorite stop on the guided bus tours that wove through the city streets.

In 1894, LeBrun was just finishing up his fifteen-year tenure as the city's dedicated firehouse architect. Working with his son Pierre and later with his younger son, Michel, he had designed about forty firehouses, each more elegant than the next. LeBrun's farewell performance was a firehouse designed to look more like a sixteenth-century Loire Valley chateau than a municipal structure.

The large three-bay structure was constructed of brick and Indiana limestone topped by a dormered slate roof lavished with intricate copper cresting, gargoyles, and spires. Designed with horses in mind, it featured three big doors that were large enough for seventeen horses to all charge out at once. In the stable at the rear of the apparatus floor were stalls featuring doors that opened automatically as the fire bell rang. There was also a large tower that masked a shaft in which Captain Smoky Joe Martin and his thirty-three men could hang their hoses to dry.

By 1924, the horses had been gone a dozen years, and the apparatus floor had been converted to accommodate the new motorized vehicles (the department's first motor-propelled water tower was tested and put into service at the Lafayette Street firehouse in 1912). The main attraction of the firehouse was not the building itself but rather a fire cat with a penchant for sliding down poles and catching rubber balls. Visitors by the hundreds could not get enough of the feline's antics.

Now, Smoke was reportedly a modest cat who didn't actively seek out publicity. She enjoyed being pampered by the firemen, sleeping beside the warm boiler, and basically living in the life of luxury. But one day a news reporter from the *New York World* learned of her tricks, and her easy life as a beloved mascot came to an end. For weeks, fans came at all hours of the night to watch her repeatedly slide down the brass pole and catch the balls. In addition to tourists and news reporters, noted scientists reportedly came to give her intelligence tests. Catnip manufacturers begged for permission to use her picture in their ads. Moving-picture companies offered her jobs. Smoke fended off the paparazzi for a while until she could take it no more. One night she walked out of the firehouse and disappeared.

A few days after Smoke ran away, Lieutenant Charles Kohlenberger and Fireman Charley Farley found the cat in poor condition near the Edison Company's plant on Lafayette Street. Workmen in the plant had been trying to tempt her with dainty morsels of liver and fish, but she refused to eat. According to a tongue-in-cheek story originally published in the *New York World* and picked up by several other newspapers, the firemen had told Smoke to stay away from the plant on previous occasions because "she had returned from there so often in a lit condition."

Apparently, some tough cats hung around the backyard of the plant, and according to the men, many of these cats were envious of Smoke and expressed their intention of making her pay for her lifestyle. The firemen thought that perhaps One-Eyed Horace, a cat with a bad reputation, had roughed her up, which then caused her to get sick and lose her appetite. The men took Smoke home, where she continued her hunger strike. At a loss for words for why their cat wouldn't eat, the firemen came up with a few other theories. Perhaps she was a sympathizer with the Irish Republicans who had gone on a hunger strike in Belfast, or maybe she just wanted to get away from all the publicity. A few other engine companies offered her better liver and more mice if she would leave Lafayette Street and become their mascot, but in the end nothing worked. The men brought Smoke to the Ellin Prince Speyer Hospital for Animals a few blocks away at 350 Lafayette Street, where, despite attempts at forced feeding, she slipped into a coma and died on August 26, 1924.

Smoke's fire company originated as Metropolitan Engine Company No. 31, which was organized on October 20, 1865, at 116 Leonard Street. This firehouse had previously been home to Fulton Engine

Company No. 21 of the volunteer fire department. Fulton Engine Company, one of the city's earliest engine companies, was organized in June 1795 and located at Burling Slip. (Burling Slip was an inlet for ships on the East River until 1835, when it was filled in to create John Street, between Front and South Streets.) The company moved to the Baptist Meeting House on Gold Street (between Fulton and John Streets) in 1796 and then to the Fireman's Hall on Fulton Street. Over the years, the company relocated numerous times until finally moving into its new house on Leonard Street in 1864, under the command of foreman Patrick Gavagan and assistant foreman Michael Buckley. A year later, Fulton Engine Company was disbanded to make way for Engine Company No. 31.

In 1893, the New York Life Insurance Company commissioned the architect Stephen Decatur Hatch to extend its headquarters building at 346 Broadway eastward toward Leonard Street. Shortly thereafter, Hatch passed away, and McKim, Mead & White was commissioned to complete the project. In exchange for the firehouse property at 116 Leonard Street, the insurance company offered the services of Stanford White as a consultant and $83,000 to build a replacement—a sum then adequate to build three standard single-bay firehouses. The city accepted the great deal, and the men of Engine Company No. 31 were temporarily relocated to the old Grammar School No. 24 at 66–68 Lafayette Street while their new castle was constructed.

About forty years after the passing of Smoke, the city took the firehouse out of service and sold the building, which by this time was due for an extensive restoration and modernization, including fireproofing. Engine Company No. 31 moved to 100 Duane Street in 1967 and then to 363 Broome Street, where it shared headquarters with Engine Company No. 55 until No. 31 was disbanded on November 25, 1972. Although the old firehouse was declared a city landmark in 1966 and placed on the National Registry of Historic Places in January 1972, it sat empty and neglected for years until 1978. That's when Jon Albert, a founder of Downtown Community Television Center (DCTV), first discovered that the building was up for auction when his dog decided to do his business in front of it. DCTV rented the building from the city for $500 a month until

Despite major renovations, the French Renaissance firehouse at 87 Lafayette Street still looks like a castle out of place in Lower Manhattan. (Photo by the author)

1983, when the nonprofit joined forces with the Chinese-American Planning Council to purchase the building for $400,000. DCTV has been slowly renovating the building over the decades, beginning with the rotted wooden support columns beneath its foundation. Today it shares the landmark firehouse with New Yorkers Against Gun Violence, an advocacy group founded in 1993 to push for legislative action to reduce gun violence.

DID YOU KNOW?

The Lafayette Street firehouse was built on land that the city had purchased from the People of the State of New York on June 27, 1850, for $30,000. More specifically, it was constructed on the site of the old State Arsenal, which was erected on top of the Collect Pond in 1808, the year the large spring-fed freshwater lake was partially drained and poorly covered over with landfill and rubbish.

The State Arsenal was a three-story brick building that sat on the southwest corner of a yard bounded by Centre, Elm (Lafayette), Franklin, and White Streets. In the early 1800s, military companies, battalions, or officers of various regiments would assemble on the yard to practice their military tactics and participate in tournaments known as trials of skill. The State Arsenal building was replaced in 1844 by the Downtown Arsenal of the First Division, a large two-story building constructed of bluestone that featured narrow windows for defense against mobs, a thirteen-foot-high ground floor that was used as a gun room and meeting room, and a thirty-foot-high second floor that served as a drill room and rendezvous point in the event of a riot. The building was occupied by three batteries of the First Artillery until 1888, which is when the building was converted for use as a center of light industry.

In 1894, the northwest corner of the old arsenal yard at Elm and White Streets consisted of vacant lots that were fenced in and rented for $100 a month to the Edison Light and Power Installation Company for storage purposes. On April 16, 1894, in a report to the Commissioners of the Sinking Fund, City Comptroller Ashbel P. Fitch stated, "From an examination made by the Engineer of the Finance Department, at my direction, it appears that the location is well suited for the purposes of the Fire Department." He could not have been more wrong, and the Sinking Fund could not have been more appropriately named.

When LeBrun began designing the firehouse in 1894, he considered the lessons learned from the Tombs prison next door, which had begun to sink just five months after its foundation was laid in 1835. His solution was to drive immense wooden pilings below the ground on which the firehouse's foundation would sit. As long as the pilings remained submerged, LeBrun believed, the building would remain stable. The problem was that the Collect Pond began drying up over the years, and the water level below the street fell to a level that caused the pilings to dry out and begin to rot. Over time, the firehouse continued sinking further into the mud. As Christopher Gray reported for the *New York Times* in 1990, by the time DCTV and the Chinese-American Planning Council purchased the building in 1983, the foundation problems were severe, with interior floors that "roll and heave like waves." Many years and $800,000 dollars in extensive renovation costs later, the story of the famous fairy-tale firehouse finally has a happy ending.

4

Artist and Editorial Cats

Of all the kinds of cats in New York City's history, the cats of writers, editors, and artists may have had it easiest. Unlike the cats attached to sailors, cops, or firemen, they were not expected to earn their keep by catching mice. Their job was simply to serve as a muse (or is that mews?) for the men who featured their feline friends in books, editorials, paintings, and photographs.

For example, consider the portrait photographer Arnold Genthe's cat Buzzer, who was once called "the most photographed cat in America." Today's feline internet sensations couldn't have held a candle to Buzzer, who was featured in more than eighty portraits of celebrated women of New York City's stage and screen in the early twentieth century. Not only did he get to pose with beautiful women, but Buzzer also spent his days in Genthe's studio at 1 West Forty-Sixth Street schmoozing with the rich and famous, including Sinclair Lewis, Babe Ruth, John Pierpont Morgan, John D. Rockefeller, and Theodore Roosevelt. In 1936, the photographer wrote about Buzzer in his autobiography, *As I Remember*: "Buzzer was certainly an important figure in my studio and even today, years after his death, he is fondly remembered by young and old. I sometimes was accused of paying more attention to that cat than to people. Possibly I enjoyed his contented purr more than the idle

In the 1930s, Buzzer was called the "Most Photographed Cat in America." (Library of Congress, Prints & Photographs Division, Arnold Genthe Collection: Negatives and Transparencies, LC-G432-0187)

chatter of an inopportune caller. I have not found another cat to take his place."

Edgar Allan Poe, who spent many years in New York City in the 1830s and 1840s—he lived in apartments at 130 Greenwich Street and 85 Amity Street (now West Third Street), in a farmhouse on the corner of West Eighty-Fourth Street and the old Bloomingdale Road (Broadway), and in an 1812 cottage in the Fordham section of the Bronx—was one of many writers of this period who received inspiration from a feline. Poe had at least two cats in his lifetime: one, a female he described as "one of the most remarkable black cats in the world," and the other, a cat named Caterina who served as his muse while he was living in New York. Caterina, described as a large tortoiseshell cat, would often sit and purr on Poe's shoulders as he wrote. She also served as a companion for Poe's wife, Virginia, during the woman's final years and would often lie in the bed with her to help keep her warm in the cold Fordham cottage.

Sadly, Caterina's tale does not have a happy ending: she reportedly died of starvation when Virginia's mother, Maria Clemm, deserted the cat after Poe died in October 1849. But considering how many cats led deplorable lives in antebellum New York City, Caterina had a good life in the Bronx while Poe was alive and caring for her. The same can be said for the cats of the author Mark Twain, the *New York Sun* editor Charles Dana, the cat artist J. H. Dolph, and the *Town Topics* publisher Colonel William d'Alton Mann. Not all of these felines had fairy-tale lives with happy endings, but while they were under the care of the men whom they inspired, life was pretty darn good.

1884

Mutilator and the Legendary Newspaper Office Cats of the *New York Sun*

A single member of this [cat] family has been known, on a "rush" night, to devour three and a half columns of presidential possibilities, seven columns of general politics, pretty much all but the head of a large and able-bodied railroad accident, and a full page of miscellaneous news, and then claw the nether garments of the managing editor, and call attention to an appetite still in good working order.

—Charles Dana, in *Concerning Cats: My Own and Some Others*

Most of us are familiar with the expression "The dog ate my home-work." Some of us may have even resorted to this excuse when we forgot or chose not to do a homework assignment. Reportedly, the expression may date to a story in a 1905 issue of the *Cambrian*, a magazine for Welsh Americans, in which William ApMadoc, the journal's music critic, related an anecdote about a minister who once asked his clerk whether his sermon that day had been long enough. Upon being assured that it was, the minister told the clerk that his dog had eaten some of the paper it was written on just before the service.

I hate to break it to dog lovers, but I think the cats trump the dogs on this expression—by about twenty years.

On July 2, 1881, President James A. Garfield was assassinated by Charles Guiteau. Guiteau reportedly killed the president because he was angry that he did not get a government position that he felt was due him. Following the assassination, President Chester Arthur pushed through legislation to put an end to civil appointments based on patronage. Two years later, on January 16, 1883, Congress passed the Civil Service Reform Act, sometimes referred to as the Pendleton Act after Senator George Hunt Pendleton of Ohio, a primary sponsor of the legislation. The Civil Service Reform Act was based on a draft written by the American lawyer Dorman Bridgeman Eaton, a staunch opponent of the spoils system, which awarded government jobs to party supporters, friends, and relatives.

So what does this have to do with a cat? Well, according to the story, the cat came into play on December 30, 1884, when New York State governor and president-elect Grover Cleveland wrote a letter to George William Curtis, president of the state's Civil Service Reform Association. The letter, which stressed Cleveland's intent to support the Pendleton Act during his administration, was submitted to several New York newspapers, including the *Evening Post*, the *New York Times*, and the *Sun*. The next morning, the letter appeared in all the newspapers but the *Sun*. Although the letter allegedly blew out an open window and was lost on Nassau Street, the *Sun*'s office cat ended up taking all the blame.

Here's what happened: When New York Supreme Court Justice Willard Bartlett inquired about the lack of publication the next day, the *Sun*'s editor, Charles Anderson Dana, remarked that it would be difficult to explain what happened to the readers, especially since it was well known that he was not all that fond of Grover Cleveland. Justice Bartlett responded, "Oh, say that the office cat ate it up." Dana apparently thought this was a good idea, so he dictated an editorial blaming the cat:

We are frequently obliged to deplore the circumstance that *The Sun* is not invariably conducted in a manner to please those of our esteemed contemporaries that do not happen to agree with us in opinion; but, sad as it is, we cannot always help it. Here are the *Evening Post* and the *New York Times*, both seasonably exercised because the *Sun* happened to publish Mr. Cleveland's letter on the civil service question on Wednesday, and not on Tuesday. The more profound of the two journals accounts for the fact on the hypothesis that we are afraid, and were "let into the astonishing journalistic blunder of trying to suppress it." This is a new conception worthy of its origin. *The Sun* is not usually suspected of being afraid of Mr. Cleveland's publications; and we solemnly declare that, so far as we can remember, we never tried to suppress a public document that came from a President. Since the *Evening Post* and *The Times* take interest in the conduct of the *Sun*, we beg to assure them that it was only through an accident that Mr. Cleveland's letter was not published by us on Tuesday. The assistant editor, who had charge of it, lost the copy from his desk, either by some person taking it or by the wind blowing it away, or the office cat eating it up; and that is all there is of it. In the name of the Prophet: Fudge!

The news about the cat went viral, so to speak, and within days almost every newspaper in the country had picked up on the story of the nameless office cat. The *New York Times* called the editorial "the most astonishing confession" and said the story shed light on the *Sun*'s political leanings during the past six months. In response to the media hoopla, Dana penned another lengthy editorial about the office cat on January 12, 1885, a portion of which follows:

The universal interest which this accomplished animal has excited throughout the country is a striking refutation that genius is not honored in its own day and generation. Perhaps no other living critic has attained the popularity and vogue now enjoyed by our cat. For years he worked in silence, unknown, perhaps, beyond the limits of the office. He is a sort of Rosicrucian cat, and his motto has been "to know all and to keep himself unknown." But he could not escape the glory his efforts deserved, and a few mornings ago he woke up, like Byron, to find himself famous.

We are glad to announce that he hasn't been puffed up by the enthusiastic praise which comes to him from all sources. He is the same industrious, conscientious, sharp-eyed, and sharp-toothed censor of copy that he has always been, nor should we have known that he is conscious of the admiration he excites among his esteemed contemporaries of the press had we not observed him in the act of dilacerating a copy of the *Graphic* containing an alleged portrait of him. . . .

We have received many requests to give a detailed account of the personal habits and peculiarities of this feline Aristarchus. His favorite food is a tariff discussion. When a big speech, full of wind and statistics, comes within his reach, he pounces upon it immediately and digests the figures at his leisure. . . . When a piece of stale news or a long-winded, prosy article comes into the office, his remarkable sense of smell instantly detects it, and it is impossible to keep it from him. He always assists with great interest at the opening of the office mail, and he files several hundred letters a day in his interior department. The favorite diversion of the office-boys is to make him jump for twelve-column articles on the restoration of the American merchant marine. . . .

We don't pretend he is perfect. We admit that he has an uncontrollable appetite for the Congressional Record. We have to keep this peculiar publication out of his reach. He will sit for hours and watch with burning eyes the iron safe in which we are obliged to shut up the Record for safe-keeping. Once in a while we let him have a number or two. He becomes uneasy without it. It is his catnip.

Many of our esteemed contemporaries are furnishing their offices with cats, but they can never hope to have the equal of the *Sun*'s venerable polyphage. He is a cat of genius.

Over the years, the *Sun*'s office cat took the blame for many news blunders. The *New York Times* especially criticized its rival's editorials—particularly those about politics—by suggesting the office cat must have chewed up the good parts or devoured all the copy written about any topic or candidate the *Sun* did not support. Some folks took the cat way too literally. For example, one day John J. Ford, while in a state of inebriation, stormed into the *Sun*'s editorial room demanding to see the cat. Ford charged the cat with failing to devour an article that appeared in the Sunday paper. Then he physically charged at the cat, causing it to cry out and scamper under a desk. When Ford became too aggressive with the editorial staff, he was knocked down by a few newspaper men and arrested by a policeman from the Twenty-Sixth Precinct station. Ford lost three teeth in the confrontation; the cat was unhurt, and a saucer of cream "soon tranquilized the emotions that had agitated the intelligent creature's bosom."

In 1897, Dr. Philip O'Hanlon, a coroner's assistant on Manhattan's Upper West Side, was asked by his eight-year-old daughter, Virginia, whether Santa Claus really existed. Dr. O'Hanlon suggested she write to the *Sun*, assuring her, "If you see it in the *Sun*, it's so." One of the paper's editors, Francis Pharcellus Church, wrote the famous editorial we still celebrate today at the holiday season. The editorial, "Yes, Virginia, There Is a Santa Claus," was published on September 21, 1897. Three weeks later, on October 17, Charles Dana passed away.

Sometime shortly before his death, Dana was approached by Helen M. Winslow, who was in the process of writing a book about famous cats. At Winslow's request, Dana furnished a lengthy description of the newspaper's many office cats. According to Dana, the first office cat was a female cat that had reportedly died after drinking the contents of an ink bottle. Fortunately, she had many kittens that were "weaned on reports from country correspondents," and one of them advanced to the duties and honors of second office cat. Mutilator, the latest office cat at the time, was a descendant of this kitten. According to Dana, the striped cat with beryl eyes was "a creditable specimen of his family" with "an appetite for copy unsurpassed in the annals of his race."

I can't say for sure that the *Sun* had any actual office cats or whether the term "office cat" was just a running joke. Winslow also appears to have doubts about the story. In fact, in her introduction to Dana's text, she notes, "I can only vouch for its veracity by quoting the famous phrase, 'If you see it in the *Sun*, it's so.'"

DID YOU KNOW?

In 1867, when Charles Dana and a group of investors purchased the *New York Sun* from the family of Moses Yale Beach for $175,000, they moved the offices into the old Tammany Hall building at 170 Nassau Street. This building had been constructed for the Tammany Society in 1812 and featured a large room that could hold up to two thousand people for political and social events. It was here, in the long, dark, barn-like room that was littered with paper and jammed with rolltop desks, that Mutilator and the other famous office cats made their home.

In July 1915, the *Sun* (then under the editorship of Dana's son, Paul) moved to 150 Nassau Street. Two years later, the newspaper moved into the former A. T. Stewart Dry Goods Store, also known as the Marble Palace, at 280 Broadway. This building was constructed in 1845 on the site of Washington Hall, the former headquarters of the Federalist Party, at the northeast corner of Broadway and Chambers Street, just north of City Hall Park. The building was declared a National Historic Landmark in 1965 and today houses the central offices for the New York City Department of Buildings.

1891

Princess, Josephine, and the 101 Feline Models of the Cat Artist J. H. Dolph

What J. G. Brown has done for the American street urchin, Mr. Dolph has done for the American cat.

—*Recorder*, 1892

Unlike many nineteenth-century New York City residents who wanted nothing to do with stray felines, John Henry Dolph welcomed them with open arms. He was also willing to pay the neighborhood children a few coins whenever they brought him baskets of homeless kittens. And if the kittens were very young and had no mother, Dolph even went as far as playing mother cat. Lifting each kitten by the scruff of the neck, he'd gingerly place them on

Sometimes a mischievous puppy would make his way into a John Henry Dolph cat painting, much to the chagrin of the feline models. *Pup, Kittens, Onions*, date unknown. (Sheldon Museum of Art, University of Nebraska–Lincoln, Gift of Mrs. Florence Dolph Warner, D-22.1916)

the workbench in the small workshop behind his summer cottage-studio. Then he'd dip a large paintbrush into a cup of milk and touch the tip of the brush to the kitten's mouth. After all the kittens had their share of milk, Dolph would take a clean sponge and warm water and wash their mouths and faces, just like a mother cat would do. Once a day he would wash them all over. "It takes some time to feed a family in this way, but I must have my models, and so I must work for them," Dolph told W. Lewis Fraser during an interview for *St. Nicholas* magazine in 1891. "It's much easier to feed them than it is to keep them clean."

Sometimes Dolph received more kittens than he needed. However, he'd always try to make them all comfortable, whether at his summer cottage in Bellport, Long Island, or in his New York City studio at 58 West Fifty-Seventh Street. After all, cats and kittens were his models and his meal ticket.

Born to Osman Dolph and Olive Horton Dolph in Fort Ann, New York, in 1835, J. H. Dolph became an apprentice to a carriage painter at the age of fourteen. Several years later, he progressed to painting portraits in Cleveland, Ohio. After moving to New York City in 1864 (three years after the death of his first wife, Flora Theresa Wiggins), he became a prominent landscape painter specializing in farm scenes. As Dolph told Fraser, it was soon after he returned from Europe, where he studied with the celebrated horse painter Louis van Kuyck, that he decided to paint his first kitten. He had a little twelve-dollar gold frame in his studio, so he thought a kitten would be perfect for that.

Dolph didn't expect anything great to come of this painting when he sent it to an auction house. So he was quite shocked when the auctioneer gave him one hundred dollars. He tried painting another cat, and then another. The more the whiskered artist painted cats, the more the public demanded his cat paintings. Soon he was known only for his cat paintings, and his human portraits and landscapes were forgotten.

Following a fire in 1889 that destroyed the contents of Dolph's studio in the YMCA building on Twenty-Third Street, he moved into the Sherwood Studio Building at 58 West Fifty-Seventh Street. As Fraser noted, the Sherwood was "one of those great, ugly houses called studio-buildings, ever so many stories high, which rich men build for artists to live in, if they can afford the high rent."

Constructed in 1880 by John H. Sherwood, a banker and boot maker turned real estate tycoon and art collector, the seven-story brick Sherwood Studio Building was the first apartment building in New York City designed specifically for artists. It featured forty-four apartments, each with a fifteen-foot-high studio and one or two bedrooms for the artists and their families. Modern amenities included electric-bell signals, speaking tubes, gas service, and an oversize elevator to accommodate giant paintings. Although the building was reportedly "plain and cold and comfortless," with row upon row of doors in hallways without carpeting, it was like something out of a fairy tale inside Dolph's studio. As Fraser described,

"Once in the studio you think that you are in one of the rooms of some old palace in Europe. Here are beautiful eastern carpets in the soft, rich colors which artists love; great high-backed chairs all carved, brought from Italy, chairs on which knights and ladies have sat hundreds of years ago; old, curious musical instruments which make you wonder what they would sound like and how they were played; a carved chest which some Venetian noble gave to his daughter." The studio was also filled with cats and the kittens, which would lounge on the old carved chests, tear and claw at the Persian rugs, and organize kitty concerts at night, which, as Dolph noted, "were a trifling distracting to [the] neighbors."

It wasn't long after Dolph started painting cats and kittens that he realized that a New York City artist's studio was no place for a feline. He gave away a few of his cats to the clubs that he belonged to, including the Salmagundi Club, Lotus Club, and the appropriately named Kit Kat Club. But giving cats away didn't solve his need to be surrounded by cats of all kinds. A summer cottage near the water, he decided, was the perfect place to house his model cats and observe them in action. And so it was at his summer studio, just a few blocks from Bellport Bay on the south shore of Long Island, that he raised hundreds of cats, including Princess, who had her very own seat at the Dolph dinner table, and Josephine, the Angora cat whom Dolph purchased in Paris.

Dolph's summer cottage in Bellport, where he lived with his wife Mary Heaney and many cats and dogs from 1875 to 1903, was reportedly built before 1850 as a carpentry shop where boats and decoys were made. The country studio was a large square room with a pointed roof and high walls covered in gray burlap-canvas. On the north side was a high studio window and a large wood-burning fireplace. The room had very little furniture, save for an old carved cabinet, a few comfortable chairs, and a few tables. In this room, the kittens (and a few puppies) were free to roll about and play as much as they pleased as Dolph sketched their every move in charcoal.

To further accommodate his models, Dolph turned his workshop behind the cottage into a cat house, so to speak. He called his workshop the cat's dormitory. Outside the cottage, Dolph built a raised floor with a grapevine trellis, where he would place his feline and canine models to sketch them as they frolicked in the sun. The floor had a little hole so that if the kittens got scared by a noise or stray dog, they could make a quick escape.

Because the cats couldn't be photographed (they were too fast for the cameras of the time), Dolph resorted to all kinds of tricks to pose them. For example, he'd wave milk-soaked bread over their heads to make them reach up or jump, or he'd put a caterpillar or toad on the floor and sketch the cats while they watched it crawl or hop across the floor. Dolph would make a very rough sketch of all the kittens in a group, and then he would draw each one separately. He'd tack the sketches all over the walls and choose his favorites to paint. Once he finished painting his models, it was always his desire "to find Christian homes" for the cats.

Yes, cats are easily spoiled if you pet them too much, and quickly become your master.

—J. H. Dolph, 1891

Princess was reportedly a very beautiful cat who was a favorite model with Dolph's customers. Rather than finding a home for her, Dolph kept her as one of his many pets at the summer cottage. According to Dolph, Princess always sat on his knee or at her own chair at dinnertime, and she would only feed from his fingers or eat bits of food put on the table just for her.

In addition to Princess, Dolph had two pet Angora cats, which he purchased during a trip to Paris. One of the cats was shot and killed by someone who mistook him for a skunk in the bushes. The other was Josephine, a huntress who could not be kept indoors at night. Josephine reportedly made a lot of noise outside, which angered all the neighbors on Academy Lane. The Dolphs would try to find her before they turned in for the night, but she would stay quiet until they gave up and turned off the lights. Then she'd begin her nightly chorus.

One summer Josephine gave birth in the carpenter shop. Her kittens were beautiful, although not pure Angora. When some little neighborhood boys started playing with them, Josephine carried them away to a safe hiding place. For days she would come to the house for meals but then run away through the fields. Then one day she brought a dead kitten to the house. Dolph told the *St. Nicholas*, "She looked at me beseechingly out of her large, lovely eyes, and licked the kitten all over, and looking at me again with an expression so human that I felt my eyes moisten." Every day after that, Josephine brought another dead kitten to Dolph, each with a fatal cut in the neck. Apparently, she had been keeping the kittens under a barn, and a weasel had gotten to them. Only one kitten survived.

In 1900, Mary Dolph passed away while the couple was staying at the New York City studio. Three years later, on September 28, 1903, Dolph died suddenly while in the apartment of Sarah E. Grenner, at 121 West Seventy-First Street (Grenner was a distant relative who told the press that she and Dolph had planned to marry). According to the *Evening World*, Dolph was sitting in a chair dressed for bed when he succumbed to complications from heart disease. Only a few days before, he had sold the cottage at Bellport. I don't know what happened to his cats after he passed, but their legacy lives on in his paintings, many of which his daughter, Flora Warner, donated to the University of Nebraska in 1923. In recent years, Dolph's paintings have sold for $5,000 or more at art auctions.

1895

Taffy, the Laird, and the Clowder of *Town Topics* Office Cats

In May 1895, James T. Hyde organized the first official "cat fancy" show at New York's Madison Square Garden. The National Cat Show attracted close to two hundred felines occupying all sorts of boxes, baskets, and cages. The entrants ranged from humble street cats rescued by the SPCA to the upper-crust cats of Mrs. John J. Astor, Mrs. Stanford White, and Mrs. Prescott Lawrence.

Although they did not take home any ribbons, a trio of black cats belonging to Colonel William d'Alton Mann, publisher of the *Town Topics* society magazine, stole the show. According to the

New York Times, the cats were named Little Billie, Leo, and David. I'm not sure that's correct, though. Helen Maria Winslow, author of *Concerning Cats: My Own and Some Others*, claims the three jet-black cats were named Taffy, The Laird, and Little Billee. I'm more prone to believe that Winslow has it right. Not only was she familiar with Colonel Mann and his office cats, but Taffy, The Laird, and Little Billee were the names of the leading male characters in a long-running play called *Trilby*, which was based on the novel by George Du Maurier. *Trilby* had opened at the Garden Theatre on the southeast corner of Madison Avenue and Twenty-Seventh Street just one month before the cat show. The *Town Topics* office, where the cats lived, was located just down the street from the theater on Fifth Avenue.

According to Winslow, Colonel Mann was a devoted lover of animals who had a standing order: should any of his employees see a starving kitten on the street, they were not to leave it to suffer and die. Hence, the *Town Topics* office was a sanctuary for unfortunate cats. As Winslow writes, "One may always see a number of happy-looking creatures there, who seem to appreciate the kindness which surrounds them."

The *Town Topics* office cats made their home on the top floor of 208 Fifth Avenue, a Renaissance Revival building designed by Berg & Clark for Alfred B. Darling in 1894. (Prior to this date, the address was a five-story brick and brownstone building occupied by the Chesterfield Hotel.) The seven-story building had frontages on Fifth Avenue and Broadway and housed stores and offices. Until the Cross Building was constructed at 210 Fifth Avenue around 1904, a narrow vacant lot separated the building from the famous Delmonico's restaurant, which was on the southwest corner of Fifth Avenue and Twenty-Sixth Street from 1876 to 1899 (from 1900 to 1913, the Delmonico's building was occupied by the Café Martin).

In the spring and summer months, Taffy, The Laird, Little Billee, and other *Town Topics* office cats would crawl out on the wide window ledge to enjoy the fresh air and the view of Madison Square Park below. Sadly, The Laird and Little Billee reportedly came to their deaths by jumping from their high perch to chase after some sparrows they saw in the park. Following this tragedy, Colonel

Colonel William d'Alton Mann rescued many cats from the streets of New York. (Library of Congress, Prints & Photographs Division, LC-DIG-ggbain-06920)

Mann put up a strong wire grating across the windows. From that point on, Taffy, described as a "monstrous, shiny black fellow," was the leader of the *Town Topics* cat colony.

William Mann, like the street cats he rescued, had a humble beginning. Born in Sandusky, Ohio, in 1839, Mann grew up on his father's farm and was one of thirteen children. From this simple start, he epitomized the American dream. Mann was a Civil War hero at Gettysburg, an entrepreneur and inventor (he invented a luxury railroad car called the "Mann Boudoir Car"), and later a business tycoon, millionaire, and publisher. He was also a family man who doted on his daughter, Emma, and a cat man who adored his office cats. Alas, Colonel Mann also was a blackmailer who extorted tens of thousands of dollars from New York's millionaires via a column called "Saunterings" in *Town Topics*. The weekly magazine had been founded in 1879 as J. R. Andrews's *American Queen, a National Society Journal*. Louis Keller, founder of the *Social Register*, took over in 1883, and under his editorship, the publication was "dedicated to art, music, literature, and society." When the publication went bankrupt in 1885, Colonel Mann's brother Eugene D. Mann purchased it and renamed it *Town Topics*. Under Eugene Mann's reign, the weekly magazine morphed into a scandal sheet that often identified high-society wrongdoers by name.

In 1891, Eugene went into hiding after being charged with sending obscene matter through the mail. Colonel Mann came to New York City and assumed ownership and editorship of the publication. Much to the dismay of the Vanderbilts, Goulds, Morgans, and other upper-crust folks, Colonel Mann took the art of scandal to a mastery level. What he did, in essence, was establish a network of paid spies comprising servants, telegraph operators, hotel employees, seamstresses, butlers, and grocers to spy on the socialites and supply the magazine with juicy gossip. The colonel would then meet with the "guilty parties" at Delmonico's, where they could negotiate for discretion. The amount of money that Colonel Mann managed to extort from America's wealthiest men—Mann called them loans—was staggering. For example, William K. Vanderbilt paid $25,000, Charles M. Schwab paid $10,000, and the Wall Street stockbroker James R. Keene "loaned" the colonel $90,000.

As time went on, the well-to-do members of New York's Gilded Age became paranoid that their own maids and butlers were supplying gossip to *Town Topics*. Sometimes they would make up gossip as a test to see if their servants or associates could be trusted. If they read this made-up gossip in *Town Topics*, they knew there was a leak somewhere within their household or circle of friends. Despite all this paranoia—or maybe because of it—*Town Topics* was the most widely read magazine in society, even though no one would ever admit to subscribing to it.

The bribery continued to escalate, leading to numerous lawsuits over the years. In 1905, Colonel Mann was arrested on charges of perjury (the complainant in this case was Robert J. Collier of *Collier's Weekly*). The colonel's daughter bailed him out by offering as collateral the vacant lots he owned at 310–328 West Thirty-Eighth Street, where he was building new offices for his new Ess Ess Publishing. Colonel Mann was ultimately cleared of perjury, but by that time *Town Topics* had lost most of its appeal. Two years after Mann's death in 1920, A. Ralph Keller organized the T. T. Publishing Company to buy *Town Topics*. The paper lingered on until eventually folding in the 1930s. Mann's estate sold the property on Thirty-Eighth Street—then the site of a garage for the United States Post Office—in 1925.

1905

Bambino, the City Cat Who Stole Away from Mark Twain

Samuel Langhorne Clemens loved cats. One might even say that the author and humorist better known as Mark Twain was a crazy cat man. As the Clemens family maid once said, "Mr. Clemens, you know, was so crazy about cats that he'd stop anything—even his writing, to speak to a cat!" And Albert Bigelow Paine, who wrote the official biography of Twain while the author was living on Fifth Avenue in New York City, said Twain had an absolute passion for cats. Even Twain's daughter Susy acknowledged her father's strong attachment to cats: "The difference between Papa and Mamma is that Mamma loves morals and Papa loves cats."

One of Twain's favorite cats was Satan, a large black cat who lived at Quarry Farm in Elmira, New York, where the Clemens family spent their summers. Satan gave birth to a gray kitten whom Twain named Sin, the daughter of Satan. Some of his other favorite felines on the family farm were Deuteronomy, Genesis, Sour Mash, Fraulein, Blatherskite, and Stray Kit. (He reportedly had up to eleven cats at one time on the farm.) Although Twain adored all of his farm cats, it was a city cat named Bambino who stole his heart.

Photograph of Bambino, New York, NY (PH 02398). (Courtesy of the Mark Twain Project, The Bancroft Library University of California, Berkeley)

The story of Mark Twain and Bambino starts shortly after the death of Twain's wife, Olivia Langdon Clemens, in June 1904. Clara Clemens, the couple's middle daughter, took Olivia's death hard and had a nervous breakdown. She spent much of the following year recovering in a Connecticut sanatorium. Completely cut off from friends and family, Clara defied the sanatorium rules and smuggled a black kitten she named Bambino into her bedroom. The cat was permitted to stay with her until he stole away one day and entered the room of a patient who hated cats. Ordered to get rid of the cat, Clara gave Bambino to her father as a gift, knowing Twain would love him. Over the next few months, Clara and her father exchanged several letters. In one letter, Twain said Bambino missed Clara so much he refused all meat and milk. However, a few days later, he contradicted his statement: "It has been discovered that the reason your cat declines milk and meat and lets on to live by miraculous intervention is, that he catches mice privately."

In the fall of 1904, Twain leased James Renwick's four-story red-brick and stone house at 21 Fifth Avenue, on the southeast corner of East Ninth Street. The family maid Katie Leary, live-in secretary Isabel Lyon, and Bambino joined him in his new city home. Although Isabel reportedly had sole rule over the staff, it was Bambino who had total rule of Twain's bedroom, which is where the author did all of his writing. For hours a day, as Twain wrote in his bed, the large black cat with wide green eyes would sleep or play at his side.

In 1905, Colonel George Harvey, Mark Twain's publisher, provided this testimonial about Twain and Bambino to the *Washington Post*:

> I think that perhaps the funniest thing about Mark Twain now is not his writing, but his bed. . . . His bed is the largest one I ever saw, and on it is the weirdest collection of objects you ever saw, enough to furnish a Harlem flat—books, writing materials, clothes, any and everything that could foregather in his vicinity. He looks quite happy rising out of the mass, and over all prowls a huge black cat of a very unhappy disposition. She snaps and snarls and claws and bites, and Mark Twain takes his turn with the rest; when she gets tired of tearing up manuscript she scratches him and he bears it with a patience wonderful to behold.

When Bambino wasn't assisting Twain with his manuscripts, he kept busy learning new tricks. The author reportedly taught his favorite feline how to turn out the lamp in the bedroom and how to put out his cigar lighter by giving Bambino special signals. Twain loved to show off Bambino's talents whenever people called at the home.

Although Bambino was quite content being an indoor cat, his instinctive wanderlust took over on the night of March 31, 1905. According to Leary, Bambino heard some cats calling from the back fence, so he went searching for a way to get outside. Finding an open window, the cat made his escape. The following day, everyone looked high and low for Bambino. Twain even placed the following ad in the *New York American* (a newspaper published from 1902 to 1937):

A CAT LOST—FIVE DOLLARS REWARD for his restoration to Mark Twain, No. 21 Fifth Avenue. Large and intensely black; thick, velvety fur; has a faint fringe of white hair across his chest; not easy to find in ordinary light.

The ad did not bring Bambino back, but many people responded to it by bringing all kinds of cats to the residence. (As Leary noted, "anything to get a glimpse of Mr. Clemens!") A few nights later, Leary heard a cat meowing across the street in General Daniel Edgar Sickles's backyard at 23 Fifth Avenue. Perhaps the general's King Charles spaniel, Bobo, had frightened the cat and chased him up the large sycamore tree on General Sickles's property, but whatever had happened, Bambino was more than happy to follow Leary back home. Although Twain gave Bambino the riot act when he returned, he was delighted to have his cat back. He withdrew the ad, "fearing a rush of black street cats 'from the common people,'" but of course that didn't stop curious New Yorkers from bringing strays to his house for several more days.

Twain lived in New York City until June 1908, when he moved to his new villa, Stormfield, in Redding, Connecticut. I do not know whether Bambino was still with the family at this time, but if he was, he would have definitely moved with them to Connecticut. According to Leary, Twain had refused to move into the villa until all his cats were eating and purring on the hearth. "When they was doin' that," she wrote, "he'd know everything was settled and he'd be ready to come, too."

The house where Mark Twain lived from 1904 to 1908 was designed by the noted architect James Renwick Jr., the son of James Renwick and Margaret Ann Brevoort Renwick, who were the original owners of 21 Fifth Avenue. The younger Renwick was a structural engineer and self-taught architect who had served as a supervisor on the city's Croton Reservoir construction project after graduating from Columbia College (later Columbia University) in 1836. He went on to achieve fame as an architect with his designs for numerous churches and other buildings, including the Grace Church (1843) on the corner of Broadway and East Tenth Street, the St. Denis Hotel on Broadway and Eleventh Street (1853), and St. Patrick's Cathedral (1858) on Fifth Avenue at Fiftieth Street.

The Renwick home was constructed sometime around 1840 on a small section of what had once been the Brevoort farm, which comprised about eighty-six acres bounded by Ninth and Eighteenth Streets, Fifth Avenue, and the Bowery. A portion of the farm dates back to December 18, 1667, which is when Bastiaen Elyessen received the land from Richard Nicolls, the first English governor of New York. It passed from Elyessen to his son-in-law, John Hendricks Kyckuyt, on November 15, 1701. By that time, Kyckuyt had changed his surname to Brevoort (sometimes written as van Brevoort). Hence, the land became known as the Brevoort farm.

In 1831, Henry Brevoort, the great-grandson of John Hendricks Brevoort, decided to build a new mansion for his family. Although he wanted to build in the exclusive Bond Street neighborhood, his father, Hendrik Brevoort, insisted that Henry build farther to the west, on undeveloped lands on Fifth Avenue above Washington Square Park. Henry agreed to build in the woods, as he called it, and erected a lavish mansion on the northwest corner of Fifth Avenue and Ninth Street in 1834. Two years later, Hendrick Brevoort deeded the land diagonally across the street to his only daughter, Margaret Ann. It was on this land that James Renwick Jr. designed the Italianate-style house at 21 Fifth Avenue for his parents.

Margaret and James Renwick lived in the home with their eldest son, Henry, his wife, Margaret, and their son, James Armstrong Renwick, who was born in the house in 1856. By the time James Armstrong graduated college in 1876, the family had left 21 Fifth Avenue; however, they continued to lease the home for use as an upscale boardinghouse with multiple tenants until the turn of the century, when the home was returned to a single-family residence.

During the early 1900s, the home was owned by James A. Renwick and his cousin Elizabeth Brevoort Whittingham. In August 1923, Whittingham's son, Edward Renwick Whittingham, took sole possession of the house. Although the young lawyer insisted that the home would not be torn down as long as he was alive, change was inevitable as the lower Fifth Avenue mansions continued to succumb to high-rise apartment buildings. In 1925, Whittingham converted the grand old home into ten one- and two-room apartments. In 1929, he signed a twenty-one-year lease with the new Washington Square National Bank, pending the removal of residential zoning restrictions. At that time, Whittingham said if the restrictions were not lifted, he would be forced to tear the old house down and "erect something on the site that would bring fair return on the property." The bank deal never went through, and on July 10, 1933, the house was sold at auction in foreclosure proceedings brought by the Bank of Manhattan Company on a claim of $103,911 for unpaid taxes and other debts. The bank bought the property on a bid of $10,000. For the next twenty years, the house continued to serve as a small residential apartment building.

In 1952, the fate of 21 Fifth Avenue, the old Brevoort Hotel, and ten adjoining brownstone dwellings between Eighth and Ninth Streets was decided when Sam Minskoff & Sons signed a 105-year lease with plans of building a "tall ultramodern apartment building" on the site. The Minskoffs agreed to notify the Mark Twain Association and the New-York Historical Society well in advance of the demolition. Although several efforts were made to preserve the home, no one could raise enough funds, and the last residents were forced to leave in March 1954. The house was razed to make way for the Brevoort and Brevoort East, a large apartment complex that occupies the full block bounded by Fifth Avenue, East Eighth Street, University Place, and East Ninth Street.

DID YOU KNOW?

At the start of the nineteenth century, with Manhattan's population quickly expanding and moving northward, city officials announced plans to open Broadway on a straight line to Twenty-Third Street. The problem with this plan was that they would have had to cut Broadway right through Hendrik Brevoort's homestead and cherry grove between Tenth and Eleventh Streets. According to legend, Brevoort had no intention of partitioning his land or parting with the cherry orchard. He supposedly protested the plan by keeping a loaded blunderbuss on his porch and chaining a live bear to a tree near his watermelon patch (near the site of the present-day St. Denis Hotel). To avoid confrontations with the blunderbuss and the bear, the commissioners reportedly revised their plans by creating a dog-leg bend on Broadway at Tenth Street. One newspaper later called Brevoort a "stubborn old Knickerbocker" who "put the bend in Broadway."

Sometime around 1836, the city proposed opening Eleventh Street between Broadway and the Bowery. Hendrik Brevoort fought this plan also, because he did not want a road running so close to the old brick and frame house his father had built at 492 Bowery. Although the street was never opened, the trees were doomed after Brevoort died in 1841 at the age of ninety-four. In 1843, his son Henry sold the grove to the Grace Protestant Episcopal Church. The trees were razed, and the cornerstone was laid for a grand new Gothic Revival edifice designed by Henry's nephew James Renwick Jr.

5

Hospitality Cats

Some studies have shown that where you're born has a large impact on how far you'll go in life. I think the same holds true for cats, especially for those born in large cities. With so many hotels, bars, and restaurants to choose from, Old New York was a great birthplace for felines that aspired to become hospitality cats. For example, when a mother cat gave birth to three kittens near Times Square in 1928, she couldn't have picked a better place to bring her little ones into the world. I don't know what possessed her to give birth among the wrecking crews at the corner of Eighth Avenue and Forty-Fifth Street, but her decision paid off for one kitty named Abe, who would spend the rest of his life living in the laps, literally, of luxury.

In 1919, Bill McSorley, the owner of the renowned McSorley's Old Ale House on Seventh Street near Third Avenue, told a reporter from the *New York Evening Telegram* that cats had been a fixture at McSorley's ever since his father, John, founded the tavern in 1854. "My father wanted me to keep cats. It has been his motto that 'it costs less to feed a cat than it does to pay a plumber.' Cats keep away rats, who gnaw through lead pipes."

It's been said that Bill McSorley was gruff with his customers, but he displayed plenty of kindness toward his cats. He owned as many as eighteen barfly felines at once, and they reportedly had the run of the saloon (although they always took their catnaps in the back room). I'm not sure how motivated the cats were when it came to catching rats, because McSorley reportedly fed them bull livers that he ran through a sausage grinder every day. As Joseph Mitchell wrote in the *New Yorker* in 1940, "When it came time to feed them, he would leave the bar, no matter how brisk business was, and bang on the bottom of a tin pan; the fat cats would come loping up, like leopards, from all corners of the saloon."

In 1913, the realist painter John French Sloan memorialized McSorley's cats in an illustration he created for *Harper's Magazine*. Fifteen years later, he captured the same scene in oil on canvas with his painting *McSorley's Cats*. One of a series of five McSorley's paintings that Sloan created between 1912 and 1930, *McSorley's Cats* depicts the militant anarchist Hippolyte Havel, the cartoonist Art Young, the artist Alexander Kruse, and several other men smoking, laughing, and drinking ale at the bar. To their right, McSorley is opening an icebox as five cats huddle around him, waiting to be fed. In "McSorley's: John Sloan's Visual Commentary on Male Bonding, Prohibition, and the Working Class," Mariea Caudill Dennison writes, "The hardy camaraderie has been momentarily interrupted by Bill McSorley's call to his cats. Although the date of the painting is secure, the image seems to suggest a re-occurring event."

John "Jack" Bleeck (pronounced Blake), the owner of the Opera Café and the Artist and Writers Club, also knew the value of a cat for an establishment where food was served. He was ecstatic when an orphan kitten showed up at his door one winter night in 1920. Bleeck desperately needed a champion mouser; throughout the years, Minnie did not disappoint him. And Frank Case, the owner-manager of the Algonquin Hotel, also appreciated his hospitality cats. He couldn't believe his good fortune when a street-smart tabby took the job of hotel cat without even applying and interviewing for the position. I don't know if Rusty was a good mouser, but like all the cats in these stories, he certainly had all the people in his life wrapped around his little paws.

1920

Minnie, the Female Mouser of a Manhattan Men-Only Speakeasy

It was a cold November night in 1920 when a dusty black-and-dirty-white orphan kitten showed up at the Opera Café at 561 Seventh Avenue near Fortieth Street. Jack Bleeck, who had just taken over the place after working as a bartender there for nine years, saw the kitten outside and invited her in while he was oiling the lock on the door. He was just about to put up a "Help Wanted" sign for a good mouser, so the timing could not have been better.

Bleeck, the son of a German American St. Louis shoemaker, left his home city on a freight car sometime around 1900 to find a better life on the East Coast. He landed a job making a dollar a day at a cocktail bar in New Orleans during Mardi Gras. After arriving in New York, his first jobs included selling hats and shoes and tending bar on Coney Island. In 1920, at the start of Prohibition, Bleeck borrowed some money to purchase the Opera Café, and he turned it into a speakeasy to circumvent the law. Business was brisk, but Bleeck was no match for the rats and mice that nibbled at his customers' shoes. A cat like Minnie was the answer to his prayers.

On the night she arrived, Minnie slept well in a warm corner of the basement, her little belly full with food. She immediately paid Bleeck back by catching a mouse and placing it at his feet the next morning. As Bleeck told a reporter from the *New York Herald Tribune* just before Minnie's death in July 1934, while wiping tears from his eyes, "Minnie was made of strong stuff. She'd chase the rats into the holes and then wait three or four hours to get another crack at them. Inside of six months she had cleaned out all the rodents and the survivors never dared come back. It was a tough job. The rats used to gang her, but her paws moved like lightning and she could punch like [Jack] Dempsey."

According to Bleeck, the rats came from a rathskeller next door, which featured a men's lunch for fifteen cents that included "cheap cuts of meat" and "near beer." The meat attracted the rats, but even they didn't like it too much. Bleeck said the rats would burrow through the foundations and sneak into his establishment in search of a decent scrap of sirloin. "These rats were the biggest and boldest you ever saw," he told the reporter. "They would stand right up against the bar and gnaw at the shoes resting against the brass rail. My customers stood for this tickling just so long, and then began to complain." Bleeck said he tried putting about forty traps around the café, and he even threw gallons of ammonia into the holes they bored into the walls; but they seemed to thrive on this. "Altogether I spent $600 on those damned rats and they didn't have the courtesy to leave me alone." Bleeck said as soon as Minnie moved in, she took immediate possession of the premises and went promptly to work on the rodents.

In October 1925, Bleeck sold the Opera Café and secured a charter from Albany to open a men's-only social club in a grimy, 1910 loft building at 213 West Fortieth Street, next to the New York Herald Tribune Building. Called the Artist and Writers Club, the speakeasy-disguised-as-social-club looked and operated like a formal dining club. Bleeck was a strict disciplinarian at his club, and he was always present at a central table to keep order. If any of the club's six thousand members started singing a loud drinking song or tried to occupy a table without permission, Bleeck saw to it that he was kicked out. If a wife or girlfriend tried to get in, the entrance was blocked (during Prohibition, patrons had to enter the club through a door inside a warehouse where the Metropolitan Opera stored scenery). In the early days, the Artist and Writers Club attracted opera singers from the Metropolitan Opera House and numerous thespians and stagehands from the National Theatre (later the Billy Rose and today the Nederlander Theatre) at 208 West Forty-First Street. Later on, reporters, editors, authors, and press agents from all over the city made the club a favorite literary hangout.

One of the most famous patrons of the club was the great tenor Enrico Caruso, who would stop by with his friend Antonio Scotti, a baritone, after performing at the Metropolitan Opera. Minnie would jump on the bar and arch her back so Caruso could pet her while sipping his martinis. Although Minnie was the first female ever admitted to the club, the feisty feline enjoyed her privileges

The Ellin Prince Speyer Animal Hospital, operated by the New York Women's League for Animals, opened in 1914 at 350 Lafayette Street. The building featured a general examination room, an emergency room and padded stall for horses, operating rooms, isolation wards, quarters for birds, and an apartment for resident veterinarian, Dr. Bruce Blair. (Photo by the author)

but did not abuse them. She spent most of her waking hours policing the basement kitchen, which was where she slept in a box filled with sawdust. Every evening at the same time, she would come upstairs to pass an hour at the bar or in the card room. She loved schmoozing, but she never once meowed or complained. Over the years, Minnie reportedly had about 110 kittens. According to Bleeck, whenever she was pregnant, members of the club would form a kitten pool and bet on the litter size. Usually she had six kittens at a time, but sometimes she'd have only four or five. The mother cat made good mousers of them all, but none of her offspring ever acquired her social abilities.

Just six weeks before Minnie died, she gave birth to her final litter of only two kittens. Bleeck could sense that she was not faring well after this delivery, so he took her by taxi to the Ellin Prince Speyer

Hospital for Animals. There, she was examined by Dr. Bruce Blair, who told Bleeck that his cat had a tumor in her stomach. He said she was too weak for an operation and could not be saved. Bleeck said his last good-bye to Minnie on July 20, 1934. While leaving the hospital for the last time, Bleeck told reporters, "She has a face like a human being. She looks right up in my face as if to say to me, I know I'm sick and you're trying to help me." He raised a finger to his moist eyes and, wiping back the tears, said, "Just some soot in my eye. She's just a cat."

Following Minnie's death, Bleeck buried her in a deeded plot at the Hartsdale Pet Cemetery in Westchester County, New York. All of her newspaper friends also saw to it that she had a decent obituary. As Eleanor Booth Simmons noted in her cat column in the *New York Sun* in 1937, "When, full of years, Minnie died, she had longer newspaper obituaries than most people get." About a dozen of Minnie's kittens continued living at the club after her passing, but none of them ever gained her notoriety.

Following the repeal of Prohibition in December 1933, Bleeck had to change the name of his club to the Artist and Writers Restaurant (although most of his patrons called it Bleeck's). To the great dismay of his patrons, he also had to allow women. (It took Bleeck ten months to finally open the door to women, but even then he did his best to make most of them feel quite unwelcome for the next twenty years.) Bleeck's was the favorite drinking spot for *Herald Tribune* reporters, who would clear out every night to check their news copy as soon as the walls of the saloon began shaking, signaling that the presses next door had started their run. Magazine writers, radio executives, advertising men, Broadway actors, and press agents also spent many hours at the forty-two-foot-long bar or at the bare oak tables, where waiters with thick German accents served German American fare.

In March 1953, Bleeck sold the business to Thomas F. Fitzpatrick and Ernst Hitz. After retiring, he lived in Florida during the winter months and on Long Island in the warmer months. He died at the age of eighty-three at his home in Manhasset on April 22, 1963. His only immediate survivor was his wife, Myrtle Bennett Bleeck.

In 1981, the old loft building on Fortieth Street was destroyed in a fire. Today the six-story refurbished office building is owned by the Nederlander Organization. The former employees' entrance for the Herald Tribune Building is now the entrance to the City University of New York Graduate School of Journalism.

DID YOU KNOW?

On January 16, 1920, the Eighteenth Amendment to the US Constitution—banning the manufacture, transportation, and sale of intoxicating liquors—went into effect. In New York City, police confiscated barrels of wine and beer, smashed them, and dumped their contents into gutters or harbors. While some New Yorkers watched in horror, others began finding ways to circumvent the law by selling alcohol illegally at places called speakeasies. According to the New-York Historical Society, there were anywhere from twenty thousand to one hundred thousand speakeasies in New York City during the Prohibition era, ranging from complete dives to well-appointed establishments like Bleeck's that catered to the wealthy and elite. Mixed drinks took off during this time—in part to help mask the foul taste of homemade alcohol—with cocktail menus featuring categories like fizzes (made with lime or lemon juice and soda), flips (made with egg), punches (rum drinks), and cordials.

The city's sources of alcohol were numerous during these days. There was homemade wine made in apartments in Little Italy and Greenwich Village and whisky from Canadian distilleries that was smuggled across the porous border. Much of the booze was smuggled in from Nova Scotia, England, Mexico, and Cuba by black-market rum runners. These rumrunners would keep their boats twelve miles offshore from Montauk, Long Island, just past US territorial waters, in a lineup that became known as Rum Row. Each night, a flotilla or small craft would dodge the Coast Guard and head for the Rum Line, where it would load up on bottles to bring back to the shores. The cargo was then either transported to speakeasies in the city or on Long Island or stashed for safekeeping in Montauk's sand dunes.

Of particular interest is the rumrunner Captain William McCoy, who regularly sailed between the Bahamas and New York in his schooner *Arethusa* and who is credited with establishing Rum Row. According to legend, McCoy established his reputation by supplying pure, high-quality Scotch whisky and rye rather than watering down the liquor as other bootleggers were doing to meet the high demand. As you may have guessed, his quality products became known as "The Real McCoy."

1928

Abe, the Times Square Tiger Cat Who Refused to Scat from the Hotel Lincoln

A half-grown cat has adopted the Hotel Lincoln as its permanent home. Cats have always been regarded as a good omen, especially when they come to the door unsolicited. This kitten has a special history. He was born on the site of the present hotel, and spent his life in the debris while the hotel was in course of construction. Let us all be kind to our new mascot. His name from now on is Abe.

—James T. Clyde, manager of the Hotel Lincoln,
March 1928

In the spring of 1927, when Abe and his two siblings were born, crews were working frantically to erect a new thirty-story hotel on the east side of Eighth Avenue between Forty-Fourth and Forty-Fifth Streets. The men had already demolished the block of old brick-with-brownstone-front buildings and were now trying to set a record to build a grand hotel on the site. Before the debris was cleared and the concrete caissons were sunk, a mother cat gave birth to three male kittens.

Abe, like his mother, was a white cat with gray tiger markings. One of his brothers was black with a white star on his breast, and the other was mouse colored. For several weeks after their birth, the steel workers shared their slabs of pork and salami with the mother cat and her kittens. As news of the litter spread, people from the theater district brought milk and biscuits for the kitties. When the kittens were big enough to run over the steel girders and mama cat felt they could be left on their own, she disappeared into the city streets. The black and gray kittens also left the construction site, leaving the white and tiger-striped cat to fend for himself. As the weeks went by, the construction workers continued to share their lunches with the kitten. Pedestrians and others in the area would stop by to scratch his ears and stroke his fur. Life was good;

but winter was coming, and what was going to be the largest hotel west of Broadway was almost ready to open for business.

The $11 million Hotel Lincoln opened its large, bronze doors on January 31, 1928, just ten months after construction began. The new doorman, who took his job very seriously, was not about to let a stray cat through these doors, and so the little kitten sat on the pavement in the falling snow and waited patiently for the right moment. Luckily, it didn't take long for opportunity to knock. One day when the doorman had turned his back on the open doors, the brazen kitten jumped inside and scampered up the carpeted stairs. He found a comfy chair on the mezzanine level and took what was probably the best catnap in his life.

Life was good for Abe at the luxurious Hotel Lincoln. Not only was he adopted by a very prestigious hotel manager, but he also had a French chef who served his daily dish of meat and a parlor maid who brought him fresh milk every day. Abe loved all the attention, especially from the hotel guests. Any time a guest remarked, "Oh, what a beautiful cat!" Abe would shake the bell on his shiny red collar in appreciation. For those who offered their lap or made the effort to pet him, Abe rewarded them with a hearty purr. One news reporter theorized that the purr in human language translated to, "You can get away with anything if you try hard enough."

Abe owed his life to James T. Clyde, a prominent restaurateur and hotelier who loved animals, especially the thoroughbred horses, cattle, and other animals that lived on his farm in Columbus, Ohio. Born in Philadelphia in 1862, Clyde was an athletic man who excelled in boxing, swimming, and rowing at the University of Pittsburgh. During his early career, he traveled extensively with carnivals and circuses in Australia, the United States, and Europe. He managed numerous hotels in New York, St. Paul, Boston, Cincinnati, Seattle, and Chicago, as well as several athletic clubs in Chicago, Columbus, and New York. In January 1915, John Willy, writing in the *Hotel Monthly*, said this of Abe's hero: "Mr. Clyde is widely known as a caterer who has earned a reputation for rejuvenating hotels and clubs, changing them from losers to winners." By the time Clyde was asked to manage the Hotel Lincoln in 1928, he was approaching sixty-five years old and ready for retirement.

Two years after Abe moved in, Clyde left the hotel and returned to his farm in Ohio. I'm not sure if he took Abe with him, but I have a feeling Abe would have been too stubborn to leave his hotel life.

In 1939, the Hotel Lincoln was sold to Maria Kramer, a dancer and wife of Max J. Kramer, who owned the Hotel Edison on West Forty-Sixth Street. During this era, the hotel was under the management of Frank J. Kridel, who had taken over sometime around 1935. The hotel continued to do fairly well through the 1930s and 1940s, but less than thirty years after Abe the cat moved into the Hotel Lincoln, the once-grand hotel had become a run-down apartment hotel. By the 1950s, French chefs and parlor maids were only a faded memory in a building that was now just a shell with empty, ghostly hallways. (And I do mean ghostly: during the Great Depression years, more than a dozen people jumped from the upper floors to their deaths or hung themselves in their hotel rooms.) In 1956, the developer William Zeckendorf got permission to evict seven long-time rent-controlled tenants. These holdout residents put up quite a fight. Even when offered similar accommodations at the Knicker-bocker on West Forty-Fourth Street, the tenants refused to scat. Not until the developer offered each person $3,000 to promptly vacate did the tenants leave their home. The last to move out was Edna King, a guest since 1929 who had probably stopped to pet Abe on many occasions.

In 1958, the Hotel Lincoln reopened as the Hotel Manhattan. The hotel had a short stint as the Royal Manhattan when some English developers purchased it in 1964, but by then it was way past its prime. By the late 1970s, the hotel had been boarded up and left for dead. In 1978, Paul and Seymour Milstein purchased the Royal Manhattan and renamed it the Milford Plaza. They reportedly gave it that name because they did not want to change the huge neon "M" on the roof. The Milstein family was ready to throw in the towel following the economic downturn in 2009, but a year later Rockpoint Group and the hotel operator Highgate Holdings purchased the hotel for $250 million and began an extensive $140 million renovation. As part of the renovations, the lobby and all

1,331 guest rooms and suites were updated, and the neon sign was removed. In 2014, the hotel was renamed Row NYC.

DID YOU KNOW?

Step back in time 250 years, long before Thomas Edison's invention turned Broadway and Times Square into the "Great White Way." In those days, the land bounded by the old Bloomingdale Road (Broadway) and the Hudson River from about Forty-Second to Forty-Sixth Streets was owned by an English brewer-turned-farmer named Medcef Eden. Eden never had much luck with his onion and potato crops; hence, he was still in debt when he died in 1798.

Sometime around 1803, a well-to-do German American fur merchant and a lawyer named William Cutting purchased a one-third interest in an outstanding mortgage on the Eden farm. The men foreclosed on the mortgage and purchased for $25,000 a property that was worth close to $30 million one hundred years later. Cutting took the undeveloped western portion of the land near the Hudson River, and the fur merchant took the eastern section along the Bloomingdale Road, which also included two dwelling houses and two barns. Although Eden's heirs brought a suit against Cutting and the fur merchant—which dragged on for twenty years—the buyers prevailed in the end. After all, Cutting was the sheriff of the city and county of New York, and the fur merchant was John Jacob Astor.

Astor called his twenty-two-acre farm the "Farm at Bloomingdale" for the main road that formed the farm's eastern boundary. Opened under the Act of June 19, 1703, the Bloomingdale Road was the continuation of what was once called Bowery or New York Lane. The road began at Fourteenth Street and Fourth Avenue, crossed diagonally across present Union Square, and proceeded northerly to the junction of the Old Post Road at present Madison Square. From there it was laid out northwesterly "the breadth of four rods" beginning from the house of John Horn at Twenty-Third Street and Fifth Avenue and terminating at the house of Adrian Hooglandt and the barn of Nicholas de Peyster near 116th Street (now the site of Columbia University). Astor's farm was located at the road's four-mile stone, meaning it was four miles from Federal Hall on Wall Street.

Whenever I pass by the towering Row NYC hotel on Eighth Avenue today, I try to imagine what it was like when an English farmer grew onions and potatoes on the land we call Times Square and where long ago a mother cat gave birth to a special kitten named Abe.

1936

Rusty, the Famous Feline Host of the Algonquin Hotel

Rusty, the Algonquin's "snooty cat" . . . ignores more celebrities than the Social Register. . . . It's whispered around by those who claim to know that he really runs the place.
                    —Dorothy Kilgallen, "Voice of Broadway"

In 1936, a disheveled kitten about seven months old stepped into the lobby of New York City's Algonquin Hotel on Forty-Fourth Street. Like most stray cats, he was fighting for survival on the streets, and a hotel lobby was as good a place as any to beg for food and shelter. Frank Case, the legendary owner of the Algonquin, welcomed this feline hotel guest, even though the interloper was just a ragamuffin street cat. Somehow, he knew there was something special about this orange cat with perfect tabby markings. Plus, the hotel needed a new cat to replace hotel cat Billy, who had arrived at the Algonquin around 1921 and had died just three days earlier. As Case wrote in his memoir *Please Don't Disturb*, "Three days later a new cat came in and without so much as by your leave took up right where Billy left off. It was as if he had heard there was an opening and came in and applied for it, only he didn't apply, he just took the job." Case named the cat Rusty, and the rest, as they say, is history.

Over the years, Rusty grew into a very distinguished cat, weighing eighteen pounds at his prime. He was a favorite among the actors, artists, and writers who frequented the hotel, and he especially loved new guests. Rusty would greet and nudge each new guest warmly and incorrigibly—he'd often have to be pushed off the register so they could sign it. (What's with cats lying on newspapers and books?) He also loved to nap smack in the center of the lobby during the lunch hour, which would force all the guests to detour around him as he dozed.

Rusty had a daily routine, which began every morning in the tenth-floor suite occupied by Frank and Bertha Case. Here, Bertha would prepare him for the hotel guests by grooming him. Rusty loved this ritual and would run to Bertha as soon as he saw the brush in her hands. Once presentable, Rusty would take the passenger elevator down to assist the Algonquin staff. For Rusty's convenience, a little swinging door between the lobby and the kitchen was installed so he could help with the kitchen staff and call on his dear friend the chef.

Sometimes Rusty would make a detour and get off the elevator on a specific floor to call on one of his favorite guests. According to Frank Case, Rusty knew exactly what floor he wanted to get off, and so if he wished to get off on the eighth floor, no persuasion or coaxing would get him to exit at the seventh floor. He also knew whether the elevator was going his way. "If he is on the eighth floor wishing to go down and the operator on the way up stops and opens the door for him, the cat just sits and looks at him," Case wrote in *Do Not Disturb*. "He is not going to ride all the way up to the top floor; no indeed. So the car goes on up without him and on the return trip the patient elevator man stops again, opens the door, his royal catness steps in and descends with dignity to the ground floor."

Rusty spent much of the day with Louie the bartender in the Blue Bar, where the cat had a special stool reserved just for him. He'd show up for duty before noon, when guests began arriving, and following his catnap, he'd return to keep guard until early afternoon, when the lunch crowd thinned out. When he finally had the bar and Louie to himself, Rusty would drum his front paws on the counter to demand his daily shot of milk. Rusty would only drink the milk if Louie served it in a champagne glass; a wine glass, beer glass, or highball glass would not do. Sometimes Louie would whistle songs, and Rusty would sort of sway to the music as if dancing. Then promptly at 4:00 p.m. he'd jump off his stool and get back on the elevator with his guardian, Germaine Legrand, the Case family's housekeeper. Back in the Case suite, Rusty would get another snifter of milk in a champagne glass and then take a late-afternoon nap. Following the dinner hour, he'd appear at the bar again for his next tour of duty, and then he'd head back upstairs for the night around 10:00 p.m.

Life at the Algonquin Hotel wasn't always easy for Rusty, especially during the early years, when the hotel allowed temporary residents to have dogs. Rusty had quite a few run-ins with canines over the years. One time a French poodle that was staying at the hotel gave Rusty quite a tussle, and the poor cat hid under a bed for several days. He also suffered from a bout of pneumonia and had to be placed in an oxygen tent at the Ellin Prince Speyer Hospital for Animals. According to one news report, "The news of his desperate illness spread rapidly and the Algonquin phone was kept busy." A local radio station reportedly put out bulletins to keep the public informed of his status.

Summers were extra special for Rusty, because he got to take a break from the city and spend weekends at the Case family's summer home, Shore Acre Farm. The home was located on Actors Colony Road and Cedar Avenue in the Village of North Haven, on a small island just off Sag Harbor on the eastern end of Long Island. Case had purchased the waterfront summer home in June 1919 from Lilian Backus, the widow of Eben Y. Backus, who was the stage manager for the Empire Theatre on Forty-Second Street. The home was located in a cottage colony of actors, and many famous thespians who also lived or vacationed at the colony, including Douglass Fairbanks and Mary Pickford, would often visit the family and Rusty.

On February 21, 1946, five years after Rusty won his long battle with pneumonia, Bertha Case succumbed to a year-long illness and died in the Cases' hotel suite. Four months later, on June 7, Frank Case died in the hotel. Following his death, Frank's body was laid in state in the suite. John Martin, manager of the hotel, held Rusty in his arms and let him take a last look at his master. Martin told the press that as he held Rusty, a shudder appeared to go through the cat's body. He also uttered a strange cry.

For several days, Rusty refused to eat or roam the premises. He no longer visited Martin on Sundays, as he had done for years. Martin took him to the Ellin Prince Speyer Hospital for Animals, where the depressed cat was diagnosed with jaundice complicated by leukemia. Less than two weeks after Frank Case's death, Martin

Hamlet, the newest Algonquin cat, arrived at the hotel in 2017. (Photo courtesy of the Algonquin Hotel)

found Rusty in the suite, curled beside the bed of his old master. Rusty was buried in the Cases' garden at their summer home in North Haven.

Although complications from the jaundice and feline leukemia were no doubt the cause of Rusty's death, for those who knew him, he simply died of a broken heart. "Rusty was sick from missing the two people he loved best," Legrand told the *Sun*. "Always he was looking at the door as if he wondered why they didn't come."

More than eighty years following Rusty's passing, the iconic twelve-story hotel at 59 West Forty-Fourth Street still has a resident cat. In fact, in all these years, the Algonquin has never been without a feline host or hostess. The three female cats have all been named Matilda, and the male cats, other than Rusty and Billy, have all been named Hamlet in honor of the Shakespearian actor John Barrymore. (Barrymore, who was best known for his portrayal of Hamlet in London and on Broadway, had tried to give Rusty the name Hamlet, but the name apparently didn't catch on with Frank Case or the New York press.) All but one of the Algonquin cats have been rescues.

Hamlet (Hammy), the newest Algonquin cat, is the hotel's twelfth cat and its first male mascot in forty years. He replaced Matilda III, a regal long-haired ragdoll who was rescued after being abandoned in a box outside the North Shore Animal League in Port Washington, New York, in 2010 and who passed away in 2017. Hamlet came to the Algonquin via the Bideawee animal rescue in Wantagh, Long Island, which had taken in the former feral-colony cat with a clipped left ear when he showed up at its door. When the employees found out the Algonquin was looking for a short-haired orange tabby like Rusty, they knew this adorable kitty would make the perfect Hamlet. Having had the pleasure of meeting Hamlet in person, I can personally vouch for his perfection.

Although most of the Algonquin cats have had full run of the hotel, that freedom was taken away in 2011 with a directive from the New York City Department of Health, which required the hotel cat to remain in areas where food is not prepared or served. The hotel installed an electric fence to keep the cat out of the dining areas, but that did not satisfy the Department of Health. Because of this directive, there is no longer a special stool at the bar reserved for the hotel's feline and no longer a kitty door to the kitchen for Hamlet or any future Algonquin cats.

6

Theatrical and
Show Cats

Although James T. Hyde's National Cat Show in 1895 is often cited as the first cat show in America, there were actually quite a few cat exhibits in New York City and other American cities before this first proper cat fancy show took place at Madison Square Garden. During the late 1800s, New York poultry and pet-stock shows often included a cat exhibit as a secondary attraction. Groups such as the New York Poultry, Pig, and Stock Association managed the shows, which often attracted thousands of entries, including hundreds of cats. While some owners at these events described their cats as Persian, Angora, or Maltese, most of the cats on display were domestic house cats and back-fence hoodlums that were remarkable for their size, color, weight, or talents. In the 1870s and 1880s, many of these exhibitions took place at dime museums, where the cats would sometimes be on display in stacked wooden boxes or cages for up to a week as part of a cat-themed event. These shows often included performing cats on stage or a taxidermy display of cats posed in anthropomorphic settings such as a tea party or photography session.

One hundred years before the hit musical *Cats* made its debut on Broadway, performing cats were also popular at places like Tony Pastor's Opera House on the Bowery and Oscar Hammerstein's Olympia Theatre on Broadway. One of the most popular cat trainers on the New York City vaudeville circuit in the late 1800s was Herr Professor George Techow of Hamburg, Germany, whose performing felines could do a wide range of tricks that ranged from walking on two front paws to jumping through hoops of fire on tightropes.

For those vagrant cats without talent or the right connections, there were also opportunities to vicariously enjoy stardom by working as a theater mouser or by schmoozing with the actors of stage and screen at New York City's various social clubs. Sometimes these mascot cats, like Union Square Jim of the Union Square Theatre and Tommy Casanova Lamb of The Lambs theatrical club, were even offered cameo opportunities that brought down the house.

1877–1881

The Felines of the Cat Congress on Bowery and Broadway

In 1877, an impromptu Cat Congress took place at George B. Bunnell's New American Museum, a popular dime museum located at 103–105 Bowery. The December exhibit featured several hundred cats, including, as one newspaper reported, "some of the greatest curiosities to be found." Among the entrants were two albino cats, an eighteen-year-old toothless cat, a cat from Egypt weighing only four ounces, and a double-toed, web-footed cat from Germany. There were reportedly also cats with six and seven toes; cats with three, six, and even eight legs; and a few fat cats from New Jersey, including a nineteen-pound cat from Jersey City and a thirty-pound cat from Hudson City. One of the most valuable entries was a show cat that had traveled with P. T. Barnum's circus for seven years. There were also several "silver-spoon" felines, including a Brooklyn hero cat that had aroused and saved his family when their house caught fire.

The *Brooklyn Standard Union* summarized the show as follows:

The New York cat show appears to be a sort of asylum for purse-proud, aristocratic cats, or those which exhibit some exceptional intelligence or tail or something. The real old corsairs of the dark nights, whose voices have tunefully mingled with the clash of boot-jacks, tin dippers and No. 4 shot, are not there. Neither is there present the nervous old rounder who has escaped from the midnight melee with knotty protuberances on his head and a tail resembling a hair-mounted joint of stove-pipe. The show is very incomplete.

Four years later, to kick off the 1881 Cat Congress, George Bunnell announced he would offer a ten-dollar prize for the best short essay on cats. The response was overwhelming. Within days, his office floor was covered with 557 funny, serious, and poetic essays about cats. The briefest entry came from a man who said he hadn't had a good night's sleep in a long time. "Damn all cats anyway" was all he wrote. The winning essay was written by the *New York World* journalist Walter C. Quevedo of Brooklyn, who attached his page-long ode to felines to a little wooden "tipcat" game piece. In his essay, "This Is a Cat," Quevedo compared cats to the average German band and the fiddle and had some fun playing on words: "The cat is a cuss that mews and purrs, be-cuss, perhaps, it a-mew-ses him. He is covered with fur, filled with deceitfulness and abounds in cheek. I said that on-purr-puss."

One of the favorite felines featured at the 1881 Cat Congress was a thirteen-year-old tomcat named Humpty Dumpty. According to the *New York Times*, Humpty had previously been owned by the late George L. Fox, an American actor and comedian who created a comical clown character called Humpty Dumpty in 1867. The cat had reportedly won a lifesaving medal for saving Fox's life during a house fire. According to the anecdote, Humpty Dumpty jumped up on Fox's bed and started scratching his face to awake him and alert him to the fire. Over the years, Fox trained Humpty to do several tricks; the veteran cat was still able to perform a few of them in his old age.

Another crowd-pleaser was a cat named General Washington. The *New York Times* said General Washington "was a black and white gentleman cat, with an intellectual breadth of forehead and a frank open face. His great-grandfather is alleged to have witnessed the surrender of [British General Charles] Cornwallis some years ago. There may be some mistake about his ancestry, but it will not be denied that he himself is a handsome specimen."

Here's how the *Times* summed up the 1881 show:

> Manager Bunnell stood in the center of his museum on Broadway, his hands in his hair, utterly perplexed. . . . He was surrounded by cats in cages, cats in wooden boxes, cats in band-boxes, cats in bags, half of them yelling, spitting, and scratching, as mad as cats can be in uncomfortable quarters and in a strange place. . . . Some of the cats are remarkable for their size, color, stripes, and weight. By far the greater number possess all the characteristics of the back-fence tenors.

When most of us hear the name P. T. Barnum, we think of the circus and "The Greatest Show on Earth." But many years before P. T. Barnum's Grand Traveling Museum, Menagerie, Caravan, and Circus made its debut in 1871—and forty years before he partnered with James A. Bailey—Phineas Taylor Barnum rose to fame during the era of the American dime museum. Popular between the 1840s and about 1900, dime museums featured an eclectic range of entertainment and scientific exhibits, including human and animal "freaks of nature," wax-figure displays, and vaudeville performances. Barnum's dime museum, which he established in 1841 on the southeast corner of Broadway and Ann Street, featured a large collection of artificial and natural curiosities from around the world, including whales, eels, kangaroos, "mermaids," and about five hundred thousand other objects of curiosity. The cost of admission was twenty-five cents.

In 1876, eleven years after Barnum's American Museum burned to the ground in a horrific fire that killed almost all the animals on display, George Bunnell entered the dime-museum business in

On June 1, 1879, all of the contents of George Bunnell's Great American Museum at 298 Bowery (middle building), including "an educated pig," were destroyed by a fire that completely gutted the building's interior. Today the building is home to Chef Restaurant Supplies. (Photo by the author)

New York. He purchased the collection of George Wood's Museum and Metropolitan Theatre at 1221 Broadway and opened his own New American Museum at 103–105 Bowery, which is where the Cat Congress of 1877 took place. In March 1879, he opened a combination museum, music hall, and lodging house in a new five-story brick building at 298 Bowery, then owned by Georgiana B. English. (This site was formerly occupied by an eighteenth-century farmhouse and ale house that later became the Bowery Cottage and Harry B. Venn's Gotham Saloon [aka Gotham Cottage], which was headquarters for the city's volunteer firefighters in the 1840s and the Gotham Base Ball Club in the 1850s). As with many theaters and museums of that era, Bunnell's museum caught fire soon after it opened, forcing him to find another location. In December 1880, he moved his museum to 771 Broadway, a four-story brick building owned by the Felix Effray estate. This building had previously been home to Effray's French chocolate shop and L. Leroy's apothecary (1850s) and, later, O'Sullivan & Greig's clothing and dry-goods store

(1860s–1870s). It was in this building, which featured six rooms of curiosities, that the Cat Congress of 1881 took place.

Although the New American Museum was quite successful, it didn't last long at 771 Broadway. In 1883, the Sailor's Snug Harbor Corporation, which owned much of the surrounding property, purchased the building and replaced the dime museum with a six-story brick-and-iron building for retail purposes. Bunnell headed north and established a dime museum in Buffalo, New York. After this building was destroyed in a fatal fire in March 1887, he took his museum to New Haven, Connecticut, which is where he stayed until his death on May 3, 1911.

DID YOU KNOW?

In 1955, a fourteen-story apartment building called the Randall House was constructed on the northwest corner of Broadway and Ninth Street, on the very spot where George Bunnell operated his dime museum from 1880 to 1883. The Randall House was named for Captain Robert Richard Randall, a Revolutionary War soldier and former sea captain who owned most of the land bounded by Tenth Street, Waverly Place, Fifth Avenue, and the Bowery Lane (present-day Fourth Avenue) in what is now Greenwich Village.

Born in New Jersey in about 1740, Robert Richard Randall inherited his father's vast estate in downtown Manhattan when Captain Thomas Randall, a daring privateer, died in 1797. In 1790, Robert Richard Randall paid £5,000 to purchase the old Minto estate on what was then called Sandy Hill from Frederick Charles Hans Bruno Poelnitz (also known as Baron Poelnitz), who had been using the land for "fancy farming." The twenty-one-acre Minto estate had previously been owned by Andrew Elliot, the last royal governor of the Province of New York (1780). Elliot had begun purchasing the land, which extended from the Bowery westward to the present Sixth Avenue, in 1776. He named the estate in honor of his father, Sir Gilbert Elliott, who was the Second Baronet of Minto, a village in Scotland. Baron Poelnitz acquired Minto shortly after Andrew Elliott fled the city during the British evacuation in 1783.

When Captain Randall purchased Minto from Baron Poelnitz in 1790, Randall was a "retiring old bachelor" who was living "a quiet and lonely life." At the suggestion of his attorney, Alexander Hamilton (who reportedly drew up Randall's will), Randall requested that upon his death, the Minto farm be used as a snug harbor, in other words, "an asylum, or Marine

Hospital to maintain and to support aged, decrepit, and worn-out sailors." The land was good for farming, so Randall thought the residents living at the Sailors' Snug Harbor would be able to sustain themselves by growing their own grain and vegetables.

Following Randall's death in 1801, his relatives immediately contested the will. It was not until 1831 that the matter was settled by the Supreme Court of the United States. By this time, the property—which included the northern edge of Washington Square Park—had become so valuable that the Trustees of the Sailors' Snug Harbor thought it better to subdivide the land into 253 leasable lots. The trustees used the lease money to purchase from Isaac Houseman a 130-acre farm on the north shore of Staten Island for about $10,000.

The Sailors' Snug Harbor on Staten Island, the country's first home for retired merchant seaman, opened on August 1, 1833. Over the next century, the institution expanded from three buildings to fifty structures and nine hundred residents from every corner of the world. In 1975, the Snug Harbor Cultural Center was formed to operate the buildings. The Staten Island Botanical Gardens stepped in to manage the gardens. The two organizations merged in 2008, which created the Snug Harbor Cultural Center & Botanical Garden. The Sailors' Snug Harbor Trust, considered to be one of the oldest secular philanthropies in the country, continues to assist eligible mariners throughout the country.

1888

Union Square Jim, the Mascot Cat of the Union Square Theatre

Like most cats that became the popular mascots of New York City police stations, fire stations, hotels, and theaters in the 1800s and 1900s, Jim began his life as a vagrant cat without friends or influence. It didn't take him long, however, to win the hearts of the managers, actors, and patrons of the old Union Square Theatre. In fact, one might say he literally stole the show.

A reporter for the *Detroit Free Press* wrote in a feature story about the theater's blue-eyed, orange tabby mascot cat on August 14, 1887, "Union Square Jim is either an exceptional cat or a proof of my ignorance concerning the kind." The reporter noted that the large sorrel cat was first and foremost a sociable cat with an expressive face who loved human companionship.

Jim made his home under the stage of the Union Square Theatre at 58 East Fourteenth Street, between Broadway and Fourth Avenue. At that time, the theater was under the management of James M. Hill. Jim's favorite person was the janitor Mike Sweeney, but he also enjoyed visiting all the members of the acting companies in their dressing rooms before every performance. He was quite talented— for example, he could "sing," shake paws, stand on his hind legs, "and otherwise distinguish himself in a remarkable way from the ordinary race of cats"—and he found himself in the spotlight on more than one occasion. One might say that Jim had a knack for turning a sorrowful and serious drama scene into a comedy act that brought down the house with laughter and howls of delight.

Our story begins in 1886, in an unused dressing room of the theater. There, according to Harmon Lee Ensign, author of *Lady Lee and Other Animal Stories*, a quiet brindle cat named Roxy gave birth to five kittens. The kittens were discovered by a gasman named George (more probably janitor Mike Sweeney), who cared for the mother cat for several weeks so she in turn could feed her kittens. According to Ensign's version of the story, one night the mother cat was severely injured when a disgruntled actor kicked her against a corridor wall. Although she suffered greatly from broken ribs and other injuries, Roxy cared for her kittens for five more days until she passed away. Although the gasman tried to save them all, only one of the five survived after their mother's death. A few weeks later, the smallest of the litter was a strong and mischievous kitten named Jim.

As a kitten, Jim spent most of the day under the stage, either in the dark passageways or in the dressing rooms. At night, after the final curtain had come down and the crowds dispersed, Jim would follow Sweeney on his janitorial rounds. Every night man and cat would walk together from the cellar, where the scenery was stored, to the roof, where the moonlight came streaming through the skylights. During their time together, Sweeney taught Jim many tricks, like standing erect, walking and "boxing" on his hind legs, and flicking his tail to the left or right on command. Jim was quite intelligent, and over time he also learned how to put on a show by weeping in mock mews, posing like different actors, and performing numerous acrobatic tricks.

A few months after his first birthday, Jim was introduced to the theater proper. There, he mingled with stagehands, actors, and other prominent people of the New York theater world. He was cuddled and coddled by his admirers and friends, who all considered him the mascot of the institution. One of Jim's biggest fans was Madame Helena Modjeska, a well-known actress who specialized in Shakespearean and tragic roles. She gave him a wicker cradle stuffed with rich bedding materials. Jim was quite partial to this bed and supposedly would not sleep on anything else. Jim also had a lady admirer in Bangor, Maine, who once sent him a plump package of catnip. According to the *New York Times*, Jim enjoyed the catnip "with the relish of an epicure." He was also welcomed by the theater manager, James Hill, who considered him a good-luck charm for the theater. Hill valued the cat so much that he would reportedly fire any employee who tried to harm Jim—but not after giving the employee a lecture on animal cruelty.

One afternoon during the summer of 1887, a skylight on the roof sprung a leak during a heavy rainstorm. Sweeney reportedly went on the roof to fix it, and he took his feline friend along to get some fresh air and sunshine. As the janitor was in the progress of repairing the skylight, he heard a loud crash. Looking up from what he was doing, he saw that Jim had fallen through another skylight and was frantically trying to hang onto the framework with one paw. Right before Sweeney's eyes, Jim lost his claw-grip and fell about eighty feet to the center of the auditorium below. Sweeney rushed down the stairs and ran into the auditorium, where he found Jim lying motionless between two rows of iron-backed chairs. He carried the unconscious cat into his room and tended to Jim as best he could with alcohol and bandages. Sharing the story with the author Harmon Lee Ensign, Sweeney said, "Poor Jim! I know I'm a good deal better man for his influence. I aint ashamed to own that his life has been a good example for me. Many's the time I've been tempted to swear, and Jim's innocent blue eyes would come up before me and choke the words on my lips."

Two weeks after his fall, Jim was alert and miraculously back on his feet again, making the rounds with Sweeney as if the plunge from the roof had never happened. In fact, on September 26, 1887, Jim was well enough to make his accidental stage debut during opening night of *The Henrietta*, a romantic comedy written by Bronson Howard and produced by the comedians Stuart Robson and William Henry Crane. According to accounts of the incident in the *New York Times*, Jim got a bit frisky onstage and almost spoiled a scene, but the audience appreciated his antics. Robson and Crane were angry at the large orange tabby at first, but they came to love Jim over the next few months. They even tried to buy Jim from Hill and change his name to Henrietta. Hill had to decline the offer because, one, Jim was a male and, two, the mascot cat brought good luck to the theater (at least up to that point in time).

On the afternoon of February 28, 1888, a fire broke out in a loft between the ceiling and roof of the auditorium of the theater. The flames were discovered by stage carpenters and painters, who had been working on the stage with Ben Teal, the stage manager. Hill was also in the building at the time; one of the stagehands ran into his office to warn him of the fire. Union Square Jim was in the basement of the building, but no one came to warn the cat as he slept peacefully in his wicker basket.

The large fire caused extensive damage as it burned through the partitions that separated the theater from the surrounding Morton House hotel (all the hotel guests had been safely evacuated before it reached this point). The two upper stories of the hotel caught fire, and the roof of the theater was demolished. Six firemen were critically injured when they were buried under the debris of a staircase that collapsed. Remarkably, when the firemen got the fire under control about three hours later, the walls of the hotel and theater were still intact even though the interior of the theater was gutted.

"Has anyone seen Jim?" Sweeney asked everyone when he arrived on the scene later that afternoon. When no one answered, he asked one of the firemen to help him find the mascot cat. Carrying lanterns, the two men made their way through the smoky basement corridor to the dressing room where Jim spent his days sleeping. There, in the flooded room, they found Jim perched on top of his basket, trying to stay dry with no means of escape in sight.

That evening, there was a reception in honor of Jim's rescue followed by a "general jollification" at the Hotel Hungaria "when Jim had been thoroughly dried out and recovered from his scare." Hill told everyone that he planned to reopen the theater in March; however, it took almost a year for the Union Square Theatre to open again. No immediate plans were made for Jim, so he continued to live by himself at the ruined theater for several months while the cleanup and rebuilding commenced.

Three months after the fire, the *New York Times* reported,

> Blonde Jim, the far-famed cat of the Union-Square Theatre, is in troubled spirits these days, and moves about his wonted haunts with an air of dejection almost human. . . . The chaotic and unsafe condition of the old Union-Square since the fire has driven the petted darling Jim to the narrow confines of the property room, . . . as dark and uninviting as a tomb, and here he has had the exercising swing of about 15 feet of chain and the silent company of himself. Accustomed to excitement and fond of the popular gaze, he has been slowly withering in spirit and flesh in this chilly back room, and last week refused to eat at all. This alarmed the old stage hands, and after a solemn council it was decided to take Jim each night at least to the Madison Square Theatre in the hope that the plan would revive his dropping spirits and health.

Jim's mood did change as soon as he saw his old friends at the Madison Square Theatre on Twenty-Fourth Street and Broadway. According to the article, "He purred incessantly, jumped upon chair and table, frisked about the carpet, and peeked through the curtain from time to time to watch the assembling audience." He even decided to take the stage again, this time in a brief appearance during the performance of *A Possible Cause* by Sydney Rosenfeld. In this cameo role, Jim reportedly leapt onto the lead actor during a dramatic scene and brought the house down with laughter as he purred and licked the actor's head and forehead in "a delirium of delight."

Although he was led offstage, there were many bursts of laughter from the crowd as the drama progressed, and after the last curtain, repeated calls were made for the theatrical cat to come out and take a bow.

I do not know for sure what happened to Jim in the end. One story suggests that he died at the Madison Square Theatre in a dramatic fashion after pouncing on a starlet's dress that had caught fire as she walked too close to the gas lights. But a small news article picked up by several daily newspapers in 1890 suggests that Jim died from an incurable illness and had been under the care of Benjamin G. Dovey, a veterinarian with a hospital for dogs and cats at 26 West Fourth Street, for some time.

The Union Square Theatre occupied a parcel of land that was once part of a large farm owned by Petrus (Peter) Stuyvesant, the last Dutch director-general of the colony of New Netherland. Stuyvesant's farm extended from the Bowery to the East River between present-day Third and Thirtieth Streets. In 1748, Cornelius Tiebout, a New York merchant, purchased part of this farm from one of Stuyvesant's heirs. Tiebout built a farmhouse near the intersection of present-day Eighteenth Street and Park Avenue South and named his estate Roxborough. One hundred years later, in 1849, the Union Place Hotel was built on the former Roxborough estate, on the south side of Fourteenth Street between Broadway and Fourth Avenue.

In 1871, Sheridan Shook, a butter and cheese merchant and former collector for the Thirty-Second Internal Revenue District of New York, signed a ten-year lease with Courtlandt Palmer, a wealthy hardware merchant and real estate speculator who owned the Union Place Hotel at this time. Shook renamed the hotel the Maison Dorée and hired chief constructor H. M. Simons to build a variety theater within the walls of the hotel. The main entrance to the theater was on Fourteenth Street; a separate entrance to the gallery and stage was on Fourth Avenue. The new theater opened on September 11, 1871, under the management of Robert W. Butler, a variety manager and former proprietor of the American

Concert Saloon at 414 Broadway. One year later, Albert Marshall Palmer, Shook's former clerk, took over the theater. Under Palmer's management, the theater operated as the Union Square Theatre Stock Company. Fifteen years later, when Jim the cat entered the scene, the Maison Dorée was a refurbished hotel called the Morton House, and the theater within the hotel was called the Union Square Theatre.

A year after the fire of 1888, the Union Square Theatre was completely rebuilt. The revamped theater featured a horseshoe balcony that rose in the center to make good use of the high, narrow space. The interior was painted in old gold and ivory, and the surviving proscenium arch (the frame in front of the curtain that separates the stage from the auditorium) was embellished with a large medallion featuring a portrait of Shakespeare. The hand-carved cherry chairs were upholstered in electric blue.

In 1893, Benjamin Franklin Keith and Edward Franklin Albee, the most powerful and successful vaudeville producers of their time, purchased the lease for the Union Square Theatre and remodeled it again. They offered continuous vaudeville at their new venue—in fact, the song-and-dance man George M. Cohan made his New York debut on its stage. In 1906, the theater—now called B. F. Keith's Theatre—exhibited some early motion pictures, and in 1908, it was converted once again to showcase only films. The theater also dabbled in "the most dubious activities that a picture house can indulge in," according to the *New York Herald Tribune*, referring to racy films and lectures about sex. B. F. Keith's Theatre and the old Morton House hotel were sold at auction in May 1920 for the benefit of the Palmer heirs. The theater was renamed the Acme in 1921, and it continued to run films until 1936. That year, the ground floor, where the orchestra section of the theater's auditorium was located, was sealed off and divided to create space for offices and some dry-goods stores.

In 1986, the Philips International Corporation acquired the site and vacated the buildings. Six years later, as the exterior of the building was peeled away during the demolition process, the last ruined remnants of the old Union Square Theatre were revealed. Although many features of the old theater were still intact, including the proscenium arch, the fire-ravaged finishes, still brown with smoke, held the lost memories of a fire that almost took the life of Union Square Jim.

1895

Nicodemus, the Prize-Winning Alley Cat of the Prankster Brian G. Hughes

Mr. Brian Hughes died the other day at his farm in Monroe, N.Y., and with his passing New York lost its master jokesmith, the originator of countless practical jokes that made everybody laugh, even their victims. Although a successful banker and manufacturer, he was more widely known for his ability to joke than for his commercial successes. His entire career was one of devastating jocularity. He lived to be 75 years old, and almost to the day of his death he was getting as much fun out of life as was possible.

—Philadelphia Inquirer Magazine, January 4, 1925

Brian G. Hughes was a paper-box manufacturer and real estate investor who leased offices in the north end of the Centre Market building at 242 Centre Street. Although his businesses were successful, Hughes was associated more with his signature pranks on New York socialites than with his boxes and real estate holdings.

One of Hughes's biggest jokes involved a stray cat that he had purchased for a dime in 1895 from a young bootblack on Hester Street. The bootblack was just about to drown the cat in the East River when Hughes noticed that the stray had six toes. He figured a cat with six toes would probably make a great mouser for his box factory. As it turns out, the cat wasn't much of a mouser (probably because Hughes fed him too well). The dark-gray cat did, however, hold his head at what Hughes called an "aristocratic angle." That gave Hughes an idea for a prank. He took the cat home and had him carefully washed and brushed. Then he paid the one-dollar fee and entered the cat in the first National Cat Show as a "brindled Dublin tomcat."

He told the judges the cat's name was Nicodemus, by Bowery, out of Dust-Pan, by Sweeper, by Ragtag-and-Bobtail. He also said the cat's pedigree went back to a mummified cat that was found in an Egyptian tomb.

At the show, Nicodemus was placed on display on a silk cushion inside a gold-plated cage surrounded by roses and attended to by a woman in a nurse's gown. Every day, a livery footman by the name of Sam Smith would arrive with ice cream and chicken packed in the boxes of a celebrated caterer. A florist would also deliver flowers to the alley cat every day. The other cats, including those belonging to Mrs. Stanford White, Miss Louisa Morgan, and Mrs. John J. Astor, could only look on in envy.

Naturally, Nicodemus created a great sensation at the show, especially among cat fanciers who saw great potential in the six-toed cat. Even though Hughes advertised Nicodemus as a $1,000 cat who was not for sale, he received several offers of $2,000 and more for the former street urchin. Hughes told the press, "It seems to me, though, from the offers I've had, there must be a cat famine in New York, and a chance for someone to go into the cat business." The judges voted Nicodemus the sole winner in the class for brown and dark-gray tomcats, which earned him a blue ribbon and a $50 prize.

Despite all the attention and great food, Nicodemus apparently did not like the high life. According to news reports, he broke away from his attendant on the last day of the show and disappeared into the city streets. A few days later, however, the hungry cat showed up at Hughes's offices in the old Centre Street market.

A year later, at the 1896 National Cat Show, Hughes pulled the stunt again with the same cat. But this time, the joke was on him when it was discovered that his "male" cat was a female who was pregnant with kittens. According to the *Philadelphia Times*, Nicodemus had been placed in a class for "he" cats with short hair. When the only other entry in this class, a cat named Dot, was disqualified for having white whiskers, Nicodemus won the only prize. When the owner of Dot lodged a protest, the committee asked him why he had contested the winner. The *Philadelphia Times* reported the conversation and incident as follows:

"The class calls for he cats, don't it?" said the owner of Dot. "It does," replied the committee in chorus. "Well, Nicodemus is not that kind of a cat." The committee members looked surprised and the judges pooh-poohed. "Come and see for yourselves," said the owner of Dot. Forthwith the committee attended the inspection in a body. One of the judges looked over Nicodemus critically, and there, sure enough, Nicodemus was discovered to be of the feminine gender. The committee was somewhat amused at the mistake, and of course disqualified Nicodemus.

Still determined to have the last laugh and make a huge joke of the pedigree cat business, Hughes pulled the trick again in 1899 at the International Cat Show. This time he disguised his name as Nairb G. Sehguh. He also disguised Nicodemus by completely shaving her (save for her head and the tip of her tail). Hughes told the show organizers that his new female cat, Eulata, was a native of Hindustan who was once a mascot on the Spanish ship *Vizcaya*. When the ship sank in 1898 during the Spanish-American War, Brian explained, Eulata swam to the USS *Oregon* and was rescued by sailors. As if that story wasn't good enough, Hughes also said the cat had been presented to the king of Spain by a Bombay merchant, who in turn presented her to Captain Don Antonio Eulate of the *Vizcaya*.

During the 1899 show, Eulata dined from silver dishes, slept on velvet cushions, and was occasionally sprayed with violet perfume. Her gilded cage, which was carried in by four attendants, was bedecked with fresh roses, violets, hyacinths, and carnations. On top were US and Spanish flags, a doll's trunk labeled "Eulata," and an assortment of food in a box stamped "From Sherry's." The floor of the cage was covered with a velvet carpet, and the pampered cat had her own silver brush, comb, and toothbrush for her toilet. Although the cat was like nothing the judges had ever seen before, they eventually realized it was all a joke again when they figured out that Nairb G. Sehguh was Brian G. Hughes spelled backward.

Since the cat pranks got so many laughs, Hughes decided to try something similar with a horse in 1900. A few months before the National Horse Show opened at Madison Square Garden, he purchased an old streetcar mare from the Metropolitan Street Railway Company for $11.50. Hughes got such a great deal because the horse was about to lose her job pulling a car on the Fifty-Ninth Street line. An old horse was simply no match for an electric trolley car.

Hughes sent the horse to his farm, Brightside, in Monroe, New York, and told his head stable man that he was entering her in the horse show. Hughes said every cent of the $500 prize money would go to the man who was able to get the horse into condition to compete. For the next two months, the old car horse got the lion's share of attention in the stable, including tonic pills and consultations with a veterinary surgeon. Satisfied that the horse was ready to compete and win, Hughes entered her in the National Horse Show as "Puldeka Orphan, by Metropolitan, dam Electricity."

At Madison Square Garden, Puldeka was placed in a stall surrounded by flowers and attended to by two livery grooms. She looked majestic in the arena, with Hughes's eighteen-year-old daughter, Clara, at the reins. Everything would have gone smoothly, and Puldeka may have even won the $500 prize, had the judges failed to notice the small bell placed under her saddle. You see, Puldeka was a streetcar horse who was accustomed to responding to bells (one bell for *start* and two bells for *stop*). Unlike the pedigree horses, she didn't know any other signals or "giddy up." Clara Hughes had to use the bells several times, which Hughes said was what cost him the blue ribbon. The funny thing is, although the judges noticed the bell, nobody noticed until the event was over that the name of the horse could be read, "Pulled a car often, by Metropolitan. Damn electricity."

Brian Hughes was born in Ireland in May 1849. He arrived in America in 1858, and eighteen years later he married Josephine White of Boston. The couple had three children: Gertrude Marie (later Mrs. John Joseph Burrell), Clara, and Arthur (who legally changed his name to Brian G. Hughes Jr. in 1909). They lived for a time in Brooklyn and later at 49 East 126th Street, at the Fifth Avenue Hotel, and at 1984 Madison Avenue in Harlem.

Little is known about Hughes's earlier life in New York or how he came to work in the box-manufacturing industry. However, he became one of the most prosperous box makers in the city, and everyone seemed to know him, even though the only address he ever used was "America." Even when he moved his offices to 135–137 Mulberry Street (the site of the former African Free School #2) sometime around 1904 when the old Centre Market was torn down to make way for the new police headquarters building, almost any piece of mail that originated in New York and was addressed "Brian G. Hughes, America" found its way to his desk.

On August 1, 1915, Hughes's wife succumbed to a long illness at the age of fifty-seven. Only six weeks earlier, she had left their home in Harlem with the hopes of recuperating in the fresh air at their Brightside farm in Monroe. Three years after her death, Hughes became president of the Dollar Savings Bank in the Bronx. With his wife's recent death, his new position at the bank, and World War I, Hughes was no longer in the mood to joke around. He told the public he was finally putting an end to the pranks.

Brian Hughes died at his home in Monroe on December 8, 1924. More than four hundred people attended the services at the All Saints Church on Madison Avenue in Harlem. The Reverend Patrick F. MacAran, founder of the Parish of St. Anastasia in Harriman, New York, officiated the mass. Hughes was buried at Calvary Cemetery in Queens. Four years later, his son shot himself with a pistol in the Hughes's Mulberry Street office just minutes after talking to his young bride, Margaret. His wife and secretary thought he was just taking after his father and pulling a practical joke, but when they went in to check on him, they found him dead on the floor. To this day, the motive remains a mystery.

1932

Tommy Casanova, the Lady-Killer Cat Mascot of The Lambs

Tommy C. Lamb . . . was truly a remarkable cat. Merely an alley cat when he first came to The Lambs, he blossomed forth as one of the most beautiful cats you have ever seen. There wasn't a pregnant cat within a radius of six blocks that didn't blame it on Tom. He really was remarkable.

—Joe Laurie Jr., 1953

Tommy Casanova Lamb, a husky gray-and-white cat from the Hell's Kitchen neighborhood on Manhattan's west side, wandered into The Lambs' clubhouse in 1932 when he was just a kitten. There, at 128 West Forty-Fourth Street, he took up his station at the bar, where he spent most of his waking hours schmoozing with the celebrity members of America's first professional theatrical club. As the club's designated bouncer, it was Tommy's job to kick out any other cats that tried to create disorder at the club. His paycheck consisted of beer, stuffed olives, and free lunches. Although the *New York Times* called Tommy the Feline Bar Fly, he did keep good order at the establishment. For example, one time a black tom with green eyes from Sixth Avenue crashed into the bar and tried to steal some bologna from the counter. Tommy reportedly "evicted him with a few accurate and destructive lefts."

Tommy was a very smart feline. Not only did he know when anyone in the dining room ordered fish, but he was also quite aware that The Lambs' clubhouse was his forever home. In December 1935, the vaudeville singer and pianist Herb Williams (Herbert Schussler Billerbeck) borrowed Tommy for his trick piano skit at the Waldorf-Astoria Hotel on Park Avenue and Forty-Ninth Street. (The act was captured on film, which can be viewed on YouTube.) During the finale, as the piano fell apart, Tommy popped out, let out a loud meow, jumped over the footlights, and ran down the aisle and out the door. So much for his stage debut. Two hours later,

Tommy Casanova Lamb. (Photo courtesy of The
Lambs collection)

drenched from the rain, he appeared at the entrance to The Lambs'
clubhouse, meowing to be let inside. Mind you, the clubhouse was
almost ten city blocks away from the hotel.

One of the reasons Tommy may have felt so at home with The
Lambs is that, according to the club members—tongue in cheek—
he was a direct descendant of one of the performing cats in Charles
Swain's Rats and Cats vaudeville act. This act featured rats dressed
as jockeys that would ride on the cats' backs around a little race-
track. The climax of the act was a comedy skit featuring two cats
boxing each other. Not only did Tommy reportedly mimic the
boxer John L. Sullivan by drinking a lot of beer, but he also had a
bad habit of flirting with the other tomcats' wives. Many a boxing
match took place when Tommy tried to add another female to his
harem, earning him the titles of "Great Lover of the Forties" and
"New York's Toughest Tomcat."

One time, Tommy got into a fight with Felix Adelphi, the neutered tuxedo cat of the Alpha Delta Phi Club at 136 West Forty-Fourth Street. Another time, after an all-night battle in the winter of 1936, he limped home in such a shocking state of disrepair that he was put in a taxicab and rushed to the Ellin Prince Speyer Hospital for Animals. He spent several days there—at a cost of three dollars a day—healing from his wounds. James R. Kinney, chief vet, said it was one of the worst cases of mayhem and mussing up that he had ever seen. Although the vet thought Tommy's wounds would lead to gangrene, the tough cat pulled through, albeit with quite a few more battle scars.

To celebrate Tommy's recovery from the big fight, the Gallery Boys, as the younger set of The Lambs was known, decided to hold a testimonial dinner for Tommy Lamb in March 1936. On March 21, the headline in the *New York Post* read, "Lambs Club's Tough Tomcat to Take Girlfriend to Party." (Right above this story, the headline read, "Hitler Is Asked for Counter-Plan.") According to the article, Joe Laurie Jr., super president of the Gallery Boys, came up with the idea for the special dinner. It featured all of Tommy's favorite dishes, including scallops, stuffed olives, cantaloupe, and beer. Tails and white tie were compulsory, and it was agreed that Tommy would sit at the head of the table (although no one wanted to volunteer to make him sit there). Tommy's girlfriend, a little "black and white cutie" who lived at the nearby Central Union Bus Terminal under the Hotel Dixie on West Forty-Second Street (the precursor to the Port Authority Bus Terminal), was invited to be his escort for the evening. The Alpha Delta Phi fraternity asked if Felix could attend, but that request was shot down by the Gallery Boys.

Laurie, who wrote about the event in *Vaudeville from the Honky-Tonks to the Palace*, reported that everyone wore evening clothes, many great speeches were made, and Tommy took it all in stride as he stretched out on a special throne surrounded by catnip. When people read about the dinner, they sent him gifts, including catnip, hand-knit sweaters and booties, dishes, and more. The professional boxer Edward Patrick "Mickey" Walker gave him a set of boxing gloves, and the New York artist James Montgomery Flagg sketched a portrait of him among all his fellow Lambs.

A month after the dinner, Diana Belais, president of the New York Anti-Vivisection Society, presented a silver medal to Tommy. The medal was accompanied by this inscription: "Thomas Casanova Lamb crept into the Lambs' club four years ago when he was an orphan and took up residence in the bar, fattening on the beer and free lunches until now he is a great, husky gray and white cat who is to receive our medal for his super-intelligence and devotion." Tommy attended the medal ceremony with the club members Joseph Keegan and Colonel John Fitz Madden. The newspapers reported that Tommy showed his "alleged super-intelligence and devotion by yielding with serene dignity to this latest tribute."

Although Tommy was long since gone when Laurie published his vaudeville book in 1953, he did have a talented grandson who took over as bouncer and mascot. This cat was trained by Willie, The Lambs' longtime waiter, to sit up with a cigarette in his mouth while wearing glasses and holding a newspaper in his paws. According to Laurie, when Tommy III (I don't know his real name) was on the pool table, nobody was allowed to chase him off—the players simply had to shoot around him. No doubt, Tommy III was made a life member of The Lambs.

The Lambs club was formed by the English matinée star Henry J. Montague in December 1874 in the Blue Room at Delmonico's restaurant on Fourteenth Street. The club was named after a London establishment—of which Montague was a member—that honored the essayist and poet Charles Lamb. After Shepherd Montague passed away (the club steward is called the Shepherd, the members are the Flock, and the clubhouse is the Fold), the newly incorporated club met on a regular basis for dinner at the Maison Dorée Hotel, and later at the Union Square Hotel, to glorify the late essayist.

The Lambs moved into a brownstone at 19 East Sixteenth Street in 1878 and then into a four-story brownstone at 34 West Twenty-Sixth Street in 1880, which served as its headquarters until about 1892. The brownstone had a large backyard with a marquee illuminated with Chinese lanterns, where some of the younger members would have boisterous parties in the summer months. Apparently, the neighbors were not fond of these late-night summer gatherings. Although the parties quieted down after Washington Irving Bishop, a professional mind reader, died at the club in 1888, the noise levels picked up within a year of his death. In 1890, several neighbors complained that The Lambs members were carrying "their bleatings so far into the early morning hours that they become intolerable." Miss M. L. Thomas and her ninety-year-old mother told police of the Nineteenth Precinct that the bleating was more like the bellowing of the Bull of Bashan. Another neighbor, Mr. J. L. Reed, who lived on the third floor of the clubhouse, threatened to turn a water hose on the men when they were outside in the yard making noise.

The neighbors were finally successful in silencing The Lambs when the club moved out and the New York Press Club moved in. For the next few years, The Lambs moved around a bit, trying its luck at 8 West Twenty-Ninth Street until a neighbor complained about the noise (the men allegedly made quite a ruckus playing pool) and, later, at 26 West Thirty-First Street. In 1897, it finally settled in for a few years at 70 West Thirty-Sixth Street in the Herald Square Theater District, which is where Sir Oliver, a parrot mascot, joined the Fold. In June 1902, The Lambs purchased a large lot at 128–130 West Forty-Fourth Street from Minnie Lespinasse. The membership approached the architects McKim, Mead, and White, all of whom were members of the club, to design the new clubhouse. The six-story marble Georgian building was completed in 1905.

In 1915, The Lambs' clubhouse was doubled in size by the architect George A. Freeman, who added a mirror-image addition. The building was designated a New York City Landmark in 1974 and was added to the National Register of Historic Places in 1982. The Church of the Nazarene purchased the building in 1975 for use as a mission, but today it is home to the Chatwal Hotel. Since 1976, The Lambs has made its home at 3 West Fifty-First Street, which is where a framed photograph of Tommy Casanova Lamb graces a wall in the pool room.

7

Civil Servant Cats

In 1893, the United States celebrated the four hundredth anniversary of Christopher Columbus's arrival in the New World at the World's Columbian Exposition in Chicago. One of the many guests of honor at the opening ceremonies was Cristóbal Colón de la Cerda, a descendant of Christopher Columbus and the Fourteenth Duke of Veragua. The duke had traveled to Chicago by way of New York City, where he spent several days touring the city with Mayor Thomas Francis Gilroy and other members of the city's Columbus Reception Committee of One Hundred.

The duke and his family arrived in New York on April 15, 1893, aboard the American Line steamship SS *New York*. The first person to greet Duke de la Cerda to America was Navy Commander Francis W. Dickins, who had been selected to represent the United States government. Commander Dickins presented the duke with the Freedom of the City (today we call this the Key to the City) and then escorted the royal family to the new Waldorf Hotel on Fifth Avenue, which had opened only one month earlier. During the duke's time in Manhattan, he and his family were guests at numerous grand receptions throughout the city. They also visited Mayor Gilroy at his home at 7 West 121st Street.

A year later, on February 14, 1894, a slatted pine box arrived at New York City Hall. Inside the box was a cat and a letter from Commander Dickins, a portion of which follows:

My Dear Mayor Gilroy:

Last August I sailed from the United States . . . for Queenstown, Ireland. Upon our arrival and during our stay there we received the most hearty welcome and gracious hospitality from all the Irish people, and particularly so from the gallant Mayor of Cork, the Hon. Augustine M. Roche. Remembering your kindness to me in New York . . . I wanted to bring back to you some token from that beautiful country, and the Mayor of Cork kindly gave me—not a tiger—but a gentle cat with a heart whose warmth is only exceeded by those of her countrymen. Hence, I send to you today, by express, Miss Bridget Cork, accompanied by appropriate verses . . . with a chorus set to music. The clever lines I hope will please you, and that you will accept Miss Bridget with my profound gratitude, and with the best wishes for her welfare as well as your own, believe me to be, very sincerely yours, F. W. Dickins, Commander U.S.N.

Described as a small, good-natured purring cat with a soft coat of dark gray and stripes of a darker hue, Bridget Cork had traveled with Commander Dickins on the SS *Essex*, which arrived at the Norfolk Naval Shipyard in Virginia on February 11, 1894. She then traveled by train to New York City in the pine box. Mayor Gilroy was reportedly quite pleased with the cat—and Bridget was quite pleased to be out of the box—but Bridget was not destined to be one of the many government cats in New York City's history. As much as the mayor would have loved his own City Hall mascot cat, he knew there was no way Bridget could stay in his office. After all, City Hall already had Old Tom, and Tom would never have accepted another cat in his territory. Brooklyn City Hall was also taken, by a cat named Jerry Fox, and the nearby New York City Post Office had more cats than it needed; so those options were also out of the question for Bridget. So Mayor Gilroy sent Bridget to his home in Harlem, where I'm sure she received plenty of love and attention from his many children.

1891

Old Tom, the Brazen, Pampered Pet of New York City Hall

It was a cold and wet day in 1891 when a homely tabby kitten with white paws first tried to make City Hall his manor home. Somehow, he got the nerve to march up the steps and enter the front door, saunter down the long hallway, and calmly begin to lick his fur. Martin J. Keese, the City Hall custodian, tried to shoo the little cat outside, but the cat returned. Keese tossed the kitten from a window, but again the cat came back. No matter what he did, Keese, the man who once fought with the First Fire Zouaves in the Civil War and who, as a deputy sheriff, had arrested William "Boss" Tweed, couldn't keep the defiant kitty away. As the children's camp song goes, "the cat came back the very next day, the cat came back, he just wouldn't stay away."

Keese was no stranger to the many cats that hunted for sparrows in City Hall Park. By the time Tom arrived, Keese had been living with his children on the top floor of City Hall for ten years. His youngest daughter loved cats and would feed the many forlorn felines that temporarily evaded Keese's keen eyes and escaped inside City Hall. Tom must have been very determined, because he was the first cat to earn a permanent spot on the City Hall roster. A reporter for the *New York Times* who called Tom "a looter of the city feed bag" said he was "a fine example of the self-made American cat." For the next seventeen years, City Hall was Tom's kingdom.

In 1891, Hugh J. Grant was in his third year as the eighty-eighth mayor of New York. A graduate of Manhattan College and a Tammany Hall Democrat who began his political career as a city alderman in 1883, he was the youngest mayor in the city's history when he took office at the age of thirty-one. Grant was the first of six mayors to serve during Tom's long reign as the city's official mascot. During his tenure, Tom also shared his home with mayors Thomas F. Gilroy, William L. Strong, Robert A. Van Wyck, Seth Low, and George B. McClellan Jr. As the *New York Times* reporter noted on Tom's fifteenth anniversary, "what the ancient cat does not know about City Hall politics the Sphinx does not know about Pharaoh."

Life was good for the City Hall pet cat. Over the years, the tabby befriended many of the men on the Board of Aldermen and City Council. He often fell asleep in the aldermen chambers during board meetings, and he loved sitting on the desk of City Council President Randolph Guggenheimer. Tom was especially fond of the council president, and the feelings were mutual: Guggenheimer spent fifty cents on a special dinner for Tom every Christmas.

In winters, Tom slept by a radiator in the basement or passed the time in the city marshal's office. When spring arrived, he'd deliver the authoritative message that winter was over by ambling down the City Hall steps and sunning himself on the asphalt pavement of the plaza. In warm weather, Tom liked to visit his girlfriend cats who worked on the feline police force at the General Post Office. He also enjoyed taking dips in the park fountain and hunting for sparrows. Men and boys would often make bets on whether cat or bird would prevail. When Tom won the fight, he'd bring the dead bird to the mayor's office—Mayor Strong was one of his favorite recipients.

Life was also good for the City Hall custodian. Consider that at night and on weekends and holidays, City Hall was the private mansion for Keese, his mother-in-law, Isabella Dunn, and his four children, William R., Elizabeth A. (Lillie; later Mrs. James A. Maxwell), Charles W., and Marie L. (Dolly). They made their home in the custodian's apartment under the City Hall dome, which was located at the top of thirty-eight stairs in the building's third-floor rotunda. Lace curtains on the windows and flowering plants gave the odd space "a homelike look." (In later years, Keese shared the apartment with a maid-servant named Julia Kelly, who once mistook the City Hall flagpole halyard for a clothesline.)

On June 25, 1906, Keese and some of the aldermen celebrated Tom's birthday and anniversary. Keese picked up the fifteen-year-old tabby from the rear steps and escorted him to the hall, where Alderman Frank Dowling and a committee of veterans were waiting for him. Each man shook Tom's paw, and then they served him a porterhouse steak. Alderman Dowling said the occasion was "worthy a resolution of the Board of Alderman, but Tom wouldn't

Martin Keese and family members in the custodian's apartment on the third floor of City Hall. (Collection of Margaret Gayle, Public Design Commission of the City of New York)

like to leave his real age exposed to his lady friends in the Post Office Building."

By this time, old Tom was deaf and feeble and could no longer hunt sparrows. Keese had taken over feeding him, and the City Hall reporters kept a bowl of water in their room for him to drink. Keese was also starting to feel his age, and he often struggled making his way up the iron spiral staircase to his apartment. As they aged together, Tom and Keese enjoyed sunning themselves on the steps of City Hall while watching the city continue to grow all around them.

On July 22, 1908, Keese knew it was time to put Tom out of his misery. He called for the SPCA, but no one was available to help. Then he called on Policeman Joseph Cahill of the City Hall Park Police, who led the old cat into the park and, as humanely as possible, ended Tom's life. Keese and several politicians stood by to pay tribute to the famous sparrow hunter and City Hall mascot.

Eleven months after Tom passed, and a day before what would have been Keese's seventy-second birthday, the custodian died from complications of acute bronchitis at St. John's Hospital in Long Island City. His half brother, Edmund Rogers, was at his side when he died. At the time of his death, Keese's apartment in City Hall was filled with relics, scrapbooks, and several cats that had probably moved in after Tom's death.

On June 28, 1909, a day after Keese's death, the *New York Times* wrote the following about him in a lengthy memorial to the famous custodian: "Marty Keese, as the aged janitor of the City Hall has been known to mayors, aldermen, politicians, and newspaper men who have come and gone there for more than a quarter of a century, had a most interesting history. He was probably more closely identified with the important events of the city in the last fifty years than any other man living."

Keese was born on June 27, 1837, in a little brick house at the corner of Grand Street and Laurens Street (later called South Fifth Avenue and now West Broadway). He attended school at Mrs. Weston's frame schoolhouse on Orange Street (now Baxter Street), which cost his mother one penny a day. (Keese's school days did not last long: with five younger siblings to care for, his mother could not afford to send him to school for many years.) When they weren't at school, Keese and his older brother, Billy, liked to ride on the pigs that roamed freely through City Hall Park.

As the *New York Times* noted, Keese celebrated some major events in New York City's history. On April 30, 1839, when he was only two, his mother took him to the Middle Dutch Church and held him up high so he could see former president John Quincy Adams speak at the semicentennial anniversary of the first inauguration of George Washington. On June 23, 1842, he and his mother attended an event at City Hall to celebrate fresh water flowing from the Croton Aqueduct into New York City for the first time. Keese was also a fire buff who loved following the volunteer firemen of United States Engine Company No. 23, which was then located on Anthony Street (now Worth Street), just west of Broadway. He and his friends would trail the firemen on their calls, whooping and hollering after their idols. Keese was a young buff in 1845, the year the third Great Fire of New York City killed four volunteer firefighters and twenty-six civilians and destroyed more than 345 buildings in lower Manhattan.

Following schooling, Keese was trained in brass polishing and finishing. He got his first job at the William F. Ford surgical instrument factory on what is now Lafayette Street in the early 1850s, and he later started his own business manufacturing plumbers' materials. He also officially joined New York's Volunteer Fire Department, first as a runner with Fulton Engine Company No. 21 and then as a member of the M. T. Brennan Hose Company No. 60 (named in honor of New York's Sheriff Matthew T. Brennan). In 1860, he married his wife, Elizabeth Starr Dunn of Halifax, Nova Scotia. According to federal census records, they lived at 117 White Street and then at 621 Pearl Street.

In the spring of 1861, Keese enlisted in Company F of Colonel Elmer Ephraim Ellsworth's First Fire Zouaves, formally known as the Eleventh New York Volunteer Infantry Regiment. This regiment of twelve hundred New York City volunteer firemen was attacked during the First Battle of Bull Run in July 1861 as it guarded the retreating Army of the Potomac. Keese was seriously injured in this battle by a shot to his side; his brother Billy and his friend Tommy Curry both died of injuries sustained in the war. Despite Keese's injuries, he returned to New York and fought with the soldiers and firemen during the city's Draft Riots in 1863. He was elected foreman of M. T. Brennan Hose Company, a position he held until the volunteer fire service was disbanded in 1865. And he also accepted the position of deputy sheriff under Sheriff Brennan.

By 1871, according to Keese, New York City had sunken down to such a low moral level that "she'd need a stepladder to climb into hell." On December 16 of that year, Special Deputy Sheriff Keese arrested Tammany Hall's William "Boss" Tweed in Suite 114–118 of the Metropolitan Hotel on Broadway at Prince Street. Tweed had just returned to the city from his country home in Greenwich, Connecticut. According to Keese, Tweed said he couldn't keep away from the bright store windows during the holidays, even though he had a feeling he was going to be arrested. Two years later, Tweed was tried and convicted on fifty out of fifty-five charges against him and sentenced to twelve years in debtors' prison plus a $3,000 fine. (Tweed later escaped and traveled the world in exile, only to die in prison after giving up the fight in April 1878.) "I was always sorry for him," Keese told reporters many years later.

Keese also made the headlines when he became one of the first New Yorkers not associated with the construction of the Brooklyn Bridge to pay the penny toll to cross it. At midnight on May 24, 1893, when the bridge first opened to the public, Keese and several news reporters raced to cross the bridge. Keese, wearing his best suit for the occasion, came in second place. As the story goes, Keese and one of the reporters forgot about the toll going back and had to borrow a penny to cross back to Manhattan.

Keese's legacy with the firefighting services is also commendable. He was one of the principal organizers of the Exempt Firemen's Association and president of the city's Volunteer Firemen's Association. Together with George W. Anderson, who rode with the Phoenix Hose Company No. 22, he also helped found the Fireman's Home for sick, disabled, and indigent firefighters in Hudson, New York. Today, the Firemen's Home is a certified residential health-care facility and serves as the grounds for the Museum of Firefighting as well as the Firefighter's Memorial.

Throughout his life, Keese witnessed the names on the city's business signs change from old Dutch to English, and he watched in dismay as "the little buildings that then rimmed City Hall" were replaced by "giants of brick and iron that leapt to the clouds." As he once told a reporter for the *New York Sun*, "I was proud of the high buildings when they first began, as all New York was proud of them, but now when I get old enough to have sense I'm sorry they ever put them up. It was prettier years ago when the little buildings rimmed my square, buildings that were dwarfs compared even to that."

Following Keese's death in 1909, he was buried in Brooklyn's Green-Wood Cemetery. In his will dated May 28, 1909, he asked to be buried as close to the plot of the Volunteer Firemen's Association as possible. His final wish was fulfilled.

1904

The Feline Police Squad of New York's General Post Office

On November 5, 1904, the New York City postal clerk George W. Cook celebrated his eighty-first birthday and his fifty-fourth anniversary working for the US Post Office Department with a special dinner. The banquet took place in the basement of the General Post Office building—colloquially known as the Mullet Post Office or Mullet's Monstrosity (after its architect, Alfred B. Mullet)—which was then located at the intersection of Broadway and Park Row in City Hall Park. The menu was simple and included raw calves' liver and lambs' kidney heaped high in piles and served on clean white paper. Each guest "helped himself or herself with nature's implements." In attendance were Cook; two sergeant cats, named Bill and Richard; one bowlegged, brindled roundsman cat; and fifty-seven able-bodied patrolman cats. The entire dinner was funded by the federal government.

When Cook wasn't sorting letters in the Mailing Department, he was also (unofficially) the Superintendent of Federal Cats. Under Postmaster Edward Morgan, it was Cook's responsibility to feed the almost one hundred New York mousers who were employed by the US Post Office Department to kill the rats that were attracted to the glue used on envelopes and packages. Cook was provided a budget of five dollars a month—allocated through the department's Salaries and Allowance Division—which he used to purchase cat's meat from the Washington Market. The budget allowed for one meal a day. (Cook told reporters he thought the budget should have been at least ten dollars a month in order to accommodate his growing feline police force.) The budget was apparently necessary: many of the cats had become lazy and started nibbling on leather mail bags and stealing postal clerks' lunches, so the meat kept those bad habits at bay.

According to federal census records, Cook was a father of five daughters (Carrie, Jennie, Lilly, Laura, and Annie) and a resident of Ludlow Street on the Lower East Side. He began working for the Post Office Department in 1850, when New York's general post office was located in the former Middle Dutch Reformed Church on the corner of Liberty and Nassau Streets. (The circa 1729 church served as the city's main post office from 1844 to 1875.) When the new General Post Office at City Hall Park opened in August 1875, Cook brought one female postal tabby with him and put her to work as the new building's first mouser.

"That darned low critter would never stay on post," Cook told several reporters during his grand anniversary dinner. "She used to go a stravagin' all over town. I tell you, mister, in a few months there were more cats in this office than letters. Every corner I turned it seemed as if I stumbled on a nest o' kittens." According to Cook, the superintendent of mails once asked him to get six strong mail bags. "He just stuffed them bags full o' big and little cats and registered them, yes, mister, an' sent 'em to a little post office in New Jersey. Gosh! I wonder what th' feller said when he got 'em."

As you can imagine, transferring a few cats across the river did not solve the problem. By 1897, there were about sixty cats in the General Post Office. Most of them were born in the building, but others came from the restaurants on Park Row or gave up catching sparrows in City Hall Park for a more secure job on the postal feline police force. That year, the SPCA was called in to remove about thirty of the cats and have them humanely destroyed. Some of the cats taken away included Fitzsimmons, a long-legged cat who could stand on his hind legs; and Tim McCarthy, a big, gray cat who was a known lady-killer. Cook spared several of his favorites from the death wagon, including Nellie, a champion mouser, and Jim Corbett, a large black-and-white cat. Whitey, who was a kitten at this time, also survived to eventually become the mother of some of the best cats on the force.

Of course, in addition to Whitey, the surviving cats continued to breed, so every now and then the post office allowed employees to take their favorite cats home when the ranks were full. If the population got out of control, the postal clerks would "mail" some cats in the newspaper mail sacks. The sacks were carefully placed on the wagon with the other mail and deposited at other substations that needed a mouser. (Occasionally, a cat would accidentally get into a mail bag and be delivered to a distant city if the railway postal clerks didn't intercept.) The SPCA also continued to raid the cat colony when things got out of hand. The old rat catchers that were born in the building knew to stay away from the cat catchers. But the kittens and the cats from the restaurants, which were used to being petted, were often captured and taken away to the gas chamber.

On December 10, 1906, an article in several newspapers reported that due to overpopulation, the post office was laying off some employees in the "Department of Mouse Catching." The public was invited to come to the post office to adopt some first-class cats. According to the article, some of the cats were descendants of the original tabby from the Nassau Street post office. "Never was a greater variety of breeds under one roof than that which may be found in the basement of the Post Office," the article stated.

At the General Post Office building, most of the cats started their policing careers at the ground level or, more specifically, the newspaper department. This department, which was responsible for sorting and distributing newspaper mail (second class) and mail from the ocean steamships, took up the entire basement of the enormous building. The basement offered numerous patrol and napping posts for the cats, including hundreds of lockers where the employees stored their street clothes and a large storage area for all the mail bags not in use. Each patrol cat had a favorite spot to sit for hours and wait for a rat to pass. It was estimated that each cat caught about two rodents a week.

Hardworking cats that went above and beyond the call of duty could be promoted to the Registry Division on the top floor. Registered mail required extra care to safeguard it, and all persons handling this mail had to account for it as it passed through their hands along its route. The postal cats had to be extra diligent in their rat-catching efforts to protect this valuable class of mail.

Cook explained that he used "a two-platoon system" in order to ensure that there were always enough cats on duty at one time to catch the vermin. He said he set up this system one day when he didn't have enough cats on reserve to handle a massive rat attack.

Apparently, a cheese house had mailed samples of its most powerful Limburger cheese, and the mail bags were attacked by the rats. A riot ensued, but there were not enough cats on duty to arrest all the perpetrators.

Every day at around 2:00 p.m., Cook, like the Pied Piper, would blow a whistle to summon the second-class cats to their lunch. Cats would come running to the feeding area near the lockers from everywhere they were actively mousing or sleeping on the job. They'd scramble under and over hand trucks, through people's legs, over counters, or whatever they had to do to get to the food the fastest. The cats ate in assigned groups of six; if a cat from another table went to the wrong place by mistake, the boss of the group would box his ears and chase him back to where he belonged. In addition to strips of meat (usually lamb, beef, or calves' livers and hearts), sometimes the cats would get fresh catnip for dessert or some green grass from outdoors.

In order to keep the second-class and first-class cats separate so they wouldn't fight, Cook would serve the top-floor cats separately. All those cats detailed for duty in the Registry Department would gather around the elevator door at the designated hour and take it down to the basement. When they were done eating, they'd take the elevator back up to work. In the summer months, the newspaper department cats were allowed to take an afternoon furlough outdoors in City Hall Park. They'd catch some sparrows and maybe swap stories while soaking up the sun with the park cats or with Old Tom at City Hall. After sunning themselves, the post office cats would stroll back to the basement and resume their duties.

In 1910, there were about two hundred postal cats on Uncle Sam's payroll in New York City. Most of these felines worked in the General Post Office building, and the rest were employed at the various substations. Although Cook was still working as a clerk this year, a much-younger man named William W. Dixon was now in charge of the cat police force. Dixon made $700 a year as a laborer, but one of his primary duties was caring for the mousers. His fellow employees called him "King of the Cats."

One of the people who kept in contact with Dixon was Policeman John Foley of the City Hall Park Police. Policeman Foley looked out for the park cats, and he would always try to persuade Dixon to take one of them whenever there was an opening on the postal force. He once told a reporter for the *New York Press* that a black-and-white cat named Mollie was at the head of the civil service list. Her specialty was hunting sparrows by hiding under newspapers. She held the record with two sparrow kills in an hour and twelve in a week.

Construction of a new General Post Office on Eighth Avenue between Thirty-First and Thirty-Third Streets began in 1910. (That year, the eighty-seven-year-old George Cook still listed his occupation as "postal clerk" on the census report.) Postal services continued on the first floor of the City Hall postal building through the 1920s, but the building was demolished in 1938 as part of the city's efforts to beautify the downtown district for the 1939 New York World's Fair. In the 1920s, the cats went on strike, so to speak, and began hunting for sparrows in the park rather than hunting for mice in mailbags. This mass killing inspired a benefactor named Elizabeth Wittke to come to the park every morning "armed with bags of food, bottles of milk and cream, wooden plates and cups." I have not found any mention of New York's post office cats after 1924, so one might assume that their skills were either no longer required in the new building or that they no longer had a public relations spokesperson.

DID YOU KNOW?

From 1897 to 1953, the New York City Post Office used an intricate pneumatic-tube system to move mail across the city. At the peak of its operation, the tubes carried around ninety-five thousand letters a day, which was about 30 percent of all the mail routed daily in the city.

Put into operation by the New York Mail and Newspaper Transportation Company (a subsidiary of the American Pneumatic Service Company), the twenty-seven-mile system connected twenty-two post offices in Manhattan and the General Post Office in Brooklyn. The cast-iron tubes ran four to twelve feet underground; in some places, they ran alongside the subway tunnels on the Lexington Avenue line. The system used twenty-one-pound steel cylinders, each twenty-four inches long and eight inches in diameter, to transport first-class letters and second-, third-, and fourth-class items such as clothing and books. The canisters were shot through the tubes via air pressure at a rate of thirty miles per hour. It took about one and a half minutes to make the one-way trip from the General Post Office in City Hall Park to the Produce Exchange Building at Bowling Green—a distance of three-quarters of a mile.

On October 7, 1897, a ceremonial demonstration took place at the General Post Office to celebrate the new tube system. According to the postal supervisor Howard Wallace Connelly, about one hundred friends and postal officials watched as the first canister arrived from Station P in the Produce Exchange Building. Inside was a Bible wrapped in an American flag, a copy of the United States Constitution, a copy of President William McKinley's inaugural speech, and several other papers. Subsequent canisters carried a peach, a suit of clothes, and a live tortoiseshell cat in a cotton sack (the cat was probably on the postal feline police squad).

"How [the cat] could live after being shot at terrific speed from Station P in the Produce Exchange Building, making several turns before reaching Broadway and Park Row, I cannot conceive, but it did," Connelly notes in his 1931 autobiography. "It seemed to be dazed for a minute or two but started to run and was quickly secured and placed in a basket that had been provided for that purpose."

In addition to transporting the postal cat, the tubes were also reportedly used one time to rush a sick cat to the animal hospital. Postal employees said the cat leaped from the open container and put up quite a fight before finally being captured. Other animals sent through the tubes included dogs, mice, guinea pigs, roosters, and monkeys. And in 1908, to celebrate the opening of a new tube line from the Broad Street Station to Station C at Nineteenth Street and Columbia Avenue, a thin glass globe containing water and live goldfish was successfully sent through the tubes.

1904

Jerry Fox, the Spectacled Cat of Brooklyn Who Saved Borough Hall

Old Tom, the mascot of New York City Hall, may have thought he was the king cat of New York, but that's probably because he didn't know about his feline counterpart in Brooklyn. Jerry Fox, an enormous tiger cat of striking appearance who performed heroic deeds during his twenty-eight-year reign as Brooklyn's official cat (yes, twenty-eight years!), would have given Old Tom a run for his money.

Jerry Fox was originally the pet of the undertaker Jacob M. Hopper, whose establishment was in the Washington Building at the southeast corner of Court and Joralemon Streets. When a large black cat forced Jerry out of that building, he moved into a popular café run by T. F. Fox next to what was then Brooklyn City Hall (it was not until January 1898, when the City of Brooklyn merged with the City of New York, and Kings County became the Borough of Brooklyn, that City Hall became Brooklyn Borough Hall). On Sundays and Monday mornings, when the café was closed, Jerry attracted much attention by sitting in the windows and watching passersby. But during the rest of the week, when the café was open, he spent his days making scheduled rounds in the neighborhood. According to the *New-York Tribune*, he seemed to be able to read time, and "promptly at 1 o'clock every morning," he would make his rounds to make sure everything was fine. It was said that only once in his early years did he fail to show up in all the places on his beat at about the same time.

Jerry took his job patrolling the City Hall neighborhood very seriously and was often credited for preventing crimes or alerting humans to danger. While making the rounds of the café each day, for example, he would always alert the owner if he found a door or window ajar. One time a thief reportedly tried to break into the back window of the café. Jerry's loud howls attracted a policeman, who chased the would-be thief away. Another time Jerry chased a mad dog out of Hopper's establishment.

For more than a quarter of a century, Jerry made his presence known at City Hall and the Municipal Building. As the press reported, he did not have any political principles—he simply gave his support to whichever party was in power. He was a smart and dignified cat who made friends with the men building the Brooklyn Bridge and who loved to play dominoes with the Brooklyn politician "Boss" Hugh McLaughlin in the Exempt Firemen's Rooms in City Hall on summer nights.

Brooklyn Under Sheriff Hugh McLaughlin was one
of Jerry's many male friends. (Brooklyn Eagle Photographs, Brooklyn Public Library, Brooklyn Collection)

Sometime around 1903, Jerry started to lose his teeth. Then he
lost much of his sight. Lucky for Jerry, he was a friend of Charles F.
Hughes, an optometrist who reportedly made a special pair of
glasses for the cat. According to the *New York Times*, the glasses
gave Jerry Fox "a certain quaint dignity." Jerry's friends would often
give him a newspaper so he could sit on the steps of the Municipal
Building and pretend he was reading like the "bums" all around
him. Even with the glasses, poor Jerry would often stumble on the
trolley tracks. The motormen would stop their trolleys when he
was in sight because they knew he couldn't see them coming.

On the afternoon of May 22, 1904, nearly blind Jerry was wandering about the third floor of Brooklyn Borough Hall when he

came upon the vacant office of Judge Almet F. Jenks of the Appellate Division of the Supreme Court. Papers on the judge's desk had caught fire by what was reported to be a misplaced lit cigar. Judge Jenks was across the street at the law library in the County Courthouse at the time. Upon smelling the fire, Jerry rushed out into the chambers and started to howl. Policeman Harry Staton, who was stationed in Borough Hall, knew something bad had happened, because Jerry was not known to complain unless something was wrong. He located the fire and alerted Policeman John Kessell, who was stationed in the office of Borough President Martin W. Littleton. One news report said the policemen turned in an alarm and then attacked the flames with a fire-extinguisher grenade. Other reports suggested the judge returned to his office and filled one of the officer's hats with water to pour on the fire. In any event, if it hadn't been for Jerry's meows, the damage to the circa 1848 building may have been much more extensive, and the city would have lost more than a desk and some papers.

By the time Jerry had saved City Hall, he was already on a downward spiral. The reporters blamed Jerry's decrepit condition on Murphy Park, a popular and dangerous hangout for "benchers" (homeless men) and teenage gangs. The *Brooklyn Standard Union* said the following on August 17, 1899:

> Jerry Fox was decent and respectable and carried himself well until Murphy Park adjoining the Municipal Building was opened as a summer resort for the hobos and the Knights of Ease. Since then Jerry has become utterly disreputable, neglects his home, pays no attention to his master, stays out at nights, and acts generally in a way that is a shame and a disgrace to his former record. He now lounges on the benches, makes friends with unsavory looking Weary Waggleses, snoozes all day, neglects his baths, drinks [ale] like a fish, does not eat regularly, and is rapidly becoming a wreck of his old self.

One winter night in 1905, Jerry strolled away from Borough Hall and fell down a subway shaft that had been shut down because of trouble with a water main. For months, everyone assumed Jerry had run away. Unfortunately, when the shaft was reopened in April 1905, workers found his remains. They brought him out by dirt cart. Jerry's death was reported in the *New York Times* on April 7, 1905: "Had each of the several hundred city officeholders, judges, lawyers, volunteer firemen, war veterans, and business men in Borough Hall Square lost an old college chum there could not have been sorrow more profound than that which greeted the death of Jerry."

Several of Jerry's old friends paid tribute to the cat upon learning of his death. "He was a student as well as a great cat," said Dr. Hughes. "I had known him since I was a boy," said an elderly Brooklyn Heights doctor, who had once extracted Jerry's lower tusks because they were cutting his upper lip. "Jerry was an epoch in himself," said Assemblyman Patrick Burns, adding, "In an earlier day he would have been to Brooklyn as the codfish is to Boston."

DID YOU KNOW?

When Jerry Fox was in his youth, the buildings on his neighborhood watch included Brooklyn City Hall, the Municipal Building, Collegiate and Polytechnic Institution, the Court House, and the Reformed Dutch Church. All of these buildings, save for City Hall, were within one large block bounded by Joralemon Street, Livingston Street, Court Street, and Boerum Place. This block had once been part of Philip Livingston's farm before he turned it over to Brooklyn sometime prior to 1801. (City Hall was on the north side of Joralemon Street, which had formerly been part of the Remsen farm.)

In 1807, the First Dutch Reformed Church of Brooklyn built its third church on the lot between Joralemon, Court, and Livingston Streets. This church was replaced in 1835 by a much-larger building that faced Livingston Street. In the 1880s, efforts were made either to move the church to the other end of the lot and use it as a lecture hall or to sell the site to the federal government for Brooklyn's new post office. Both ideas fell through. The lot was sold on March 1, 1886, to Charles L. Willoughby, a Chicago capitalist, for $250,000. The church was demolished in May 1886. Willoughby replaced the church with a cyclorama building, which "reared its head where the descendants of the ancient Dutch used to kneel and pray."

The octagonal, corrugated-iron cyclorama was 139 feet in diameter and 75 feet high with a glass roof. Inside the building was a 360-degree trompe l'oeil painting, 50 feet wide and 400 feet in length, depicting George

Pickett's *Charge at the Battle of Gettysburg* by the French artist Paul Philip-poteaux. A viewing platform accommodated about fifty people at a time, who each paid twenty-five or fifty cents for admission. The Gettysburg cyclorama painting was on display from October 15, 1886, to August 8, 1887. The exhibit was then moved to Fourth Avenue and Nineteenth Street in Manhattan and the cyclorama building was demolished.

The lot sat empty for a while until George Murphy, a Department of Public Works employee, created a park on the site at the cost of only $500. (Some sources say the park was named after Henry C. Murphy, the mayor of the City of Brooklyn, but a *Brooklyn Daily Eagle* article in May 1894 claims that the honor goes to George Murphy.) Although the park was quite lovely in early years, by 1900 its benches were filled by men who could not afford a bed in one of the Fulton Street and Washington Street boardinghouses. It was also a panhandler's paradise for what the press called "loafers, bums, tramps, and thieves." As one article noted, "The scoundrels who infest the park every day . . . have turned a pretty place into a little hell on earth." In 1906, insult was added to injury when the park was converted into a storage yard for subway contractors working on the Borough Hall subway station.

In 1915, citizens asked Borough President Lewis H. Pounds and Public Works Commissioner Edmond W. Voorhies to turn the lots once occupied by the old Municipal Building and Murphy Park into a parking lot for all the vehicles clogging the streets adjoining Borough Hall. Three years after residents begged for a parking lot, the empty lots remained an eyesore. In September 1918, by orders of the United States War Department, the lots were put into use as an exercise and drill ground to prepare student soldiers for World War I.

In 1921, there was a proposal to turn Jerry Fox's old stomping grounds into a practice golf-putting course for the judges in order to help clear their minds for better rendering of judgments. That suggestion also received a subpar response. Finally, on August 13, 1924, Borough President Edward J. Riegelmann broke ground for the erection of Brooklyn's new fifteen-story Municipal Building, designed by the architectural firm of McKenzie, Voorhees & Gmelin. I think Jerry Fox would have been overwhelmed by the $6 million neoclassical building, had he lived to see it.

1930

Tammany, the Democratic Boss Cat of New York City Hall

Although several other cats took over for Old Tom at City Hall after he died in 1908, none of these felines were as popular as Tammany, who occupied City Hall during the administrations of James J. Walker and Fiorello H. LaGuardia in the 1930s.

Tammany's life of luxury as the City Hall cat began sometime around 1930, when Mayor Walker found him near Hamilton Fish Park on the Lower East Side. Mayor Walker named the cat Tammany and brought him to City Hall to help get rid of rats in the building. Tammany was apparently quite the charmer, because during the remainder of Mayor Walker's reign, his rat diet was supplemented by calves' livers paid for with city funds and by a daily bag of food provided by Patrolman John Helmuth.

According to the *New York Times*, Tammany was a cat of "honest Democratic parentage." The *Sun* called him "a bold, swashbuckling lad" who never allowed a rat to escape from his claws. In addition to rat-catching, Tammany spent his days checking in on Board of Estimate meetings and council sessions or dropping by to visit the mayor, whose door was always open for him. Between visits, he'd stretch out in the main corridor and check out the visitors. If the visitor was feline, he'd chase the cat out of the building without mercy. When his work was done, he enjoyed sleeping in his dank cellar retreat.

Tammany was also a great friend of the City Hall reporters—well, he didn't really like them, but he spent a lot of time in Room 9, the reporters' room, sleeping on their desks. The reporters loved to pose Tammany for pictures (a favorite pose was the "Library Lion" pose in the corridor of City Hall), but he didn't love the publicity. Sometimes after being photographed sitting on a reporter's desk, stalking the halls of City Hall, or looking out the window, he'd spend the rest of the day sulking in the cellar. Following one especially long photo shoot with Deputy Mayor Henry Hastings Curran, the *New York Times* reported, "What with all the hullabaloo and the popping of flashlight bulbs, the wretched beast appeared very downcast." James E. Assing, a veterinarian with the Health Department, was actually called in to check on Tammany following that photo shoot, but the only trouble the vet could find was an excess of fish heads in the cat's stomach.

The aldermen also enjoyed Tammany's company, especially if he did something to break up a meeting. One day in the winter of 1934, the cat created quite a stir when he stared down Alderman Edward Curley of the Bronx, who was angrily denouncing Mayor LaGuardia. While Alderman Curley was calling the mayor "a self-declared monarch of all he surveys," Tammany woke up from his nap on a chair near the dais and began nudging the alderman and staring into his face. As the other men's laughter drowned out Alderman Curley's oration, Aldermanic President Bernard S. Deutsch said, "I think the sergeant-at-arms had better escort the silent member to the back of the room." The aldermen responded, "No, no, let him alone!" Alderman Walter R. Hart of Brooklyn then leapt to his feet and said, "I move that the privileges of the floor be extended to the City Hall cat." All the members who were able to stop laughing shouted "Aye!" as Tammany ran out of the room with the news photographers in hot pursuit.

Although Tammany's job was quite secure under Mayor Walker, his fate was questioned by the New York press when Mayor LaGuardia took office in 1934. After all, the anti-Tammany "reform" mayor was not a member of the Democratic Party—he ran on the Republican-Fusion ticket. Right from day one, Mayor LaGuardia reorganized the city cabinet with nonpartisan officials in his quest to develop a clean and honest city government. As Tammany watched many of his old friends leave City Hall, he may have also pondered his own fate under Mayor LaGuardia.

Mayor LaGuardia apparently had no intention of evicting Tammany from City Hall. On January 6, 1934, the headline on the front page of the *New York Sun* read, "City Hall Cat's Job Safe under LaGuardia." Shortly thereafter, Tammany was given a collar that read, "City Hall Custodian" in case he should get lost.

Tammany with his hero, Deputy Mayor Henry
Hastings Curran. (The New York Times / Redux)

Although the new mayor had no intention of sending Tammany
back to the streets of the Lower East Side, life did get a little more
challenging for the cat under the "Fusion frugality." No longer were
his meals a line item on the city budget; now he had to rely on
Tom Halton, a watchman at City Hall, and John Helmuth, the night
patrolman, who paid for Tammany's evening meal out of their own
pockets. He also had to deal with a cat named Fusion who tried
to move in on his territory. This silent battle for control lasted for
three weeks, until Fusion disappeared one night during a storm.

Tammany also had to contend with Commissioner Edward M.
Markham of the Department of Public Buildings, who, according
to rumors, was conspiring with the ASPCA to evict the cat from
City Hall. Luckily, he had an ally in Deputy Mayor Curran, who
declared that City Hall was under siege when he found out about

the plan. On June 13, 1938, Deputy Mayor Curran wrote a letter to Commissioner Markham in which he pleaded for the cat's clemency, noting that Tammany was "the wisest and bravest of all cats" who had disposed of all the rats in City Hall. Curran said the cat had fifty thousand friends at City Hall who would fight for him if the ASPCA tried to take him away. "The carnage will be cheerful, instantaneous, and complete," he wrote. "Let them come!" No one ever came.

On April 9, 1939, Tom Halton could not find Tammany when he went to feed him. The next day around noon, the City Hall reporters spotted Tammany in a telephone booth in their room. He had keeled over and was whimpering in pain. Deputy Mayor Curran immediately called the Ellin Prince Speyer Hospital for Animals to let the vet know he was coming with the cat. Then he commandeered a car belonging to Council President Newbold Morris and, escorted by two policemen, rushed Tammany to the animal hospital. On the ride to the hospital, with Tammany "quiet and trustful in the arms of friends, there was just one little cry as the passing scenes of Lafayette Street told of a journey far from home. For Tammany knew it was the last journey."

At the hospital, Dr. James R. Kinney gave Tammany a fluoroscopic exam, which showed that the cat was suffering from uremic poisoning and stones in the bladder. Dr. Kinney and his assistants stayed with the cat all night, but at 7:30 a.m. the next day, Tammany passed away. City Hall workers and reporters were notified of his death as they came to work. More than two hundred calls came into City Hall that day from people who wanted to give Curran and LaGuardia their condolences. James Speyer, the husband of the late Ellin Prince Speyer, offered to bury Tammany in a little pet cemetery at Waldheim, his 130-acre country estate on the Albany Post Road in Scarborough-on-Hudson. The inscription on the grave read, "Tammany—In Fond Memory of Our Cat—Room 9, City Hall."

Following Tammany's death, Deputy Mayor Curran told the press,

Some say Tammany was just a cat, a clean-limbed, two-fisted, hard-hitting cat to be sure, but after all only a cat. Do these superficial persons know the unspoken wisdom behind those redoubtable whiskers? The cool estimate of human nature screened by the yellow luster of those unreadable eyes? Tammany was the guardian, the center, the sage of City Hall. . . . So now all the familiar unpreaching of the head to be stroked, the rumble of the purring accompaniment, the lightning, playful swing of the velvet paw—all the stray tokens of welcome to the human friends will be missing.

1939

Snooky, the Sophisticated, Salmon-Loving Cat of New York City Hall

On May 3, 1939, one month after the City Hall cat Tammany died at the Ellin Prince Speyer Hospital, an eleven-month-old female calico cat from Queens made her debut at City Hall. The cat was the pet of the night watchman Tom Halton, who had been greatly saddened by the passing of Tammany. Upon the new cat's arrival, the City Hall reporters named her Fusion, both for her tortoiseshell coloring and for the newly formed City Fusion Party, a coalition of progressive Republicans, liberal Democrats, good-government types, and independent socialists who helped put Fiorello H. LaGuardia in the mayoral office. (A few reporters wanted to call her Confusion.) The reporters also welcomed the white, rust, and black cat with catnip and a dish of ice cream. Although the name fit her well, Halton insisted that her name—the name he had already given her—was Snooky. To prove that her name was Snooky, he even produced a white collar for her on which was printed "Snooky—City Hall." Some reporters obliged, but for years many newsmen continued to call her Fusion.

Snooky immediately fell into a daily routine, which included wandering from room to room with a rather proprietary air, stretching out on the city budget report (a large volume kept in the press room), and attending conferences in Mayor LaGuardia's office and meetings of the Board of Estimate. Every night at 5:00 p.m., Halton would feed her dinner of canned salmon or tuna fish, which he kept cold in the press-room watercooler. Snooky was, after all, "the apple of Tom's eye."

Soon after the United States entered World War II, it became apparent that voluntary conservation of goods would not be adequate, so numerous restrictions were put in place. On January 30, 1942, the Emergency Price Control Act granted the Office of Price Administration (OPA) the authority to set price limits and ration food and other commodities to discourage hoarding and to ensure equal access to scarce resources. Sugar was the first item to be rationed (and was only available for purchase via government-issued food coupons), followed by coffee, meat, cheese, fats, canned fish, canned milk, and other processed foods.

When the initial freeze on canned fish went into effect in 1943 (a freeze preceded rationing for canned fish), Halton had only one can of salmon in reserve for Snooky. As he told a reporter for the *New York Times*, he feared that Snooky would resort to killing the sparrows and pigeons in City Hall Park if she did not approve of the fish substitutes. Slippers, a cat who lived with Constance Merrall in Lawrence, Long Island, read the story and sent Snooky a can of pilchards with a note stating that she too was saddened to hear that the OPA had applied a freeze to salmon. "The dehydrated sawdust we are given now is singularly unpalatable—only fit for dogs, who have no sense of discrimination," she wrote (the letter was stamped with Slippers's paw prints).

On October 31, 1944, Snooky ran away from City Hall after reportedly getting into a tiff with a black cat that had been trying to take her place. Someone at City Hall called the police, who were instructed to leave no stone unturned in their search for the missing cat. Halton also conducted his own search in places he knew Snooky might be expected to hide. For some reason, she wasn't wearing her collar and ID tag, but Halton held onto them with hopes that the prodigal cat would return to him. A few days after Snooky's disappearance, the black cat had the nerve to return to City Hall and try taking over Snooky's territory again. The cat actually made it as far as the lobby of City Hall, but Halton, who had just arrived for his shift, gave the interloper the boot. "I bet someone stole Snooky and put this black cat in here," he told the City Hall reporters.

On November 25, four weeks after Snooky's disappearance, Patrolman William Mahoney of the Fourth Precinct police station at 9 Oak Street spotted her near the intersection of Oak and Roosevelt Streets while on patrol. (Oak and Roosevelt were two of the many streets that were demapped in 1947 and 1950 to make way for the Alfred E. Smith Houses and the Chatham Green apartments.) The officer triumphantly returned Snooky to Patrolman James Byrnes at City Hall, where the cat was welcomed back with a ceremony fit for a queen (in other words, a large can of rationed salmon). Even the stodgy City Council president and acting mayor Augustus Newbold Morris attempted to welcome the female cat back, saying, "Glad to see you back, old boy."

In May 1944, six months after Snooky's disappearing act, she celebrated her fifth anniversary at City Hall sporting a new collar and dining on her favorite fish meal. As several newspapers reported, "When Snooky first arrived she was dirty, disdainful, and debonair. Today, she is dirty, disdainful, and debonair."

Snooky went AWOL one last time in September 1945. Halton, then sixty-seven years old, feared that someone had stolen the cat whom he had adored for almost seven years. Snooky never did return. A year later, a new cat had taken her place at City Hall. This new cat was presented to Halton and Councilman Joseph T. Sharkey on January 29, 1946, by Dorothy Mills, a stewardess for Pan-American World Airways. The cat, first named O'Clipper, had been discovered as a stowaway aboard a clipper flight from Shannon, Ireland, to LaGuardia Airport. City Hall reporters renamed the reddish-brown tabby Kitty Kouncil and, later, Kitty Hall. Halton was happy to receive the new cat and immediately took to feeding her salmon and instructing her on her new duties at City Hall. Halton relegated the cat to a small room on the second floor and did not let her roam the building's marble corridors until a new collar with a name tag had been obtained.

8

Good-Luck Cats

If you've ever been to the Louis Armstrong New Orleans Airport in Louisiana, you may have wondered why the identifier for this airport is MSY. You might be interested to learn that the identifier stands for Moisant Stock Yards. What's even more interesting, though, is that the story surrounding these stock yards involves a handsome young aviator and an adorable flying mascot cat who made several flights over New York City in the early twentieth century.

The daredevil pilot John Bevins Moisant was rarely without his beloved good-luck cat, Paris-London (aka Paree or Mademoiselle Fifi). Whether he was performing aerial maneuvers over Long Island or setting new records in his monoplane, Moisant always had his bright-eyed tabby kitten at his side. Moisant adored his cat, and he did everything possible to make her comfortable in flight. Whether she was nestled in his pocket or under his sweater, Paris-London seemed to enjoy her copilot role.

According to reports, Paris-London brought good luck to Moisant on at least fourteen documented flights, including the first-ever recorded flight with a passenger across the English Channel on August 23, 1910. She was also along for the ride on October 30, 1910, when close to one million spectators in New York City came out to

Luckily for Paris-London, she was not copiloting John Moisant's fatal flight. (Library of Congress, Prints & Photographs Division, LC-DIG-ggbain-08636)

watch Moisant and other pilots race from Belmont Park on Long Island to the Statue of Liberty. But as fate would have it, she was not his copilot on December 30, 1910, when Moisant's aircraft got caught in a gust of wind during a preparatory flight for a competition in Kenner, Louisiana. Moisant was catapulted from the plane as it nose-dived from an altitude of about one hundred feet into a field occupied by cattle stock yards. Shortly after the fatal crash, the field was renamed the Moisant Stock Yards (MSY). Thirty years later, a new international airport was constructed on the site.

I tell this story not because I believe the outcome would have been different had Moisant's good-luck cat been on the plane but because many people do have superstitious beliefs involving cats or other animals. Most do not take these superstitions seriously; however, many men of Old New York, including sailors, pilots, and ballplayers, were serious when they attributed their good luck to their feline mascots. In fact, some men, like the miners working in the Joralemon-Battery Tunnel in Brooklyn, even believed that a cat could be responsible for lifesaving miracles.

1905

Bright Eyes, the Good-Luck Kitten of the Battery-Joralemon Street Tunnel

Then all of a sudden I strikes water and opens my eyes. I was flying through the air, and before I comes down I had a fine view of the city.

—tunnel worker Richard Creeden, March 27, 1905

In May 1900, a committee of fifty Brooklyn men appeared before New York's Rapid Transit Commission to advocate for a full extension of the subway system to Brooklyn. The committee suggested a route that would extend down Broadway to the Battery in Manhattan, then traverse under the East River and Joralemon Street in Brooklyn, past Borough Hall, up Fulton Street to Flatbush Avenue, and then to the Long Island Railroad Station at the junction of Flatbush and Atlantic Avenues. On July 24, 1902, the contract (Contract #2) to build this extension and a tunnel under the East River—called the Battery-Joralemon Street Tunnel or sometimes just the East River Tunnel—was awarded to the Rapid Transit Subway Construction Company. This company was owned by the pioneers of New York's first subway line (Contract #1): August Belmont Jr., president and founder of the Interborough Rapid Transit Company (IRT), and John B. McDonald, general superintendent of the Croton Dam. The contract was signed on September 11, 1902. Ground was broken in January 1903.

Work on the first underwater tunnels between Manhattan and Brooklyn took place between 1903 and 1907, starting simultaneously from excavated shafts at South Ferry in Manhattan and Henry Street in Brooklyn Heights. Engineers had originally wanted to build the dual tunnels out in the open and float them into place. However, the War Department—which required the water level atop the tunnels to be forty-five feet at low tide—and the great volume of traffic in the East River put an end to that idea. The work was instead done by a method called shield and compressed-air tunneling, in which the miners worked in a protective shield or temporary support structure and an inrush of water was prevented by compressed air

By March 1905, the excavation work on the Brooklyn end of the tunnels had reached just beyond Piers 17 and 18, then owned by the New York Dock Company. For Richard Ambrose Creeden, a twenty-five-year-old tunnel worker from Jersey City, New Jersey, it was sheer luck that the excavation work had cleared the long wooden docks.

At about 8:00 a.m. on March 27, 1905, Creeden and Jack Sheehy were on the apron, which was a platform for the workers to help them reach the top of the mechanical shield. Three other laborers—John Hughes of Manhattan, John Priody of Hoboken, New Jersey, and John Eagan of Jersey City—were also working in the north tunnel air chamber on the Brooklyn side. Creeden, described as a "small, pale, wiry Irishman" with blue eyes and brown hair, noticed a small fissure at the top of the tunnel. He immediately ran to a pile of bags filled with sawdust and shouted out a warning to his fellow workers to abandon the apron. Then he climbed a ladder and attempted to push two bags against the widening aperture as the air pressure continued to build.

Up to this point, Creeden had not had much luck in his life. Born August 27, 1880, in Jersey City, he was the fourth child of Bridget Welsh and John Creeden, both Irish immigrants. He had two older sisters, Margaret (Maggie) and Mary, and one older brother, Cornelius. His father supported the large family by working as a laborer. By 1895, Richard and his mother were the only surviving members of the family. According to census and death records, Mary died on October 11, 1884, when she was just eight years old. Cornelius died on October 29, 1884, at the age of six. (The cause of death is unknown, but the fact that two young children died only two weeks apart leads me to believe that they succumbed to either an illness or an accident.) Then on April 26, 1890, when Richard was only ten, his twenty-year-old sister Maggie passed away. His father passed sometime before 1895, and his mother died sometime before March 1905.

As the pressure in the tunnel increased, Creeden was pinned to the roof. Within seconds, the roofing and earth gave way, creating a four-foot-wide hole. Creeden was pushed through the hole and into the earthen riverbed, where he had to struggle with shoring timbers while choking on mud and stones. With the compressed air keeping the water back and Creeden's body blocking the hole like a cork, the other workers were able to escape. Knowing he would be killed within a minute, Creeden kicked and pushed at the shoring timbers. Finally, the pressure propelled Creeden like a rocket through the seventeen feet of riverbed silt and ten feet of water, sending him through the four-foot aperture "like a pea through a putty blower." The Brooklyn businessman A. G. Valentine, the New York Dock Company superintendent C. H. Phillips, and other witnesses on the docks said they saw the two bags come out, followed by a geyser of water and Creeden. They said he shot up about twenty feet and performed acrobatics in the air for a few seconds before falling into the river near the piers.

Following his amazing flight, Creeden came to rest just beyond the *Floating Bethel*, a former Erie Canal boat that had been converted into a place of worship for sailors and that had been moored at Pier 18 since 1893. Although he was wearing heavy overalls and boots, Creeden was a good swimmer and was able to stay afloat while awaiting rescue from two fishermen and Policeman Patrick Cooney of the Forty-Eighth Precinct. Cold and wet, Creeden made his way to the sandhouse (engine room and storeroom) at the corner of Furman and Joralemon Streets, where he was attended to by an ambulance surgeon from the Long Island College Hospital (the hospital had introduced the first ambulance service in Brooklyn in 1873). There, he joked with the press, stating that he had just asked the boss for a raise that day but never expected it to come so quick. Although he refused to go to the hospital, Creeden reportedly asked to smoke his pipe before a carriage took him to the home he shared with his aunt, Ellen Driscoll. He asked to return to work the next day, but he spent several days at home recovering from shock.

According to the *Brooklyn Daily Standard Union*, it was while Creeden was smoking his pipe in the sandhouse that Bright Eyes first made his appearance at the Battery-Joralemon Tunnel. The tiny black kitten, about three months old, peered sixty feet down the shaft and decided to go exploring by skinning down the shaft shoring. The workmen tried shooing him away, "but, law sakes!" as one workman told the reporter, "dat coon kitten jist cocks his tail and keeps agwine down." Several workmen who were going down on the elevator cage also tried to shoo the kitten away, but he simply jumped into the cage and gave a farewell meow to the world above. The tunnel workers agreed to adopt the kitten, believing the cat was a lucky charm who had helped save the lives of the four men who miraculously survived the blowout.

No one knew where the brave kitten came from, but the fact that he was well groomed led the men to believe that he had been living the good life in Brooklyn Heights. Bright Eyes adapted well to tunnel life, and for the next eight months, until Subway Nellie the dog appeared on the scene, he was the only mascot of the tunnel workers. The cat took this job seriously, especially the requirement to beg for his portions of the workers' food rations.

Two months after what most people would consider a life-changing event, Creeden sued the company, claiming that he had not been able to work since the accident occurred. I don't know if he won the lawsuit, but he did eventually go back to work. According to his World War I draft registration card, Creeden claimed to be working as a pipe fitter for P. McGovern & Co. (the contractor for the Sixtieth Street tunnel, which connects Manhattan to Roosevelt Island) and living at 1126 Third Avenue in Manhattan. From New York, he moved to Detroit, where he worked as a laborer in the compressed-air industry in the 1920s and 1930s. When he registered for the draft during World War II at the age of sixty-one, he was retired and living in San Francisco. I guess one could say he had finally found the light at the end of the tunnel.

DID YOU KNOW?

On November 27, 1907, the first subway train from Manhattan to Brooklyn via the new Battery-Joralemon Tunnel left the Wall Street station at 12:30 p.m. This train carried about two hundred men, including IRT officials, engineers, reporters, and other invited guests, including some personal friends. One of those guests may have been a mixed-breed dog named Subway Nellie, who only a few months earlier had accommodated a news reporter, photographer, and timekeeper on an exploratory trip of the tunnel.

Nellie had arrived at the tunnel during a severe snowstorm in 1905, after seeking shelter in the offices of John B. McDonald near Brooklyn's Borough Hall. The shaggy-haired puppy, half starved and frozen, drank some warm milk that the men offered her and then crawled under a stove for warmth. The men didn't have the heart to kick her out, so they decided to keep her and call her Nellie, an extremely popular name for female dogs in those days. Although the offices were warm and comfortable, Nellie was also interested in all the digging and shoveling outside (maybe she imagined the men were burying a giant bone). As the tunnel expanded and she was able to wander around without getting in the way of shovels and picks, she started to spend most of her time supervising the workers in the excavation area. The five hundred or so men who were working far below the streets grew quite fond of the little dog.

When the excavation project was big enough for people to begin calling it "the subway," the men christened Nellie with the name "Subway Nellie" in order to make sure that no one confused her with all the other dogs named Nellie in the neighborhood. As time progressed, the subway mascot became well known around downtown Brooklyn. She reportedly had charming manners and could show up at any restaurant around Borough Hall and be sure of a good meal. "Here comes Subway Nellie," the restaurant proprietors would say while the employees prepared a plate for her.

On the inaugural trip from Manhattan to Brooklyn, the conductor was the chief motorman G. W. Morrison. He drove the three-car train around the South Ferry loop, back up to the Bowling Green station, and then through the north tunnel (the south tunnel hadn't been completed yet). At 12:55 p.m., the train arrived at Brooklyn Borough Hall, where a large crowd had gathered inside and outside the station to greet the train (they had been attracted to the station by the ringing of the bell on top of Borough Hall, as ordered by Borough President Bird S. Coler). Throughout the day, throngs of enthusiastic "citizens and their wives and sisters" (I guess women were not considered citizens then) greeted the train and gathered at the station all day long. Horns blew, bells rung, and everyone took a ride under the river in trains packed from morning until night.

After this test run, the first experimental train was a West Farms Express that left Bowling Green on January 6, 1908. Three days later, the first official train, a standard eight-car express train conducted by Grant Cooper, left the West Farms Square station (East Tremont Avenue) at 11:50 a.m. and arrived at Borough Hall with eight hundred passengers at 12:53 p.m. Shortly thereafter, the train began the hour-long, five-cent return trip to the Bronx.

I don't know whatever happened to Nellie or Bright Eyes, but I do know that the workmen who spent a few years underground with Nellie told the press they would make sure she lived in luxury for the rest of her life after the subway was completed. Hopefully, Bright Eyes the good-luck kitten also had a similar fate.

1910

Trent, the Airship Mascot Cat Who Wowed the Crowd at Gimbels

On October 22, 1910, a month after the new Gimbel Brothers Department Store opened at Greeley Square in New York City, a large orange tabby cat was the guest of honor in an exhibition on the store's fourth floor. Lying atop comfy pillows in a gilded cage, Trent attracted crowds of sightseers who couldn't wait to meet the famous cat who had survived a failed transatlantic crossing in a hydrogen airship. As a continuous line of people tried to pet and woo him, Trent ignored them and declined to be sociable. I'm going out on a limb here, but maybe the poor cat was ignoring everyone because he had just gone through a harrowing experience that would have traumatized most cats for the rest of their nine lives.

On October 15, 1910, the journalist and pioneer airman Walter Wellman and five crew members set out from Atlantic City, New Jersey, in *America*, a 165-foot nonrigid airship. The plan was to cross the Atlantic Ocean and reach some point in Europe by following the ocean-steamer tracks. As the saying goes, the best-laid plans of mice and men often go awry. In this case, we could say it was the plans of cat and men that went awry.

In addition to Wellman, the crew included chief engineer Melvin Vaniman, assistant engineers John Aubert and Albert Louis Loud, navigator Frederick Murray Simon, and Marconi wireless radio operator John "Jack" R. Irwin. Navigator Simon decided it would

Melvin Vaniman and his good-luck cat aboard the steamship *Trent* in October 1910. (Library of Congress, Prints & Photographs Division, LC-DIG-ggbain-08627)

be good luck to have a cat on board the historic flight, so he chose a stray cat that had been living in the airship's hangar in Atlantic City. The cat had reportedly been rescued by the night watchman at the hangar after he and his litter-mate had been tossed from an automobile. A dog killed one of the cats; the men called the surviving male cat Kiddo. They placed Kiddo at radio operator Irwin's post in the airship's lifeboat, which was attached under the framework of the airship.

Not surprisingly, Kiddo was not too fond of his predicament, and he put on a great display of anger and terror by meowing and running around the lifeboat in hysterics. Chief Engineer Vaniman was reportedly so annoyed by the antics of Kiddo that he made the first-ever inflight radio transmission to Wellman's secretary back on land. "Roy, come and get this goddamn cat!" he yelled. Simon insisted that it would be bad luck to let the cat leave the ship, but the decision was left to Vaniman.

Vaniman proposed lowering the cat in a canvas bag to a *New York Times* motorboat running beneath the airship. Unfortunately, there was dense fog and the seas were too rough for the reporter on the boat to catch the bag, so Kiddo was forced to continue the journey. As Simon reported in the airship's log, "Cat seemed unhappy, and Vaniman determined to lower her to motor boat containing *Times* reporter, following *America* to sea. Boat failed to get kitty, and she was hauled aboard again. Vaniman wished we hadn't brought her but I said unless we should keep her we wouldn't have a bit of luck."

It took twenty hours of flying before Kiddo consented to eat, but he eventually settled down and took his job as feline copilot quite seriously. One of his duties was to keep the catnapping men awake by trying to lounge on their faces. He also acted as airship barometer by sleeping through the calm parts of the journey and howling just prior to bouts of high winds.

Although the airship set several new records by staying aloft for almost seventy-two hours and traveling over one thousand miles, weather and other problems forced the crew to ditch the airship and join Irwin and Kiddo in the lifeboat on October 18. Somewhere west of Bermuda, they sighted the Royal Mail Steamship *Trent*, which was making its way toward New York. After using Morse code to attract the ship's attention, Irwin made the first aerial distress call by radio, now recorded as the first message sent ashore from an airship over the ocean: "We are in distress; have lost control of our airship; we need help; am on the airship *'America.'* I have wireless on board. Use your wireless. In distress. We are drifting; not under control. Come ahead full speed, but keep astern, as we have a heavy trail dragging. . . . Come in close and put bow of your ship under us. We will drop you a line, but do not stop your ship or you will capsize us."

In preparation for abandoning the airship, the crew stored Kiddo in a forward air chamber in the lifeboat. As the passengers on the steamship cheered and the airship drifted out of sight—never to be seen again—the crew of the *Trent* rescued all the men and their cat by hauling *America*'s lifeboat aboard their ship. When they opened the air chamber, the men found Kiddo curled up and sound asleep. According to Simon's log, Kiddo immediately started scratching and howling when he woke up in the strange place, but he soon settled down to breakfast. Simon again reminded the crew that it had been a good idea to bring Kiddo on the journey, because "cats have nine lives!" The last words in Simon's log were, "We sacrificed our airship but saved our lives. . . . We have gathered a vast amount of useful knowledge. . . . And we also saved the cat!"

Upon arriving in New York, the human and feline crew members of *America* were transported by hansom cab to the editorial offices of the *New York Times* in the Times Tower at One Times Square. After telling their amazing stories to the reporters, they were wined and dined at the Waldorf-Astoria on the northwest corner of Fifth Avenue and Thirty-Third Street (now the site of the Empire State Building) and honored in a ticker-tape parade. Vaniman and the airship cat—now called Trent in honor of the boat that rescued them—were also invited to help the Gimbel brothers celebrate the opening of their New York store on Broadway and Thirty-Second Street.

In the two years following Wellman and Vaniman's failed attempt to cross the Atlantic Ocean in *America*, Vaniman exhibited Trent and the airship's lifeboat at numerous department stores to help raise money for a new airship. Vaniman must have become quite fond of the cat during this time; in addition to posing for the public in department stores, Trent reportedly made some test trips with Vaniman on his new airship *Akron*, the first airship manufactured by the Goodyear Tire & Rubber Company.

On July 2, 1912, during a trial run without their good-luck cat, Vaniman and his crew were killed when the *Akron* exploded two thousand feet above the water as the men's wives and families watched in horror from the Atlantic City pier. The gas bag was torn to shreds, and the car of the airship tipped sideways and fell to the water like a lead balloon. In addition to Vaniman, steersman Calvin Vaniman (Melvin's brother), mechanic George Bourtillion, deck-hand Fred Elmer, and deckhand Walter Guest were killed in the disaster. Arrangements were immediately made to display Trent and the wreck of the airship in the exposition building on Atlantic City's boardwalk. All the proceeds from the exhibition and other related benefits were used to create a relief fund for the families of the dead men. When the benefit tour ended, Trent reportedly lived out the rest of his eight remaining lives on land with Edith Wellman, the daughter of Walter Wellman, in Washington, DC.

DID YOU KNOW?

Although Gimbel Brothers New York officially opened on September 29, 1910, the history of this particular store at Greeley Square goes back to 1874, when the Hudson Tunnel Railroad Company initiated plans to construct a railroad connecting New Jersey and New York City via a tunnel under the mile-wide Hudson River (today's Port Authority Trans-Hudson or PATH train). Construction began in 1874, but litigation and lack of funding caused numerous delays over the years. Finally, in February 1902, the New York and Jersey Railroad Company, under the direction of William Gibbs McAdoo, took over all the railroad company's tunnels and lines of railway, including four thousand feet of tunnel already constructed. The McAdoo Tunnel, or Hudson Tubes, as it was then called, accommodated electrified surface rail cars that operated from the Journal Square terminal in Jersey City to terminals in Manhattan at Christopher, Tenth, Greenwich, and Hudson Streets.

In 1904, the newly formed Hudson and Manhattan Railroad Company (H&M) filed an application to extend the McAdoo Tunnel to a larger underground terminal on Sixth Avenue at Thirty-Third Street. The proposed site was occupied by several Broadway landmarks, including Trainor's hotel and restaurant and the Manhattan Theatre (formerly the Standard Theatre), all of which were condemned and demolished in 1905. Many smaller old buildings on West Thirty-Second and Thirty-Third Streets were also condemned, including a brothel called the House of All Nations and six other properties owned by Albert J. Adams. Incidentally, Adams also had grand plans for the same site: In 1905 he had proposed erecting a forty-two-story hotel on the site, which was to be the tallest building in the world—more than 125 feet taller than the Times Tower and the Park Row Building, then the world's tallest buildings.

On April 23, 1909, five years after the site was cleared to make way for the McAdoo Tunnel concourse at Thirty-Third Street, the Gimbel brothers— Jacob, Isaac, Charles, Daniel, Ellis, and Louis—signed a twenty-one-year lease with the Greeley Square Realty Company for the land atop the proposed terminal (the Thirty-Third Street station opened in November 1910). The Chicago architect Daniel Burnham, who had designed the city's landmarked Flatiron Building, was hired to design the new department store. The *New York Times* reported that the twelve-story department store with three basements would "be the terminal of the McAdoo tunnel system, or Manhattan tunnels, which, by the time the store building is completed, will connect with the Pennsylvania Railroad, Central Railroad of New Jersey, the Erie system, and the Lackawanna & Western Railroad, handling, it is estimated, 1,000,000 persons daily." On December 8, 1909, a copper box containing a history of Gimbels and other data was placed in the cornerstone. The $12 million building at 100 West Thirty-Third Street and Broadway was completed ahead of schedule on June 11, 1910.

On June 6, 1986, the Associated Press reported that Gimbels was going out of business. Today, the building that once paid tribute to a hero cat named Trent houses a large advertising agency, other office tenants, and the Manhattan Mall.

1927

Ranger I and Ranger III, the Mascot Cats of the New York Rangers

The love of a man for a dog is as nothing compared to a hockey player's love for his cat.
—Harold C. Burr, *Brooklyn Daily Eagle*, February 6, 1931

If you're a New York Rangers fan or just a hockey fan in general, you may have heard of the Curse of 1940, also called Dutton's Curse. The curse was a superstitious explanation for why the team did not win the National Hockey League's championship trophy for fifty-four years after last winning in 1940. Some people say the curse was caused when the management of the Madison Square Garden Corporation symbolically burned the mortgage for the arena in the bowl of the Stanley Cup after the 1939–1940 season. Others say the curse is the fault of Mervyn "Red" Dutton, the manager of the competing New York Americans, who said in 1940, "The Rangers will never win the Cup again in my lifetime." I say there was no curse at all. The reason the Rangers didn't win the Stanley Cup during all those years was because the team no longer had their black cat mascots, Ranger I and Ranger III.

❧❧

In June 1923, the boxing promoter George Lewis "Tex" Rickard and a team of wealthy businessmen formed the New Madison Square Garden Corporation. The corporation comprised Rickard (president), the circus man John Ringling (chairman of the board), and William F. Carey (vice president and treasurer). The men proposed building a twenty-six-story office building and "the largest indoor arena in the world" on a site bounded by Sixth and Seventh Avenues and Fiftieth and Fifty-First Streets, which was then occupied by the car barns of the Broadway-Seventh Avenue Railway Company.

Around the same time, the circus man Frank Bailey, who was chairman of the board of directors of Realty Associates, was making plans with Bing & Bing of Brooklyn to build the largest amphitheater in the world on the same site. Unfortunately for Rickard, the sale was held up in ongoing litigation. So, when the New York Life Insurance Company announced plans on June 17, 1924, to demolish the old Madison Square Garden II—giving Rickard until August 1, 1925, to vacate the premises—the men decided they needed to move ahead with a new plan rather than wait for a settlement. That day, Rickard announced that his corporation had purchased the old trolley barn from the Eighth Avenue Railway Company for $2 million. Plans for the new Madison Square Garden III included a mammoth swimming pool, the most modern ice hockey equipment, ice-skating carnivals, an annual six-day bicycle race, circuses, horse shows, and many other expositions.

On January 9, 1925, workmen began wrecking the old trolley depot to make way for the new Madison Square Garden III. The new Garden's gala opening took place December 15, 1925, with a hockey game pitting the New York Americans against the Montreal Canadiens. The Americans (also known as the Amerks) proved to be a great success at the new arena, which encouraged Rickard to seek his own hockey franchise. He originally planned to name his new team the New York Giants, but when the franchise was granted in April 1926, the official name was the New York Rangers Professional Hockey Club. The origin of the name is often attributed to Rickard, who once served as a marshal of Henrietta, Texas. People dubbed the team "Tex's Rangers," and the name stuck with the New York press.

❧

In the winter of 1927, the New York Rangers trainer Harry Westerby came to the rescue of a small female cat he had found whimpering outside the steel door of the hockey dressing room. When team manager Lester Patrick saw the cat in the dressing room, he asked Westerby about it. "Don't you think a black cat's unlucky?" he asked. "Why should it be, sir?" Westerby responded. Unable to answer the question, Patrick agreed to let the cat stay. He never regretted the decision.

Ranger I was described as a fighting hockey cat who snarled and used her claws while boxing with feline opponents (the cat equivalent to throwing off the gloves). She was also quite charming—a good-luck charm, that is—for the Rangers during their successful 1927–1928 season. That season, ten teams played forty-four games each, with the New York Rangers winning the Stanley Cup by beating the Montreal Maroons three games to two. The team was so successful, in fact, that many of the players became minor celebrities in New York. Playing so close to Times Square also earned the Rangers their now-famous nickname, "The Broadway Blueshirts." Although the Rangers did not take the Cup during the next two seasons, the guys still considered Ranger I to be their good-luck mascot (Patrick reportedly would not permit the players to begin dressing for a game until they rubbed her down the back three times). As long as Ranger I was patrolling the Garden, the Rangers were always in the playoffs.

Ranger I was not just a good-luck charm for the Rangers. She apparently brought good fortune to visiting college hockey teams that used the Rangers' locker room. In March 1927, right after she first arrived at the Garden, Ranger I helped both Dartmouth College and Toronto University beat Princeton University. (The press attributed Princeton's losses to the fact that Ranger I did not visit their locker room, but maybe Princeton's players were simply in need of more practice.) Bob McAllister, also known as "the flying cop," also befriended the black cat with hopes of winning the sixty-yard dash at the Knights of Columbus indoor track meet that same month. After trailing behind, McAllister won the race and took second place in the point series. He credited the win to Ranger I, who had appeared in his dressing room and meowed at him before the race.

Ranger I stayed with the team for about three years, but she remained fairly wild, except with a few players and Westerby, who always fed her. During that time, she had several litters of all-black kittens (she gave birth to her first litter in 1928 in a corner locker belonging to the goalie Lorne Chabot), but as soon as the kittens grew up, she'd shoo them away from the Garden to fend for themselves on the cold streets. It was as if she knew she was the mascot and didn't want any competition. Sometimes she'd receive a feline visitor from one of the neighborhood's back fences, but as soon as she thought the cat was trying to take her place, she'd put up quite the fight. As the reporter Harold C. Burr noted in the *Brooklyn Daily Eagle*, "More than one aspirant was sent to the cleaners, in the argot of her adopted sport."

Sometime around October 1930, Ranger I started refusing to eat and drink. Westerby would lock her in a room and bring milk and raw meat, but she'd barely take a bite. Then one night in January 1931, as Westerby was coming back from his own supper, a group of employees called him over to the same steel door where he had found Ranger I three years earlier. He dropped to his knees and started petting and cooing the poor cat and then called for some brandy so she wouldn't suffer. The day Ranger I died—January 10, 1931—all the hockey players, ticket takers, and doorkeepers at the Garden mourned her passing. After losing a game the following night, Bill Cook, the team's first captain, told the press, "That's why we lost to the Black Hawks Sunday night. We'd already lost our mascot."

"She wouldn't let anyone feed her for months," Westerby told the *Brooklyn Daily Eagle* a few days later as he started packing for the team's trip to Boston, where they were scheduled to play the Bruins. "And to think, if I hadn't gone out to supper I might have saved her," he said. Harry noted the team hadn't beaten the Bruins for more than two years, and they couldn't expect to win the upcoming game since they had lost their beloved mascot.

Ranger I was cremated in the big furnace at the Garden—the same furnace where she had kept warm on winter nights. The

Rangers went without a win for more than a week, either losing or tying the score in the eight games after her death. By this time, the cat-less Rangers were way back in fourth place in the league. "You'd better get a new mascot in here in a hurry," Cook told management. "If you don't, I'll go out on the back fences, looking for one myself."

Cook didn't have to look on the fences to find the team's next mascot. As luck would have it, one of Ranger's youngest offspring, whom the team called Ranger III, was living with the Rangers' publicity man, Willis "Jersey" Jones. (Another of her kittens, Ranger II, was living in Nutley, New Jersey, but was too old at the time to be a mascot.) Jersey Jones told the team that he'd bring the kitten to the Garden via a private car so that she could serve as the new mascot.

"Ranger III is a carbon copy of the old lady," Jones told the press on February 3, 1931. "It's marked the same kind of a way and is the same fresh kind of a cat—all claws and scratchy disposition. It's grown up, too, since I took it home. The other day it killed her first mouse." Some of the men wanted to name the kitten Play Off, but those who had experienced the luck that Ranger I brought to the team would not consent to it.

Westerby gave extra-special attention to the handsome new kitten, especially when it came to his diet. For the soup course, he served Ranger III fresh cream, followed by a daily entrée of "chicken livers à la Westerby." Despite this pampering from Westerby, Ranger III adored the rookie player Cecil Dillon the most (perhaps because Dillon had a thick mop of black hair). Dillon in turn loved the good luck that the kitten brought him. On February 5, 1931, Dillon scored both goals to help the Rangers beat the Americans. Following the game, Ranger III looked quite smug as he gave himself a bath under a table in the dressing room, while Pete, the black Newfoundland mascot of the Americans, moped about his team's locker room. The players warned the reporters not to accidentally step on their cat after the game. "If you do there's going to be a couple of dead reporters around here," Murray Murdoch said. (Of course, the players also blamed the cat for everything that went wrong in a losing game.)

News of the new mascot cat quickly spread among the opposing teams' players, who no doubt wanted some of the good luck to rub off on them. During one game with the Chicago Black Hawks, opposing manager Dick Irvin stopped at a delicatessen on his walk from his hotel to the Garden to buy some fresh cream for the cat. After sniffing the bottle and tasting the cream in front of Irvin to ensure that it had not been poisoned, Westerby presented the cream to Ranger III, who lapped up the gift from the Black Hawks. Although Ranger III was ordinarily very active during the games, the extra serving of fresh cream knocked him for a loop, sending him to a corner of the locker room for a long nap that lasted through the third period. The Black Hawks took advantage of his slumber to slam a long shot from center ice that landed in the Rangers' net for the victory. Rumor has it that Irvin left the Garden with a grin on his face while Westerby was still giving Ranger III an earful for selling his team out for a bottle of cream.

Ranger III disappeared a few seasons later. No one knows where he went, and no other cat ever replaced him as the team's mascot. Madison Square Garden III disappeared when it was demolished in 1968. The space remained a parking lot for twenty years, until William Zeckendorf Jr. and the World Wide Group purchased the property to construct the Worldwide Plaza, an immense forty-nine-story office tower and 594-unit condominium development completed in 1989.

DID YOU KNOW?

Madison Square Garden III was built in 1925, shortly after the more famous Madison Square Garden II on Madison Avenue and Twenty-Sixth Street was demolished by the New York Life Insurance Company to make way for the insurance company's new headquarters. The new Garden on Eighth Avenue between Forty-Ninth and Fiftieth Streets was built on the former site of the eighteenth-century Hopper Farm, a three-hundred-acre estate that extended on an east-west diagonal from about Sixth Avenue to the Hudson River between Forty-Eighth and Fifty-Fifth Streets. The farm was also called the Great Kill farm, after the name of a small stream that emptied into the Hudson River at the foot of what is now Forty-Second Street. In fact, all the territory north of this stream was once called the Great Kill region.

Originally established by descendants of the Dutch settlers Andries (Andreas) Hoppe (no *r*) and his wife, Geertje Hendricks, who had arrived in New Amsterdam in 1652, the farm was acquired by Matthys (Matthias) Hopper in 1714. Hopper built his home just north of Hopper's Lane, a diagonal road that ran between today's Fifty-First and Fifty-Third Streets, west of Broadway. With most of the upper Great Kill region owned by the Hopper family, the area became known as Hopperville.

Sometime prior to 1759, Matthias's son, General John Hopper, a soldier in the Revolution, took possession of the farm. According to his last will and testament, dated October 12, 1778, John Hopper bequeathed to each of his sons acreage and a house (his daughter, Jemima Hopper Horn, and his grandchildren also received acreage but no reported structures). Son John inherited a home at the terminus of Hopper's Lane near the Hudson River; Yellis received a home on Fifty-First Street between Broadway and Eighth Avenue; Matthew got a stone house at the foot of Forty-Third Street (near today's Eleventh Avenue); and Andrew inherited the stone and brick homestead on the northeast corner of Fiftieth Street and Broadway. The latter was still standing in 1872 when the *New York Times* wrote about the quaint old house. At that time, it was reported that a wild, savage-looking cat could be seen on the property hunting for sparrows. (Perhaps this was one of Ranger's ancestors.)

The Hopper family had a small family graveyard along the southwest corner of today's Ninth Avenue and Fiftieth Street. In 1885, Ellsworth L. Striker, a Hopper family descendant, had the cemetery removed to build an apartment house on the site (some graves were reportedly reinterred at Trinity Cemetery uptown and Woodlawn Cemetery in the Bronx.) In later years, the nearby land on Eighth Avenue between Forty-Ninth and Fiftieth Streets was occupied by the Eighth Avenue Railroad Company stables. These wood-frame stables were constructed sometime around August 1852, when the Eighth Avenue Railroad opened its new trolley line between Fifty-First and Chambers Streets. The stables were destroyed in a horrific fire in November 1879 that started in a fourth-story hay-storage area. The fire killed approximately 130 of the 950 horses stabled there. A year later, the railroad company hired John Correga to construct a three-story brick structure on the site. It was this structure that Tex Rickard purchased in 1925 and on this site where two cats named Ranger brought good luck to a hockey team in the 1920s and 1930s and where an actress named Marilyn Monroe sang "Happy Birthday" to President John F. Kennedy in 1962.

1927

Victory, the Feline Good-Luck Charm of the Brooklyn Robins

On the evening of April 28, 1928, the manager of the Brooklyn Robins baseball team was in a bit of a conundrum. Just fourteen games into the season, the downtrodden team also known as the Flock, the Daffy Dodgers, and Uncle Robbie's Daffiness Boys had won only two games. In the past week, they had lost five straight games to the Boston Braves, New York Giants, and Philadelphia Phillies. Tasked with pulling a rabbit out of the hat, "Uncle Robbie" Wilbert Robinson was desperate for some good luck. Enter stage right not a rabbit but a three-month-old black vagrant cat that grew up in the shadows of the Brooklyn Bridge.

According to a report in the *Brooklyn Daily Eagle*, Robinson had been in his apartment parlor when he heard a tapping noise outside his chamber door. When he opened the door to investigate, he met a stranger holding a coal-black kitten. "Mr. Robinson, here is something to break the jinx," the man said. "I found it outside."

"Black cats are bad luck," Robinson said with a gasp.

"Sometimes," the stranger replied. "But it takes a thief to catch a thief and maybe it takes a jinx to lick another jinx."

The stranger convinced him. The next day, Robinson created quite a stir when he strolled into Brooklyn's Ebbets Field clubhouse with the kitten perched on his left shoulder. The players were horrified at first, but Robinson explained about the jinx and suggested that the team give the cat a three-day trial. "And you're going to treat him right in the meantime," he added.

As the team prepared for its game with the Phillies, the kitten calmly explored each corner of the clubhouse. The lefty pitcher Watty Clark prepared a little soapbox house in a corner behind some trunks and asked Babe Hamberger, the clubhouse boy, to buy milk. Clark also brought the kitten over to the southpaw pitcher Big Jim "Jumbo" Elliott, who took the cat in his hands and stroked him. In that evening's game against the Phillies, Elliott was practically

Brooklyn Robins Manager Wilbert Robinson rescued
Victory the cat in 1927. He was inducted into the
Baseball Hall of Fame in 1945. (Brooklyn Eagle Photo-
graphs, Brooklyn Public Library, Brooklyn Collection)

unhittable. Not one opposing-team player reached third base. Only
one reached second. The Robins made ten hits and beat the Phillies seven to zero. Following the shutout, the team christened the
kitten Victory, going as far as breaking a bottle of milk over a chair
and letting the milk pour down on the poor cat. The players then

carefully groomed Victory and prepared him for the third and last game in the Philadelphia series. The Robins went on to win the next four games against the Phillies and the Giants.

I don't know how long the rags-to-riches kitty remained with the Robins, but I do know he lived in luxury during his time as the team's mascot, enjoying milk every day and fish on Sundays. Alas, not every cat can be a miracle worker. The Robins finished the season in sixth place out of eight National League teams, with a record of only sixty-five wins and eighty-eight losses.

The team that has been known as the Los Angeles Dodgers since 1958 was formed as the Brooklyn Grays (aka the Brooklyns) in 1883 by the real estate tycoon and baseball enthusiast Charles H. Byrne. That year, Byrne set up a grandstand on Fifth Avenue between Third and Fifth Streets in Red Hook and named it Washington Park in honor of George Washington, who had used the old Gowanus House (extant) on the site as an impromptu headquarters during the Battle of Long Island. The Grays played in the minor Inter-State Association of Professional Baseball Clubs that first season but the following year were invited to join the American Association, where they became the Atlantics. Sometimes the team was called the Trolley Dodgers in recognition of the fans who were good at dodging the streetcars on the nearby trolley tracks on their way to watch a game.

In 1889, after winning the championship game, the team moved to the National League, where they enjoyed many successful years by absorbing key players from the defunct New York Metropolitans and Brooklyn Ward's Wonders. Ten years later, the team moved to a new Washington Park on an old landfill bounded by First Street, Third Street, and Third and Fourth Avenues (part of the left-field wall of the old stadium still stands). It merged with the Baltimore Orioles in 1899, becoming the Brooklyn Superbas under the ownership of Charles H. Ebbets, Ferdinand Abell, Harry Von der Horst, and Ned Hanlon. It wasn't until 1932, a year after the longtime manager Wilbert Robinson retired, that the team was renamed the Brooklyn Dodgers.

DID YOU KNOW?

Before the old Ebbets Field stadium took over the block bounded by Bedford Avenue, Sullivan Place, Cedar Place (today's Zenita Thompson Place), and Montgomery Street in 1913, it was a disreputable, ramshackle, wilderness neighborhood called Pigtown, Goatville, Tin-Can Alley, and Crow Hill. The barren land was home to cow paths, goat trails, and shanty dwellers who used a giant pit in the center of the block as a garbage dump. Charles Ebbets's friends told him that he was crazy to think such a miserable location could feature a modern concrete ballpark that would make Brooklyn the envy of the baseball world. But Ebbets persisted, quietly using proceeds from the sale of his great-grandfather's business at 41 Broad Street in Manhattan to buy just over four acres of parcels for a steal behind the disguise of a dummy corporation. Over the course of three years, Ebbets secretly purchased about forty small lots on the cheap until the news finally leaked out, forcing him to pay outrageous prices for the last few parcels. Although Ebbets planned to call the new stadium Washington Park, several Brooklyn sports editors suggested that he call his ballpark Ebbets Field. The stadium opened on April 5, 1913, with an exhibition game in which the Brooklyn Dodgers beat the New York Yankees.

On February 23, 1960, three years after the Dodgers moved to Los Angeles, a wrecker's ball painted to look like an enormous baseball crashed into the walls of a stadium that was once home to players like Casey Stengel, Roy Campanella, Pee Wee Reese, and Jackie Robinson. A $22 million, twenty-story, 1,377-unit housing project rose on the site. Today, on a small patch of fenced-in grass where the clubhouse used to be, signs advise residents to keep their dogs and other pets off the lawn.

9

Lucky Cats

In the winter of 1914, a stray gray cat sought shelter from the whipping winds in the old police headquarters building at 300 Mulberry Street. Although the New York City Police Department had moved its headquarters to Centre Street a few years earlier, Mr. Furlong, the building superintendent, adopted the cat to control the rat population. Three years and three litters of kittens later, the cat he named Minnie gave birth to her last litter of five kittens in the basement on another cold winter day.

Seeking more heat for her kittens, Minnie discovered an open ash pit under the boiler in the subbasement. Unaware of the live coals buried above, she carried her kittens into the back corner of the pit. The next morning, the boiler-room stoker Thomas Warren reached into the pit to stoke the coals above. Down came the hot coals, and out flashed something gray under his feet. Before Warren could recover from his surprise, Minnie ran back into the ash pit. One by one, she carried her kittens out and laid them at Warren's feet. Sadly, Warren had to use a gun to end Minnie's life (he told the newspapers that she was "just about burned to death"), but he was able to save the unharmed kittens. The publicity following Minnie's heroic deed resulted in hundreds of requests to adopt the kittens.

Four of the lucky kittens went to good homes in Pennsylvania and New Jersey. Superintendent Furlong kept his favorite fur ball.

The story of Minnie and her kittens is just one of many tales about lucky cats and their brawny heroes. In the late nineteenth and early twentieth centuries, newspaper headlines announced heroic cat rescues on a regular basis. Sometimes the story was about a police officer who stopped traffic on a busy street so a mama cat could safely cross. Other times the stories were about firemen who saved cats and kittens from burning buildings. Because of their chosen careers, policeman and firemen were naturally the most popular knights in shining armor for the feline population, but as the following stories show, average civilians and dignitaries also heeded meows for help. Two especially lucky cats from East Harlem were even fortunate enough to be rescued by President Theodore Roosevelt.

1899

Olympia, the Dewey Arch Cat, and Her Lucky Christmas Kittens

Prior to May 1898, sixty-year-old Commodore George Dewey was a little-known leader of the United States Navy's Asiatic Fleet. That all changed during the Spanish-American War, when Commodore Dewey was ordered to attack the Spanish navy in retaliation for Spain's alleged assail on the USS *Maine* in Havana Harbor. Commodore Dewey directed his command vessel, the USS *Olympia*, to Manila Bay in the Philippines, where it was victorious over the rotting wood ships of the Spanish Armada. The stunning naval victory over Spain established the United States as a global military power and Commodore Dewey as what the *New York Times* called "an ideal hero" and the "most popular idol of the masses."

When city leaders learned that Commodore Dewey was coming to New York in September, they made plans for a magnificent two-day tribute that would include a grandiose parade on September 30, fireworks, and illumination of the harbor. They also decided to

Modeled after the Arch of Titus in Rome, the Dewey Arch on Fifth Avenue was carved in about six weeks by twenty-eight renowned sculptors. (Library of Congress, Prints & Photographs Division, Detroit Publishing Company Collection, LC-D4-11508)

erect a ceremonial arch and colonnade on Fifth Avenue at Twenty-Fourth Street to permanently honor the war hero. The city hired the architect Charles R. Lamb, who, along with fellow members of the National Sculpture Society, offered to design, for free, a monumental arch for the parade reviewing area. The city accepted the offer and set aside $26,000 for construction.

Due to short notice, the planners decided to first build a temporary arch out of staff, which was made from plaster and wood shavings. Later, a permanent arch would be reproduced in white marble. (This was how the Washington Square Arch had been constructed just a few years earlier.) Modeled after the Arch of Titus in Rome, the temporary Dewey Arch was carved in about six weeks by twenty-eight renowned sculptors. The arch was topped by a quadriga sculpted by J. Q. A. Ward, featuring four seahorses pulling a ship. Lower down were portrait sculptures of naval heroes including Commodore John Paul Jones, Commodore Matthew C. Perry, and Admiral David Glasgow Farragut. The arch and six double-trophy columns were lit by electric lights at night.

Following the celebrations in September 1899, the arch quickly began to deteriorate. Passing vehicles and carriage wheels made several large holes in the base of the double columns, and souvenir seekers began chipping off pieces of the arch (bits sold for fifteen cents each). For one large gray cat who roamed the streets near Madison Square, a large hole in the corner of one of the columns was the perfect place to give birth.

According to the national headline story first reported in the *New York Herald*, the stray feline took refuge in the hole about two weeks before Christmas. One morning, cabmen stationed across from the Fifth Avenue Hotel heard mewing sounds coming from within. When they investigated, they found the mother cat, whom they named Olympia, nursing four newborn kittens. The cabmen adopted the kittens and named them Dewey, George, Manila, and Cavite. (Another news article said Olympia gave birth to seven kittens, who were cared for by Brigadier General Charles E. Furlong, a longtime resident at the Fifth Avenue Hotel. He reportedly fed them and named them Dewey, Schley, Sampson, Hobson, Sigsbee, Gridley, and Bill Anthony.)

Following the cabmen's discovery, a nearby shopkeeper provided a bed of excelsior shavings for the feline family's home. The hotel supplied some food, including raw beef and maybe even some Lobster Newberg. The cabmen also donated tidbits from their lunches to help nourish the mother cat. During the two weeks leading to Christmas, the cabmen and policemen guarded over the new cat family, protecting them from the newsboys and thousands of curious strangers who tried to grab and taunt them. The men also kept a constant lookout for Christmas shoppers who attempted to kidnap the kittens. Olympia often left the niche to stroll down Fifth Avenue on her own, although on one of her ventures she carried a kitten in her mouth and presented it to one of the cabmen.

On Christmas Day, the cabmen and policemen presented Olympia with a special holiday dinner. The *Brooklyn Daily Eagle* called her "the happiest cat in New York this Christmas," noting that her meal comprised several courses of "the most luxurious viands to be secured on Fifth Avenue." The kittens also received a present (although I'm not sure they were too thrilled by this): the cabmen said that once the kittens were old enough, they would all go for a ride in a cab.

One of the strangers who took a keen interest in the kittens was a street hustler appropriately named Hustling Pete, who made a living selling phony pieces of the arch he made from plaster and sold at his souvenir stand on Broadway. When Pete heard about the kittens, he came up with a scam to sell phony kittens too. According to an article in the *Buffalo Review*, Pete ordered his six children to scour the city streets as far as up to Harlem for stray kittens. The children reportedly found hundreds of kittens for their father, who put them in baskets and presented them to the crowds as the original kittens born in the Dewey Arch.

"Are these really the kittens that were born in the arch?" one little girl asked Pete. "Them's the identical kittens, mum," Pete told the girl's mother. "It was my old cat that went into the arch and had them kittens, and after all sorts of trouble with the city government I've been allowed to claim them my own."

According to the news article, Pete sold about five hundred kittens for a dollar or more (kittens named Dewey were sold for up to two dollars each). If this story is true (I have my doubts), Pete made a fortune—and five hundred stray kittens had the good fortune of finding homes with families that could afford to pay such a high price for a street cat.

In addition to housing Olympia and her kittens, the Dewey Arch was also home to homeless men in the warmer months. In July 1900, the *New York Times* reported that many gaping holes in the columns were occupied by transient men (the police called it the Dewey Arch Hotel). In August, the *New York Evening Post* called the unsightly and deteriorating arch a "variable eyesore and disgrace to the city" that was "becoming a public danger." Although the parade had been a success, an attempt to raise money to rebuild the arch with more durable materials failed, and Colonel William Conant Church announced that all donations would be returned.

At a meeting of the Municipal Assembly in November 1900, a resolution was passed unanimously by both houses authorizing Commissioner James P. Keating of the Department of Streets and Highways to spend the money appropriated for repairing the structure to tear it down.

On November 15, Mayor Robert A. Van Wyck signed an ordinance directing the demolition of the arch. That evening, a crew of a dozen men with pickaxes, crowbars, and shovels began to remove the columns. A few days later, the committee received an offer for the arch from Bradford Lee Gilbert, the architect for the South Carolina Inter-State and West Indian Exposition. Although a crowd of boys had punched holes in the top (making it look like "a colossal pepper box"), Gilbert took what was the left of the arch back to Charleston. In June 1902, the exposition closed in Charleston, and the remains of the arch were demolished. Although, who knows? There may still be some souvenir pieces of the arch among old keepsake boxes in someone's basement or attic.

1904 and 1908

Holey and Gittel, the Cats with Ten Lives on the Lower East Side

On June 15, 1904, the *General Slocum* caught fire and sank in the East River. An estimated 1,021 of the 1,358 passengers on board the wooden side-wheel steamboat were killed. Most of the victims were German American women and children from the Lower East Side who had all dressed in their Sunday best for a picnic excursion hosted by St. Mark's Evangelical Lutheran Church. Many of the dead, including Alfred and Louisa Ansel, Louise Kraff, Lena Giessman, and several members of the Schultz family, had been neighbors living in tenement apartments on East Fourth Street.

Five weeks after what would become New York City's worst disaster until the attacks on the World Trade Center on September 11, 2001, the residents on East Fourth Street had something happy to celebrate when their favorite cat was rescued after spending two years stuck between two tenement buildings. A brief history of Manhattan's Lower East Side will provide a clearer picture of what happened to the cats in this tale and what their heroes had to do in order to rescue them.

The Lower East Side was originally part of the Dutch West India Company's Boweries (or Bouweries) No. 2 and No. 3. These large farms, which were bounded by the Bowery Lane and the East River, passed through several owners during the Dutch colonial period. Director General Petrus Stuyvesant acquired part of Bowery No. 2 in 1651 and established his manor house near what is now East Tenth Street between Second and Third Avenues. The fifty-acre Bowery No. 3 (also known as the Schout's Bowery) was granted to Gerrit Hendricksen in 1646. Sometime around 1732, Philip Minthorne acquired Bowery No. 3. He erected his homestead a few blocks away from where this cat tale takes place, near what would become East Third Street between the Bowery and Second Avenue. The homestead was fenced in and featured a dwelling house, a barn, "and a good bearing Orchard, with about ten acres of Meadow, both fresh and salt."

Following Minthorne's death in 1756, the farm was divided into twenty-seven lots, three for each of Minthorne's nine children: Philip, a farmer; John, a cooper; Henry, a tin man; Mangle, a cooper; Hannah, the wife of Viert Banta, a house carpenter; Hilah, the wife of Abraham Cock, a cooper; Margaret, the wife of Nicholas Romaine, a carpenter; Sarah, the wife of Samuel Hallet, a carpenter; and Francyntje (Frankey), the wife of Paulus Banta, also a carpenter. Each of the siblings received a lot along the Bowery Lane, an internal meadow lot, and a salt-marsh lot near the East River. Ownership of most of the Minthorne property was eventually consolidated under New York City Alderman Mangle Minthorne, Philip's most prominent son. On March 6, 1829, a few years after Mangle's death, 220 lots on Second, Third, Fourth, and Fifth Streets were sold at auction for just under $252,000.

Development in the Lower East Side picked up during the 1830s as growth pushed the city's limits northward. During this time, many single-family Greek Revival row houses were erected on the old farm lots, making the Lower East Side one of the city's most prestigious neighborhoods. By the 1850s, however, many poor immigrants began to settle in the area as wealthier folk moved farther uptown. Developers converted the elegant row houses into multiple-family dwellings and boardinghouses, which were later replaced by four-, five-, and six-story brick tenements in the 1860s to accommodate the housing demand. These buildings were later called pre-law or pre–Old Law tenements because they predated the Tenement House Act of 1879, which required all apartment windows to open to a source of fresh air and light (as opposed to an interior hallway).

Had the tenements of the Lower East Side been constructed in the dumbbell shape adopted after 1879 (two apartments in front, two in back, with narrow air shafts between buildings), a little kitten named Holey could have been rescued immediately by opening a ground-floor window facing the air shaft. Instead, she spent the first two years of her life confined to a four-inch-wide prison.

Like many tenements of the Lower East Side, 163 and 165 East Fourth Street were, respectively, four- and five-story brick buildings with a commercial business and two rear apartments on the ground floor and four flats on each of the upper floors. Only the main room in each three-room flat had direct window access; the interior kitchen and bedroom had no windows and no ventilation. The tenements occupied the same long and narrow footprint (about twenty-five by fifty feet) as the row houses of the previous decades. Thus, they were constructed extremely close together—perhaps as close as several inches near the ground and about fourteen inches near the rooftops (the walls of the old buildings often bulged out toward the ground floor).

In September 1902, a striped kitten was living in the top rear apartment at 163 East Fourth Street with John Poppenlauer and his family. With the arrival of a new baby boy, Poppenlauer decided to isolate the kitten on the roof to keep it away from the infant.

Whether some mischievous boy pushed her or she was just curious and clumsy, the poor kitten fell into the crevice between the rooftops and landed at the bottom of the brick chasm. There was no escape; the crevice was closed off front and back, and some tin roofing that extended over the gap further limited the kitten's air and light from above.

During the early days of imprisonment, the neighbors watched from the roof with pity as the kitten tried to climb up the slippery walls, only to fall back down. The people soon became divided into two factions: those who thought the kitten should be killed and relieved of her misery and those who believed that while there was life, there was hope. George Betz and his wife, who lived on the top floor of no. 165, and Rose Kolb, who lived at no. 163, sided with those who believed in miracles.

Although cats were plentiful in this neighborhood, Holey got everyone's sympathy with her continuous howls and meows. Fishing for the kitten using hooks with meat, button hooks, nooses, miniature scaffolds, poles, and other devices became a common diversion for the residents. Men, women, and children would often sit on the roof and talk to her. Some neighbors, like Betz and Kolb, also lowered buckets of water and food, including wienerwurst, chicken, and fish. (Foodwise, Holey made out better than any of the other stray cats on the street.) The people fed her so well, in fact, that she got a bit plump and could only turn around on the wider end of the crevice.

Betz told Gustave Froelich, the owner of no. 163, that he was going to cut a hole in the cellar wall if the cat got any fatter. "Every time I looked down and saw the poor prisoner my heart was touched, and I made up my mind she would not spend another winter down there," he told reporters. For two winters, though, Holey survived in the narrow brick prison. Sometimes the snow would pile up, and no one could see her for days at a time. Although she could keep fairly dry by staying under the tin roofing, during heavy rain storms the shaft would fill up with a couple of inches of water. Betz made a raft for the cat and lowered it down to her. When it rained, Holey could float on the makeshift raft.

The cat's predicament finally got the attention of the SPCA. The agent who came to investigate was in favor of killing the cat. He suggested shooting her, but the cat's advocates argued that this might jeopardize the safety of the human residents. He also tried to send down poisoned liver, but the cat had instinctive wisdom and ignored it. As the women of the neighborhood began mobbing him and shouting that he was being unkind to Holey, the animal-cruelty agent finally gave up and left.

Finally, on July 22, 1904, a former cowboy who had learned how to use a lariat in the western states came to the rescue with a clothesline noose. He went to the roof of no. 163, and as Holey sat amazingly still, he got the noose around her and pulled her to freedom. Although Holey tried to escape, Betz was able to grab her and bring her to Kolb, who had expressed an interest in adopting the cat as a pet for her new baby. Once in Kolb's apartment, Holey drank some milk and ran under a bed. It took Holey a while to adjust to daylight. It also took some time for her to learn to walk in directions other than backward and forward along a straight line.

Three years after Holey's rescue, a white female cat moved into an apartment in the same building. The apartment was home to Mr. and Mrs. Louis Leichtman and their children, Aaron, Ruth, and Isaac. Louis, manager of the National Employment Agency at 168 East Fourth Street, named the cat Gittel, which means "good" in Yiddish. Gittel brought much luck to Leichtman; according to a story about the cat in the *Sun*, the man with a big heart "rather would have parted with three of his toes than with Gittel, the bringer of good luck."

On July 21, 1908, Gittel was on the rooftop of the tenement soaking up the sun when she fell thirty feet into an unfinished chimney that ran down to the basement. Leichtman and his family could hear Gittel howling all night long. The next day, instead of going to work, Leichtman made a rope ladder of cord and sticks and lowered it down. Of course, the cat would have none of it. Next, he tried lowering liver skewered to the rope, followed by pails of milk and bits of fish. That didn't work either. So Leichtman asked the landlord if he could make a hole in the wall in the basement. The landlord refused.

Desperate to free his beloved Gittel, Leichtman resorted to lowering his son Aaron down the chimney. "My son," he told the boy while tying a rope around him, "there lies our Gittel; here am I and here are you. I am heavy and of no great agility, you are light and full of the strength of youth. It is you who must go down there for our Gittel." Aaron got stuck halfway down the shaft, where the walls of the tenement had bulged, and some friends and neighbors had to help Leichtman extract him. Finally, four days after Gittel had fallen down the chimney, Leichtman sought help from the SPCA. Agent Thomas Freel responded and found a plumber in the neighborhood. Together, the men were able to create a hole in the wall. The cat, of course, was too frightened to come out, so Agent Freel went back up on the roof and tossed a few small pieces of brick down to encourage the cat to leave the hole. As Gittel emerged, Leichtman and his neighbors shouted in joy.

In 1955, New York State Senator MacNeil Mitchell and Assemblyman Alfred Lama sponsored a bill for providing affordable rental and cooperative housing to moderate- and middle-income families. Four years after the Mitchell-Lama bill was passed, eighteen hundred families and three hundred small businesses were evicted from the four-block area bounded by Second Street, Avenue A, Sixth Street, and First Avenue. All of the tenements were demolished over the next two years, including 163 and 165 East Fourth Street, where Holey and Gittel had been rescued fifty years earlier. In December 1960, the New York City Housing Authority broke ground for the Franklin D. Roosevelt Houses, a complex of seven buildings comprising twelve hundred apartments. Today, the sprawling complex is called Village View.

1906

The East Harlem Cats Bequeathed to President Theodore Roosevelt

To the Coroner or First Police Officer that Finds My Body Here: I beg of you to telephone to President Theodore Roosevelt. He will have my body cremated. I have written to him, have made my will, and all I have is his. He will have everything attended to just as I wish it to be, and all will be right. He knows where to find everything. Please find enclosed $5, and a thousand thanks for your kindness. Please do not let my poor kittens be frightened or annoyed. President Roosevelt will take them as soon as he receives my letter I mailed to-night to him. Please let them stay here until then. My heart is broken, so I take my own life in the familiar way I know by drinking chloroform. No one is to blame but myself. I trust my spirit and future life to a merciful and loving God, who knows and judges our sorrow.

—Lulu B. Grover, December 8, 1906

Lulu B. Grover loved her two Angora cats almost as much as she adored President Theodore Roosevelt. So, when she decided to end her life on December 8, 1906, she first made sure all the necessary preparations were in place to ensure that her cats went to a good home after her death—in other words, the White House.

According to Grover's friend Mrs. Richard H. Connor of 72 East 120th Street, Grover was the daughter of a rancher named Smith who owned the ranch adjacent to Teddy Roosevelt's Elkhorn Ranch near Medora, North Dakota. Grover allegedly married sometime around 1880, when she was seventeen, but a year later she was a widow. (I say "allegedly" because when Grover told stories about her earlier life to her friends in East Harlem, she was not of sound mind.) Described in the newspapers as a comely woman about forty-five years old at the time of her death, Grover often claimed to be a distant relative or good friend of President Roosevelt. She loved to tell people how, as a young woman in Medora, she would take long horse rides with him across the North Dakota prairies. She also claimed to have met him in New York on several occasions. Grover was also quite fond of the president's eldest son, Teddy Jr., for whom she purchased several Christmas gifts when Roosevelt was the governor of New York. According to news reports, she anonymously sent the boy a shotgun, a compass, and a watch. Roosevelt wrote back to the gift giver, requesting the person refrain from sending more presents to his son because he didn't want strangers to spoil the boy.

According to Marie Hunter, who was the caretaker of the house at 2089 Lexington Avenue where Grover was renting the parlor-floor apartment (comprising two large rooms and a bath), Grover was a magazine writer and artist who was always well dressed. She also seemed to have a generous income from an unknown source. Although she loved to paint and do needlecraft, Grover's main interest in life were her two cats, which she had named Magistrate Joseph Pool and Queen Fairy Snowdrop. (Grover reportedly named the one cat in Magistrate Joseph Pool's honor after he took her side in a court case involving her "dear little kitten" and "a horrid man and his detestable dog.") Every day she would have meat cut up into fine pieces for them, and she was always concerned about their welfare. In addition to these two cats, she reportedly kept the cremated remains of two other cats, named Golden Teddy Roosevelt and Sunbeam, in fine Tiffany vases.

On November 13, 1906, Grover wrote her last will and testament. She bequeathed her entire estate—including about $800, some jewels, and the two Angora cats—to President Roosevelt. In the will, Grover noted that the president was a "good angel" and her "only true friend in trouble." Her neighbors Edwin and Rosetta Taft (said to be related to Secretary of War William Howard Taft) signed the will as her witnesses. Two weeks after she prepared her will, Grover wrote a letter to President Roosevelt. In the letter, she told him he would find her will and a bank book sewed into the lining of her cats' basket; he'd find the jewels hidden under the fireplace hearth. Then she went into the bathroom and swallowed a vial of chloroform.

Grover may have gotten the idea to ingest a chemical poison from a previous neighbor, Adelene L. Callender, who had lived in the flat above Grover when she was living at 58 East Eighty-Fourth Street in 1898. At that time, Grover had accused Police Captain Henry Frers and Policeman Joseph A. Wasserman of the East Eighty-Eighth Street station of hounding Callender and threatening to arrest her because they said she had a bad character. Grover supposedly contacted then governor-elect Roosevelt—who had served as president of the New York City Police Department Board of Commissioners from 1895 to 1897—and told him that the constant police harassment had caused her neighbor to kill herself by drinking carbolic acid. Roosevelt apparently wrote back saying he would have the matter fully investigated.

On Sunday morning, December 9, Rosetta Taft heard groans coming from Grover's apartment. She found Grover on the bathroom floor wearing a house gown and losing consciousness. The place smelled of chloroform, and there was an empty vial on the floor. Taft called for the police at the East 126th Street station and for Dr. E. G. Maupin of 151 East 127th Street. Lying on her hospital bed at Harlem Hospital later that day, Grover was questioned about an incident that took place during the wedding of President Roosevelt's daughter, Alice, and US Representative Nicholas Longworth III in February 1906. Apparently, a "woman in blue" had tried to break into the White House, claiming she was a magazine writer. Grover denied any knowledge of the incident.

As Grover lay dying in the hospital, Detective Sergeants O'Rourke and Kammer searched her rooms. In one room, the walls were covered with pictures of President Roosevelt at almost every stage of his career. The room contained many pictures cut from newspapers and magazines, three oil paintings of him that Grover had painted (one in uniform on horseback, one standing in his Rough Riders uniform, and one in civilian clothes), a few poems she had written about him, and several tapestries in his likeness. On the bookshelves was a complete collection of his writings. The detectives also found two letters on standard writing paper—the one to the coroner that Grover wrote on December 8 (and that several newspapers published) and another to her neighbors Mrs. Taft and Mrs. Lyons. In the letter to her neighbors, Grover spoke of the pleasure she had in knowing them and apologized for any shock she may have caused by taking her own life. The detectives also found a cat basket and two Angora cats.

Grover died at Harlem Hospital on Sunday, December 10—the same day that Theodore Roosevelt was awarded the Nobel Peace Prize. Her body was taken to the undertaking shop of W. P. St. Germain at 1984 Lexington Avenue. He held the body there for three days to allow someone to claim it. During this time, all of her property was turned over to Public Administrator William M. Hoes. Grover's personal effects included a wicker cat basket lined with silk inside and out (the bank book and will were located under the inside lining) and several small diamond pieces and other jewels, which were found inside a leather bag tucked into the smoke vent of the fireplace chimney. Hoes knew he could sell the jewelry at an auction, but he was in a quandary as to what he should do with the cats. He could not give them away, he told the press, because they had been willed to President Roosevelt. Hoes appealed to Marie Hunter to relieve him of the burden. She sent a letter to President Roosevelt, who told her to send the two cats to Washington, where he and his family would take care of them.

Even though President Roosevelt vehemently denied knowing Grover, he saw to it that her last wishes were carried out. Under his orders, US Attorney Henry L. Stimson supervised the cremation of her body and burial of her ashes at Woodlawn Cemetery in the Bronx (the president was adamant that she not be buried in a pauper's grave). Only four people—her friend Mrs. Connor, Secret Service Agent Tate, and the undertaker and his daughter—attended the funeral. Following the president's request, Stimson also made arrangements to deliver the two cats to the White House. A carriage arrived at Grover's former apartment house on Lexington Avenue, and the two cats reportedly traveled with Douglass Robinson, the president's brother-in-law, to Washington. At the time, the Roosevelts had several pets at the White House, including a few guinea pigs, dogs, ponies, a cat with six toes, a parrot, and two Kansas jackrabbits. I'm sure the large pet-friendly house and vast green lawns must have seemed like paradise for two lucky Angora cats who grew up in a small apartment in Manhattan.

At an auction of Grover's estate in September 1907, one of the items sold was an eighteen-carat gold ring in which were set two small diamonds and a tooth that the auctioneer said had formerly belonged to President Roosevelt. Robert R. Jordan, who had an antique shop at 762 Lexington Avenue, bought the ring and exhibited it on a royal-purple velvet cushion in the shop window. A friend of Grover's said Roosevelt had reportedly given the tooth to Grover in North Dakota when she asked him for a keepsake. Jordan told the press that he thought he could get about twenty-five dollars for the ring.

DID YOU KNOW?

Theodore Roosevelt was born on October 27, 1858, in a three-story brownstone at 28 East Twentieth Street. This house was constructed in 1848 on the old Cornelius Tiebout Williams farm. Roosevelt lived there for fourteen years until 1873, when the family moved uptown to a mansion at 6 West Fifty-Seventh Street, just below Central Park.

During his childhood years, Roosevelt and his three siblings would often play in a screened-in back porch on the third floor. From here, he could look down and into a large fenced-in yard behind the mansion at 890 Broadway, on the northeast corner of East Nineteenth Street. The four-story-with-basement brownstone mansion, constructed by Williams around 1830, was owned by Peter Goelet (pronounced *goo-let*), who had purchased the property from Williams's daughter, Julia C. Miner, for $22,500 in 1844.

Goelet, described as an eccentric miser and one of the last great millionaires of Old New York, filled his grassy yard with exotic birds from around the world, including pheasants from India, storks from Egypt, birds of paradise, cranes, and other brilliantly plumed fowl with clipped wings. Goelet also owned hens, horses, guinea pigs, and a cow, which was reportedly the last cow to ever graze on Broadway. While throngs of people crowded around the iron fence to watch the animals (it was a standing joke among the Broadway stagecoach drivers to encourage tourists to disembark on Nineteenth Street to visit the Central Park menagerie annex), Roosevelt could watch Goelet feed his birds, collect eggs, and milk the cow from his third-story vantage point.

In 1879, the *New York Times* reported, "The extraordinary spectacle of a cow, storks, guinea-pigs, and other animals, feeding quietly in the busiest and most bustling part of Broadway, was one that attracted every stranger's curiosity, and during the fine days in Summer it was no uncommon thing to see a considerable crowd gathered in front of the house gazing through the iron railing at the unwonted sight within."

Seven years after the Roosevelts moved uptown, Goelet died in his home. The property was conveyed to his sister, Hannah Green Gerry, who continued living there with her two servants. Although many of the peacocks and other birds had long disappeared, the cow and the remaining birds were allowed to live out their lives in the yard (the cow was last seen around 1886). By the time Gerry passed away in 1895, the stone carriage house where the birds once lived had fallen into ruin, the iron fence was rusted, the window panes in the stable where Goelet kept his horses were broken, and the grass where the cow and chickens once grazed was gone. The Goelet mansion—then valued at $850,000—was demolished in April 1897 and replaced with an eight-story commercial building that currently houses a dance studio and movie theater.

1912

Kaiser, the Feline Survivor of the Great Equitable Life Building Fire

On January 9, 1912, just after 5:00 a.m., a small fire started in a rubbish can in the basement of the Equitable Life Building at 120 Broadway. Four hours later, when the fire was finally contained, the Equitable Life Building fire was one for the books in the annals of the New York Fire Department.

According to news reports and an official account from the National Fire Protection Association, the great fire was allegedly started accidentally by Philip O'Brien, the timekeeper of the Café Savarin, which was located on the Pine Street side of the Equitable Life Building. O'Brien's office, described as a small frame enclosure, was in the basement of the building among the vaults and a receiving room for supplies. O'Brien shared the basement with Kaiser, a glossy-black tuxedo cat with white nose, breast, and mittens who had been on rat patrol at the Equitable Life Building since 1907.

Not too far away from the timekeeper's office was a large shaft that housed two steam elevators and eleven dumbwaiters that served the dining rooms of the Café Savarin and the Lawyers' Club from a shared kitchen on the eighth floor. The shaft had openings on all but the fourth floor.

On this morning, O'Brien must have been distracted, because he admitted to possibly throwing a lit match into the garbage bin. Less than twenty minutes later, his office was engulfed in flames. As O'Brien and other employees tried to extinguish the flames, the fire spread to the elevators and dumbwaiters, giving it access to the entire Equitable Life Building. While the fire raged inside, the winds were gusting up to sixty-eight miles an hour outside, making the subfreezing temperatures seem even colder. At the far end of the block-long basement, Kaiser was just waking up to start a new day of rat catching.

Comprising five buildings constructed over time and connected together, the Equitable Life Building (more commonly called the Equitable Building) occupied the entire block bordered by Broadway, Nassau, Cedar, and Pine Streets. The original building of the Equitable Life Assurance Society was a seven-story granite structure with frontage only on Broadway and Cedar Street. When this building was erected in 1869–1870, it was considered the first skyscraper in New York City. The Equitable Building was also a pioneer among office buildings in that it was constructed of fireproof building materials and featured the first public elevators in an office building in the city. By 1876, the building had been enlarged to eight stories and extended through to Nassau Street. Later, the building was extended to ten stories (although the architectural treatment of the exterior gave the impression that it was only five tall stories). Four small lower buildings at the northeast and southeast corners were subsequently acquired by the society and connected to the main building via open doorways in the dividing walls.

In addition to the main tenant on the second floor, the Equitable Building was home to some of the most well-established banking, insurance, and law offices of the Gilded Age, including the Hanover Fire Insurance Company, Mercantile Trust Company, and Union Pacific. Along the mansard roof, in several towers, were the apartments of the superintendent of the building and the offices of the local forecast officials of the Department of Agriculture's Bureau of Meteorological Observations (the Weather Bureau). In the basement, where Kaiser worked as head mouser, safe boxes and vaults were filled with several billion dollars' worth of securities, stocks, bonds, and wines.

In 1909, plans were filed to replace the building with a sixty-two-story structure that was to be 909 feet above the curb, excluding the 150-foot-tall flagstaff. The new building would have been the second-tallest man-made structure at the time, just 75 feet short of the 984-foot-tall Eiffel Tower built in 1887. Those plans fell through, courtesy of a grass-roots organization called the Committee of Congestion of Population in New York. I don't think I'd be telling this story if the new building had been constructed as planned.

At 5:34 a.m. on January 9, 1912, the first fire alarm was pulled at Box 24 on the corner of Pine and Nassau Streets. The first due responding fire companies (four engines, two ladders, two battalion chiefs, and the deputy chief of the First Division) arrived within minutes. The first-in engine company, Engine Company No. 6, which was stationed at 113 Liberty Street, immediately stretched a line into the cellar and began operating. At 5:55 a.m., Deputy Chief John Binns transmitted second and third alarms. The multialarm fire brought Fire Chief John Kenlon and Fire Commissioner Joseph Johnson to the scene.

With the fire raging out of control, Brooklyn fire companies were also called in to help. It was the first time in the history of the city's fire department that Brooklyn units responded to a Manhattan fire. The newly appointed Police Commissioner Rhinelander Waldo, who had resigned as the city's fire commissioner shortly after the deadly Triangle Shirtwaist Factory fire in 1911, ordered police officers to shut down the Brooklyn Bridge to allow the responding companies to get to the fire as fast as possible. Nine engines, four hook-and-ladder trucks, a water tower, a searchlight engine, and numerous hose tenders rolled onto the scene under the command of Brooklyn Fire Chief Thomas Lally. Kaiser, oblivious to all that was going on around her, continued to patrol the vast basement.

At about 6:00 a.m., the first of six casualties occurred when three of Café Savarin's waiters were trapped on the mansard roof after trying to escape to the top floor by elevator. Firefighters tried to rescue them, but the ladders were three stories too short. By the time the firefighters, including Fireman James F. Molloy of Engine Company No. 32, tried to rescue the waiters using a rope-rifle shot from a neighboring building, the roof had begun to collapse. The trapped men jumped to their deaths onto Cedar Street.

Fire Battalion Chief William Walsh was also killed in the fire when the building caved in while he was searching the fourth floor with Captain Charles Bass of Engine Company No. 4. Fireman James G. Brown of Ladder 1, who was with Walsh and Bass, survived after being hurled through a door into another wing of the building by the air pressure created during the collapse. His efforts to retrieve Walsh failed, but not for lack of desperately trying. Bass was able to escape the building, but he succumbed to his burns and other injuries after spending many months in a Connecticut sanatorium.

At the time of the collapse, William Giblin, the president of the Mercantile Deposit Company, and two watchmen for the company —William Campion and William Sheehan—became trapped in the cellar while searching for important documents in a massive vault. For almost two hours, Fireman James Dunn of Engine Company No. 6, Firemen Brown and Young of Truck 1, and Fireman William Lark of Engine Company No. 20 took turns cutting away at the two-inch steel bars in the basement windows with a hacksaw. As hundreds of gallons of water poured down and froze in the subzero temperatures, the men worked frantically to get through the bars. While they worked, Father McGean, the fire department's chaplain, stood by to administer the sacrament for the sick and dying—the last rites—if the rescue efforts failed. Giblin and Sheehan were eventually freed and rushed to the Hudson Street Hospital for treatment. Campion collapsed while reaching for the bars of another window and was administered the last rites.

While the firemen continued to pour water into the basement and thick black smoke continued to pour from the windows, Kaiser

As firefighters battled the fire at the Equitable Life Building, the water immediately turned to ice in the subzero temperatures, creating a massive ice fortress on Broadway. (Wurts Bros. [New York, N.Y.] / Museum of the City of New York. X2010.7.1.12034)

the cat no doubt sought another location where perhaps the floor was drier and the air was less smoky. Having witnessed my own cat in a smoky room, I trust that Kaiser was terrified—perhaps she even saw all of her nine lives flash before her eyes. Outside, as the temperatures dropped even more, Broadway and nearby streets became coated with layers of ice, hoses froze solid, fire apparatuses jammed, and the firemen became covered in icicles. By the time the fire was finally contained at 9:30 a.m., the Equitable Building was an ice-covered tomb in ruins.

On January 13, four days after the Equitable fire started, workers were finally able to crack through the ice and search for the body of Battalion Chief Walsh. It took many hours to free his frozen corpse from the ruins. The following day, the body of watchman Campion, his hand still frozen to an iron bar on a window, was carefully removed from the cellar. On January 25, sixteen days after the fire started, workmen who were trying to salvage the contents of the cellar vaults and safe boxes found a "sad wreck of a cat" in the front part of the lower floor. Kaiser, who apparently had more than nine lives, had miraculously survived the conflagration. She was weak and hungry and grateful for the warm saucer of milk and beef chop that the men gave her. However, she still wasn't ready to leave the only home she had ever known or to desert her charge.

For hours, the men tried to lure Kaiser out of the building, but she wouldn't budge from her home. Even as portions of the building collapsed or were demolished, she refused to leave. She simply moved from one corner to another until there was nowhere left to hide. Eventually, the men had to force her into a crate and carry her out of the building. Edna Blanchard Lewis, a pioneer female insurance broker and former instructor at the New York Institution for the Instruction of the Deaf and Dumb, received permission to adopt the cat and take her home to Morningside Heights. Kaiser's brawny rescuers reportedly "shed real tears as they bade goodbye to their feline friend."

Kaiser was taken to her new home at 480 West 119th Street, where she was given a bath and then brushed, petted, and hugged (not necessarily in that order). She was also given a new name: Kaiser the Faithful. Over the next few years, Kaiser the Faithful enjoyed sunning herself in the window and sleeping in her own roomy basket. She appeared at several exhibits, including the Woman's Industrial Exhibition at the Grand Central Palace in March 1912 and 1914 and at the Empire Cat Club's show of cats, held in conjunction with the Empire Poultry Association in December 1912. Grace Hazen, a jeweler who taught in her studio at the National Arts Club in Gramercy Park, presented Kaiser with a new bedazzled collar featuring a hammered-silver design showing high buildings, clouds, and flames. The collar was inscribed, "Faithful, Through Fire, Water, and Air." On the back was a cat's-eye jewel, and on each side, a topaz (a topaz also hung from the buckle). The silver plate was mounted on a soft, gray, leather collar.

I do not know how long Kaiser the Faithful continued to live in the lap of luxury; but I do know that her human mom was quite well-to-do, so I'm sure she purred through her final years and never had to work for her supper again.

Incidentally, Kaiser wasn't the only lucky animal to survive the fire. A small guinea pig was also discovered during the salvage operation. Somehow, the poor critter had survived sixteen days in the extreme cold, imprisoned in a small cage without any food or water.

Miss Bacillus had been brought to the Equitable Life Building by Dr. A. S. Wolf, who had an office on the third floor of the Pine Street side of the building. Wolf was reportedly conducting some "experiments" with the guinea pig for medical insurance purposes. Although this part of the building had not been destroyed by the fire, the office had been completely damaged by water and ice, and so no one thought to look in the room for survivors, human or otherwise. It wasn't until Wolf heard a faint squeak while recovering personal items from his office that the guinea pig was discovered.

Wolf let the guinea pig out of her cage, and she immediately scampered across the office to where he stored her food. When he brought her back outside, hundreds of people who were waiting their turn to go into the building to retrieve their contents from the vaults gathered around the cage in awe. "I was certainly surprised to find the guinea pig still living," Wolf told the press. "Of course, it did not suffer by the fire, but you know how cold it has been ever since the fire." Wolf reportedly gave his guinea pig to Henry W. Ward of Washington, DC, whose young son was mourning the recent loss of his pet guinea pig. In March 1912, Ward brought Miss Bacillus back to New York City to share the spotlight with Kaiser the Faithful at the Woman's Industrial Exhibition.

In November 1912, ten months after the great fire, several leading bankers proposed turning the site of the former Equitable Life Building into a public park called Equitable Park. Ever since the demolition of the building had approached the ground level, these bankers and other workers in buildings fronting the vacant site had been enjoying the sunlight that now flooded their offices, and they wanted to preserve this open space. Meanwhile, the E. I. du Pont de Nemours Powder Company was plotting to construct a new skyscraper on the large lot, which General Thomas Coleman du Pont and his associates had purchased for close to $13.5 million in October.

Eventually, plans were approved for a new forty-two-story Equitable Building, designed by Ernest R. Graham, which was completed in 1915. Rising ramrod straight up thirty-eight stories from its property lines with no setbacks until the top two-story penthouses, the H-shaped superstructure was touted as the largest office building in the world with 1.2 million square feet of rentable office space for up to sixteen thousand office workers. Noting its fireproof elevator shafts and doors, the contractor president J. L. Horowitz said the building was "the nearest to an absolutely fireproof building in the world." As the *New York Times* "Streetscapes" columnist Christopher Gray noted in 1986, "It was, in its time, the biggest, baddest, light-blockingest, street-congestingest space-hog ever to touch down on Manhattan bedrock."

The Equitable Building still stands at 120 Broadway, where it casts a shadow one-fifth of a mile long and seven acres in size. Although the Equitable Life Assurance Society hasn't had offices in the building since 1925, the building still houses numerous banks and brokerage firms. In 1980, Larry A. Silverstein purchased the property for $60 million and spent many years and many millions renovating the building inside and out. The Equitable Building was declared a National Historic Landmark in 1978 and a New York City Landmark in 1996.

DID YOU KNOW?

The following is a summary of three articles about the history of the Equitable Building site published by the *New York Times* in 1912, the *New York Herald* in 1918, and the *New York Evening World* in 1926. As Victor H. Lawn noted in the *Evening World*, "Beyond the great pile of stone and steel and concrete . . . lies a romantic story of old New York. . . . The soil is fertile with messages from the past."

The acre of land on which the Equitable Life Building was constructed was previously just a small portion of a large farm owned by an early Dutch settler and trader named Jan Janszen Damen (or Dam). Damen had acquired the property through a Dutch land grant in 1644 from Governor

William Kieft, just nine years before the great wall along present-day Wall Street was built. The rolling property extended from today's Pine Street to Fulton Street on the west side of Broadway and from Pine Street to Maiden Lane east of Broadway. Damen owned two of the six houses that would later stand just north of the great wall along what the Dutch called de Heere Straat—the Gentleman's Street (the English renamed it Broadway). Damen's small house occupied what is now Pine Street and Broadway, and his "great house" or farmhouse was near the corner of Broadway and Cedar Street.

Following Damen's death in 1651, his land was conveyed to his widow and her heirs. Two years later, the city, now under the command of Peter Stuyvesant, erected the great wall—essentially a twelve-foot-tall stockade—across the island to fend off attacks from Native American tribes. In 1664, the widow's heirs sold the smaller house to Pieter Van Stoutenburg (aka Peter Stoutenburgh), another Dutch settler who came to New Amsterdam sometime around 1638. In 1672, the heirs sold the farmhouse to Dr. Henry Taylor. Their timing was perfect: a year later, the city ordered Stoutenburgh, Taylor, and all the other property owners north of the wall to demolish their homes because the structures were thought to be impeding the city's walled defenses.

The Tulip Garden. Pieter Stoutenburgh was the city's horticulturist, and he's credited with bringing the first tulip bulbs to New Amsterdam. His half-acre tulip garden between present-day Nassau Street and Broadway was quite an attraction in those days. As the *Sun* reported in September 1912, "From the little lane called Broadway you could look through his gate and catch a glimpse of red, white, orange and crimson flowers, blooming riotously in the spring of the year." Although Stoutenburgh was ordered to demolish his home in 1673, he held onto the land until his death in 1699, when it was conveyed to his heirs. Sometime during the early 1700s, the Stoutenburgh estate sold the former tulip-garden property to the Dutch Reformed Church. On the site, the church constructed a parsonage that served as a residence for the minister of the Middle Dutch Church, which was located on Nassau Street between Cedar and Liberty Streets.

The Vauxhall Garden. Fast-forward to 1797, when Jacque Madelaine Joseph De La Croix (aka Delacroix), a French caterer and confectioner, purchased the parsonage plot from the Dutch Reformed Church for £3,950. According to Delacroix, it was "a remarkable lot and large house . . . with large stone cistern, a very large ice house, handsome water works, and a fine garden of fruit trees." Delacroix established a confectionery shop in the old parsonage at 112 Broadway, which he shared with John and Michael Paff, dealers in musical instruments. Behind the shop, he created a pleasure garden called Ice House Garden (later Vauxhall Garden). Opened on July 4, 1797, the garden was a popular resort that featured light refreshments and simple entertainment, including vocal and instrumental concerts. The admittance fee was six shillings, which included a glass of ice cream and punch or lemonade.

In 1825, Delacroix enlarged his shop to create the National Hotel at 112–114 Broadway. Just next door, at 110 Broadway, was the Tremont Temperance House hotel. The New York Athenaeum, established in 1824, was on the corner of Broadway and Pine. (From 1821 to 1822, William Cullen Bryant edited the *New York Review and Athenaeum* in a building on this site.) And at 120 Broadway, on the corner of Cedar Street, Francis Guerin, a celebrated restaurateur, operated a shop famous for its French cordials, bonbons, preserves, tarts, and confections.

In 1836, Delacroix sold the National Hotel to Charles St. John for $100,000. Sometime before 1867, the hotel was conveyed to General Daniel Butterfield, the son of John Butterfield, a founder of the American Express Company. Butterfield sold 112–114 Broadway to the Equitable Life Assurance Society in 1876 for just under $303,000.

1925

Blackie, the Mother Mouser Who Stopped Traffic on Lafayette Street

On June 6, 1909, the New York Humane Society and the Friends of Jerry the Cat hosted a dinner for Policeman Walter C. Rosendale at the Hotel Gonfarone on the corner of Eighth and MacDougal Streets. The officer, who was attached to Traffic Squad B, was being honored for saving Jerry, the squad's mascot cat. As a member of the Traffic Squad, Policeman Rosendale was responsible for guarding the crossing at Broadway and Worth Street. One day, Jerry, a black father cat with a family of kittens, decided to walk deliberately slowly across Broadway. For seven minutes, Rosendale held up traffic until Jerry was able to cross safely. The traffic squad adopted Jerry as its mascot, and Rosendale was rewarded for his actions with the dinner.

Perhaps Policeman James Cudmore of Traffic Squad A had read this story about Jerry when he was a young boy, and it had made a lasting impression on him. It's more likely, though, that the officer

Police Officer James Cudmore stops traffic so that mother cat Blackie can safely transport her five kittens, one by one, across Lafayette Street at Walker Street. (Photo by Harry Warnecke / NY Daily News Archive via Getty Images)

was just doing his job when he took part in what would become one of the most iconic news photographs in the city's history.

On July 29, 1925, a glossy-black mother cat tried to carry her five kittens across Lafayette Street at Walker Street. The cat was the mouser and mascot for the Atwater Company on Water Street, and she was trying to bring her family home after giving birth to the kittens on the west side of Broadway. Traffic was heavy on this hot summer day, making the crossing difficult for mama cat and her kittens. Luckily for Blackie, Policeman Cudmore saw her predicament and stopped traffic until she made five safe crossings.

News of the good deed quickly reached the desk of Cliff Laube, the city editor for the *New York Daily News*. "A guy just phoned in a tip about a cat tying up traffic carrying a kitten across Lafayette Street," Laube reportedly said, as he told the newspaper photographer Harry Warnecke to respond to the scene to take a photo of the lucky cat and her kittens. Warnecke first took some standard photos of Blackie under a desk in a cardboard box with her kittens, but then he asked the shop owner for permission to restage the street crossing. The owner agreed, as long as the photographer promised not to harm the cat family. Next, Warnecke asked Officer Cudmore to stop traffic again. The policeman hesitated at first for fear of getting reprimanded, but the photographer convinced him that nobody in the city would criticize him for repeating the good deed. The officer finally agreed, and the stage was set.

First, Warnecke positioned the machine-shop owner in front of his building, and then he handed the cats to a man on the far side of the street. The plan was to have the cat's owner call for her after the man on the other side released her with one of her kittens. Cudmore held up his hand, and traffic came to a standstill. As Warnecke got ready to take the first shot, drivers began blowing their horns, which frightened Blackie and caused her to cross diagonally, away from the commotion. The cats were carried back, Cudmore stopped the cars closer to the intersection, and Warnecke crossed his fingers that the cat wouldn't cross under the cars. As onlookers cheered and irate drivers honked their horns, Blackie gingerly crossed the street with a kitten her mouth, and Warnecke took the perfect picture. (Of course, the entire procedure was repeated one more time just in case.). Within days, the picture was on the front page of newspapers across the country.

On October 29, 1925, Police Headquarters announced that Officer Cudmore had received some checks and numerous letters of commendation for stopping traffic five times in order to let the mother cat carry her family home. Jane Chamberlain of Long Island City sent him a check for five dollars—one dollar for each kitten's life. General Reeve of Minnetonka Beach, Minnesota, the former chief of police of Manila, sent ten dollars and a small note: "His kindness to this cat is greatly appreciated in an age where there is not so much humane treatment of animals as you and I would wish."

Today, the historic photo of Officer Cudmore and Blackie that graces the cover of this book is a favorite among New Yorkers and cat lovers everywhere.

DID YOU KNOW?

Traffic control has been a major issue in New York City since at least the early nineteenth century. In 1860, the Metropolitan Police Department's Broadway Squad (aka Twenty-Fifth Precinct), a unit of forty-one officers under the command of Captain Theron S. Copeland, was organized to stop horse-drawn traffic and escort pedestrians across Broadway. The squad was reportedly the city's first police unit to have a designated function in the field of traffic regulation, followed by the mounted unit, which was officially established in 1871 and played a crucial role in traffic control until the 1920s.

Regulation of street traffic was first attempted in earnest in New York City at the beginning of the twentieth century. By this time, traffic was so intolerable that it placed a large financial burden on businesses. Although mounted patrolmen were being used to control traffic direction on Fifth Avenue, this intervention was not enough to satisfy the merchants and other businessmen, who vigorously protested for the mayor, aldermen, and police department to take action and put a full system in place. In 1903, Deputy Police Commissioner Captain Alexander Ross Piper traveled to London to study its system for regulating traffic. The following year, the city's Chamber of Commerce adopted a resolution requesting Police Commissioner William Gibbs McAdoo to create a Bureau of Street Traffic to regulate sidewalk obstruction and to supervise and administer the ordinances regarding traffic. Commissioner McAdoo assigned Captain Stephen O'Brien of the City Hall police station to take charge of traffic regulation, and a plan was put in place to use additional mounted patrolmen for regulating traffic on Broadway in lower Manhattan.

By the end of 1905, the new Traffic Squad had 581 men assigned to traffic duty, including seven mounted roundsmen and sixty-nine mounted patrolmen (the horses were kept at the police stables at 17 Leonard Street), two bicycle roundsmen and nine bicycle patrolmen, and hundreds of foot patrolmen. That year, Manhattan also installed five traffic lights (at Columbus Circle, the Pennsylvania Railroad Ferry on West Twenty-Third Street, Times Square, Broadway and Seventy-Second Street, and Amsterdam Avenue and Seventy-Third Street). Iron traffic signs indicating the direction of traffic were also installed in 1905, with the first sign placed on Amsterdam Avenue at Seventy-Third Street.

In 1914, New York State Assemblyman William T. Simpson introduced a bill to increase the Traffic Squad to one thousand members. He also introduced a bill making it a misdemeanor to disobey the orders of the police in the enforcement of vehicular traffic rules. The men of the Traffic Squad also got some much-needed help in 1920 by way of ninety-eight more patrolmen and seven temporary traffic towers with manually controlled colored lights. The towers were paid for by Special Deputy Commissioner Dr. John A. Harriss and the Fifth Avenue Association and inaugurated on Fifth Avenue on March 4, 1920. Two years later, the city replaced the temporary towers with elaborate, hand-carved bronze towers standing twenty-five feet tall at the intersections of Fifth Avenue and Fourteenth, Twenty-Sixth, Thirty-Fourth, Thirty-Eighth, Forty-Second, Fiftieth, and Fifty-Seventh Streets.

In 1926, a year after this story about Blackie takes place, New York City was still relying on thousands of Traffic Squad officers to manually direct traffic, operate the signals in traffic towers, and monitor the signals from the ground in order to coordinate traffic. However, by this year, the city also had 98 electric traffic lights. A year later, the city added 1,143 more traffic lights, and in 1928, another 2,243 were installed. While the cost of installing these lights was significant, the city was able to save over $12 million annually by cutting its Traffic Squad force to five hundred men.

Although traffic signals were fully deployed throughout the city in the 1930s, the job of aiding traffic flow, enforcing parking rules, and helping people cross the streets is still the responsibility of the New York Police Department Traffic Control Division. I'm not sure if it's a job requirement, but I am sure that most of these officers would also stop traffic if a cat and her kittens needed some good luck—and a hero cat man (or cat woman) to save the day.

SUGGESTIONS FOR FURTHER READING

My primary sources for most of the cat-related stories in this book are old newspaper articles that were published in the *New York Times, Brooklyn Daily Eagle, New York Sun, New York Herald,* and other daily newspapers. The notes list all of the newspaper sources for each cat story for your reference if you're interested in reading the original articles. However, keep in mind that much of this content is in digital archives behind pay walls that restrict access via paid subscriptions (for example, the *New York Times* archives and Newspapers.com).

In addition to newspaper articles, my sources for the historical and biographical content include books from my home reference library, plus online sources such as census and other government reports from Ancestry.com, museum and association websites, old maps, magazine articles, and electronic books (e-books). The following books from my personal library provided historical context for many of the stories in this collection. I prefer turning the pages of a printed book, but many of these books are also available in e-book format at no cost should you wish to read more about specific topics in New York City's history.

Augustyn, Robert T., and Paul E. Cohen. *Manhattan in Maps.* New York: Rizzoli, 1997.

Ballon, Hilary, ed. *The Greatest Grid: The Master Plan of Manhattan, 1811–2011.* New York: Museum of the City of New York and Columbia University Press, 2012.

Brooklyn Fire Department. *Our Firemen: The Official History of the Brooklyn Fire Department, from the First Volunteer to the Latest Appointee.* Brooklyn, 1892.

Burrows, Edwin G., and Mike Wallace. *Gotham: A History of New York City to 1898.* New York: Oxford University Press, 1999.

Cook, Harry Tecumeseh. *The Borough of the Bronx, 1639–1913.* New York: H. T. Cook, 1913.

Costello, Augustine E. *Our Firemen: The History of the New York Fire Departments from 1609 to 1887.* 1887. Reprint, New York: Knickerbocker, 1997.

Costello, Augustine E. *Our Police Protectors: History of the New York Police from the Earliest Period to the Present Time*. New York: author, 1885.

Disturnell, John. *New York as It Was and as It Is: Giving an Account of the City from Its Settlement to the Present Time*. New York: D. Van Nostrand, 1876.

Hemstreet, Charles. *Nooks and Corners of Old New York*. New York: Charles Scribner's Sons, 1899.

Innes, J. H. *New Amsterdam and Its People: Studies, Social and Topographical, of the Town under Dutch and Early English Rule*. New York: Charles Scribner's Sons, 1902.

Kernan, J. Frank. *Reminiscences of the Old Fire Laddies and Volunteer Fire Departments of New York and Brooklyn*. New York: M. Crane, 1885.

Moscow, Henry. *The Street Book: An Encyclopedia of Manhattan's Street Names and Their Origins*. 1978. Reprint, New York: Fordham University Press, 1990.

Pelletreau, William Smith. *Early New York Houses: With Historical and Genealogical Notes*. New York: Francis P. Harper, 1900.

Roman, James. *Chronicles of Old New York: Exploring Manhattan's Landmark Neighborhoods*. New York: Museyon, 2016.

Stiles, Henry R. *A History of the City of Brooklyn, Including the Old Town and Village of Brooklyn, the Town of Bushwick, and the Village and City of Williamsburgh*. 1867. Reprint, Brooklyn, NY: Heritage Books, 1993.

Stokes, I. N. Phelps. *The Iconography of Manhattan Island, 1498–1909*. New York: Robert H. Dodd, 1915.

Tuttle, H. Croswell. *Abstracts of Farm Titles in the City of New York*. New York: Spectator, 1881.

Valentine, David T. *History of the City of New York*. New York: G. P. Putnam, 1853.

NOTES

INTRODUCTION

Page
1 *stray cats sent to the gas chambers:* "72,000 Cats Killed in Paralysis Fear," *New York Times,* July 26, 1916.

1 *"old boots, hats":* "Hints for Spring Gardening," *New York Daily Graphic,* March 25, 1879.

2 *"secure painless death":* Nellie Bly, "The Midnight Band of Mercy: You Ever Hear of Such Crazy Lot of Cranks as These Deluded Women?," *New York World,* December 31, 1893.

2 *"destroyed or otherwise disposed of":* "LSA—Lost and Strayed Animals 115/1894," Justia, accessed October 5, 2018, https://law.justia.com/codes/new-york/2010/lsa/.

2 *"happy 48 hours":* "Lethe for Cats and Dogs," *Brooklyn Daily Eagle,* June 17, 1900.

2 *"Every cat without a collar":* "To Catch Dogs Politely," *New York Times,* March 11, 1894.

3 *"To catch these cats":* Ibid.

3 *164,626 dogs and 315,645 cats:* "Lethe for Cats and Dogs."

3 *"trappers and hunters":* "Facts about Furs," *New York Times,* October 12, 1890.

3 *paid boys to collect stray cats:* "Fritsch Found No Work, So He Made Lucrative Disposition of Stray Cats until He Was Arrested," *New York Sun,* March 6, 1895.

3 *eight thousand dogs and seventy-two thousand cats:* "72,000 Cats Killed in Paralysis Fear," *New York Times,* July 26, 1916.

4 *"Since the beginning of the alarm":* Ibid.

4 *"When people have to economize":* Ibid.

4 *association paid five cents:* "Children in Cat Hunt," *Brooklyn Standard Union,* October 8, 1923; "Children to Round Up Homeless Cats," *New York Sun,* March 26, 1925.

4 *"for humanitarian reasons":* "75 Boxes of Cats Bagged in a Day," *New York Times,* March 29, 1925.

1. SEAFARING CATS

Page

5 *"liberate" cats:* "Cats in the Sea Services," *Naval History Blog,* US Naval Institute, April 13, 2018, www.usni.org/news-and-features/cats-and-the -sea-services.

5 *predict the weather:* "Cats and the Weather—the Folklore," *The Old Farmer's Almanac,* April 12, 2018, www.almanac.com/blog/weather-blog/ cats-and-weather%E2%80%94-folklore.

5 *bad omen:* "Sea Superstitions," *Brooklyn Daily Eagle,* November 29, 1885.

7 *McKinley appointed:* "The Next Chief Constructor," *New York Times,* November 27, 1900.

7 *not to hurt or interfere:* "Cats in the Navy Yard," *New York Times,* December 23, 1900.

8 *"She deserves a gold medal":* Ibid.

8 *"You have no idea":* Ibid.

9 *"smell a rat":* Ibid.

10 *about fifteen hundred cats:* Joy Miller, "Maybe There Was Someone Pussyfooting around Old Brooklyn Naval Yard," *Elmira (NY) Star-Gazette,* June 29, 1966.

10 *"What happened to those cats":* Ibid.

11 *Joris Jansen Rapalje:* Tunnis G. Bergen, *The Bergen Family or the Descendants of Hans Hansen Bergen* (Albany, NY: Joel Munsell, 1876), 25–26.

11 *John Jackson and his brothers acquired:* New York City Landmarks Preservation Commission, *Lefferts-Laidlaw House,* November 13, 2001, www.neighborhoodpreservationcenter.org/db/bb_files/01-LEFFERTS -LAIDLAW-HOUSE.pdf, 2; Thomas F. Berner, *The Brooklyn Navy Yard* (Chicago: Arcadia, 1999), 12.

11 *Robert McNamara closed:* Brooklyn Navy Yard, "History of the Yard," accessed October 5, 2018, https://brooklynnavyyard.org/about/history.

11 *Continental Army soldiers were taken prisoner:* J. H. French, *Gazetteer of New York State* (Syracuse, NY: R. Pearsall Smith, 1860), 372; New York City Department of Parks and Recreation, "Prison Ship Martyrs Monument," accessed October 7, 2018, www.nycgovparks.org/parks/fort-greene-park/ monuments/1222.

12 *served as a pseudo receiving and distributing station:* "Mascots on Board Our Ships of War," *New York World,* March 6, 1898.

12 *one of only about 90 crew members:* Arlington National Cemetery, "The USS *Maine* Mast Memorial," accessed October 7, 2018, www.arlington cemetery.mil/Explore/Monuments-and-Memorials/USS-Maine-Mast -Memorial.

12 *born on a farm in Pennsylvania:* "Capt. Sigsbee's Dog Peggy and the *Maine's* Black Tom," *St. Paul Globe,* March 1, 1898.

13 *first modern warships built in the United States:* Justin Sassman, "The Sinking of the USS *Maine*: 1898," St. Mary's University History Media, April 5, 2017, www.stmuhistorymedia.org/the-sinking-of-the-first-uss-maine/.

13 *not commissioned until September 17, 1895:* "USS Maine (ACR-1)," Military Factory, updated March 17, 2015, www.militaryfactory.com/ships/detail .asp?ship_id=USS-Maine-ACR1; Sassman, "Sinking of the USS *Maine.*"

13 *Captain Charles Dwight Sigsbee relieved Captain Crowninshield:* Scott Miller, *The President and the Assassin: McKinley, Terror, and Empire at the Dawn of the American Century* (New York: Random House, 2011), 115.

14 *trembling and lurching motion:* "Personal Narrative of the *'Maine,'*" *Century Magazine,* December 1898, 241–263, www.latinamericanstudies.org/ ussmaine/Century_Magazine_Dec-1898.pdf.

14 *Peggie the pug managed to find her way:* "Mascots on Board Our Ships of War."

14 *"Maine blown up in Havana Harbor":* Arlington National Cemetery, "USS *Maine* Mast Memorial."

14 *Tom was sleeping:* "Mascots on Board Our Ships of War."

14 *"Tom was wounded in one foot":* [Eliza Lockwood] Sigsbee, "Pets in the Navy," *St. Nicholas: An Illustrated Magazine for Young Folks,* November 1898–April 1899, 63.

15 *According to Mrs. Sigsbee:* Ibid.

15 *26 officers, 290 sailors, and 39 marines onboard:* Arlington National Cemetery, "USS *Maine* Mast Memorial"; "Cat Mascot of USS *Maine*'s Mess Cooks, Martyr for Animal Rights—1896," *Hampton Roads Naval Museum Blog,* December 18, 2013, http://hamptonroadsnavalmuseum.blogspot .com/2013/12/cat-mascot-of-uss-maines-mess-cooks.html.

16 *United States Naval Court of Inquiry declared:* Naval History and Heritage Command, "Report of the Naval Court of Inquiry upon the Destruction of the United States Battleship *Maine* in Havana Harbor, February 15, 1898, 3/21/1898," accessed October 5, 2018, www.history.navy.mil/research/ publications/documentary-histories/united-states-navy-s/destruction-of -the-m/report-of-the-naval-o.html.

16 *team of naval investigators:* Louis Fisher, "Destruction of the *Maine* (1898)," Law Library of Congress, August 4, 2009, https://loc.gov/law/ help/usconlaw/pdf/Maine.1898.pdf.

16 *Chelsea Pirate Cats:* "Fierce Marine Cats Haunt Hudson Piers," *New York Times,* January 22, 1917; "Thin Days for Wharf Cats," *New York Times,* December 25, 1922.

17 *"Look at them waiting":* "Fierce Marine Cats Haunt Hudson Piers."

17 *only US ship docked at the Chelsea Piers:* "To Celebrate Aboard the *Olympic* Today," *New York Times,* December 25, 1922.

18 *just returned to New York:* "*Olympic* in Port Covered with Ice," *New York Times,* December 21, 1922.

18 *busiest port in the world:* New-York Historical Society, "Exhibitions: WWII and NYC," October 27, 2013, www.nyhistory.org/exhibitions/wwii -and-nyc.

19 *horns would blast three times:* "War Ban on Ship Whistles Strands Mascots; 50 of World's Cats Roam the Chelsea Piers," *New York Times,* March 13, 1942.

19 *"A mascot there was"*: "Yarns from Seven Seas Spun as the Pipes Glow," *Hartford (CT) Courant*, October 12, 1930.

19 *old maritime superstition*: "Ship Averts Seven Years of Bad Luck by Saving Cat in Midocean," *Rochester (NY) Democrat and Chronicle*, July 6, 1929; "Liner Puts About at Sea to Save its Mascot Cat," *Plainfield (NJ) Courier-News*, July 5, 1929.

19 *"tramp traits"*: "Liner Puts About at Sea"; "Mascot Saved," *Pittsburgh Press*, July 6, 1929.

19 *eliminated his competition*: "Cat Overboard! Liner Stops to Rescue Mascot," *Chicago Tribune*, July 6, 1929.

20 *"Cat overboard!"*: "Ship Averts Seven Years of Bad Luck"; "Laugh with Olaf," *Olean (NY) Times Herald*, July 8, 1929.

20 *Captain Bjor Boettger asked*: "Laugh with Olaf." Note that some news articles spell the captain's name as Captain Bjor Boettger, while others use Thorbjorn Dottger and various other spellings.

20 *"hefty Norwegian sailors"*: "Olaf and Nine Lives Arrive in New York," *Boston Globe*, July 6, 1929.

20 *"We shall have to thank Olaf"*: Ad Schuster, "The Other Fellow," *Oakland (CA) Tribune*, July 20, 1929.

21 *victory against seven competitors*: "Lifeboat Race Won by Sud Americano," *New York Times*, September 3, 1929.

21 *"were Norsemen whose ancestors were rowing boats"*: "Boat-Race Trophy Presented by Todd," *New York Times*, September 7, 1929.

21 *cheated by spreading grease*: Ibid.; "Slide in First in Greased Boat," *Brooklyn Daily Eagle*, September 3, 1929.

21 *"Olaf is the plan"*: "Yarns from Seven Seas Spun."

22 *Tommy Mulligan was a British boxer*: Bert Randolph Sugar, *Boxing's Greatest Fighters* (Guilford, CT: Lyons, 2006), 35.

22 *adopted fifty-year-old Herbert and his wife*: William G. Hosie, "Coney Island, Diamond-Studded, Gleams in the Night, but Sea Gate's Ruby Light Outshines It by Five Miles," *Brooklyn Daily Eagle*, March 26, 1936.

22 *living at the lighthouse for fifteen years*: Ibid.; Kraig Anderson, "Coney Island Lighthouse," Lighthousefriends.com, accessed October 5, 2018, http://lighthousefriends.com/light.asp?ID=394.

22 *Born in Rhode Island*: Hosie, "Coney Island, Diamond-Studded." All additional biographical information about Herbert Greenwood was obtained through official birth, death, census, and other records retrieved from Ancestry.com.

23 *recognized as the last civilian lighthouse keeper*: Scott Schubert, "History," Coney Island Lighthouse website, accessed October 6, 2018, www.coneyislandlighthouse.com/history.html.

24 *"a barren and repulsive waste of sand"*: C. A. O'Rourke, "A Popular Seaside Resort," in *Complete Guide to the Great Watering Place of New York* (New York: American News, 1879), 5–6.

24 *majority of the island was barren*: Michael Immerso, *Coney Island, the People's Playground* (New Brunswick, NJ: Rutgers University Press, 2002), 13; O'Rourke, "Popular Seaside Resort," 5–6.

24 *Tourist development in the western part of the island:* "The Pavilion at Coney Island," *Brooklyn Daily Eagle,* July 28, 1845; Immerso, *Coney Island, the People's Playground,* 14.

24 *charged twelve and a half cents:* In 1845, Thomas Bielby ran numerous advertisements in the *Brooklyn Daily Eagle* for his ferry between Fort Hamilton and Coney Island. The ferry ran every half hour.

24 *The Point's reputation as a den of gambling and prostitution:* Edo McCullough, *Good Old Coney Island: A Sentimental Journey into the Past* (New York: Fordham University Press, 1957), 45–46; Roger P. Roess and Gene Sansone, *The Wheels That Drove New York: A History of the New York City Transit System* (New York: Springer, 2013), 114.

25 *powerful political machine:* "Tammany Hall," History, updated August 21, 2018, www.history.com/topics/us-politics/tammany-hall.

25 *used some of the Tammany extortion loot:* McCullough, *Good Old Coney Island,* 46; Townsend Percy, *Percy's Pocket Dictionary of Coney Island* (New York: F. Leypoldt, 1880), 64.

25 *Norton & Murray's Pavilion:* Percy, *Percy's Pocket Dictionary of Coney Island,* 56–57.

25 *"a large, windy frame building":* Charles Dawson Shanley, "Coney Island," *Atlantic Monthly,* September 1, 1874, 308.

25 *Norton was indicted:* "The Ring Rout," *New York Tribune,* December 23, 1873.

25 *returned to the court:* "Michael Norton's Return," *New York Daily Herald,* May 2, 1874.

26 *"to establish lights on the western end of Coney Island":* "A Coney Island Light," *New York Times,* February 3, 1889.

26 *Congress eventually approved $25,000 to build two range lights:* Anderson, "Coney Island Lighthouse."

26 *Work on the tower:* Ibid.; Schubert, "History."

26 *James J. Sangunitto was the keeper:* "J. J. Sangunitto, Oldest Coney Isle Resident, Dies at 98," *Brooklyn Daily Eagle,* November 22, 1936.

26 *He married Sarah Mann and had six children:* Biographical information about the Sangunitto family was obtained through census reports retrieved from Ancestry.com.

27 *Sarah reportedly introduced tintype studios:* "Leon P. Sangunitto, Coney Builder," obituary, *Brooklyn Daily Eagle,* September 4, 1946. The Frenchman may have been Adolphe-Alexandre Martin, who is credited with inventing the tintype in 1853.

27 *helped prevent many wrecks:* "J. J. Sangunitto, Oldest Coney Isle Resident."

2. POLICE CATS

Page

28 *Municipal Police Act of 1844:* New York City Landmarks Preservation Commission, *(Former) Firehouse, Engine Company 29,* June 28, 2016, 5, 12, http://s-media.nyc.gov/agencies/lpc/lp/2564.pdf.

28 *most station houses occupied leased buildings:* Ibid., 5.

28 *appointed Nathaniel D. Bush:* Augustine F. Costello, *Our Police Protectors: History of the New York Police from the Earliest Period to the Present Time* (New York: author, 1885), 452.

29 *more than one hundred cats on active duty:* "100 Cats Guard New York Police," *New York Times,* May 7, 1915.

29 *station houses would have been overrun:* Ibid.

30 *"Old Nig, my friend, comes every day":* Published in "The Tombs Cat Is Dead," *Syracuse Evening Telegram,* June 1, 1901.

30 *arrested for the murder of his young bride:* "Harris Is Found Guilty," *New York Times,* February 3, 1892; "The Six Capsules," Murder by Gaslight, December 3, 2011, www.murderbygaslight.com/2011/11/six-capsules.html.

30 *Helen was an eighteen-year-old student: The Trial of Carlyle W. Harris for the Poisoning of His Wife, Helen Potts, at New York* (New York: Court of General Sessions, 1892), 11, 37.

30 *"My God, what can they do to me?": Trial of Carlyle W. Harris,* 47.

30 *jury found Harris guilty of murder:* "Harris Is Found Guilty"; "Six Capsules"; "Carlyle W. Harris Is Dead," *New York Times,* May 9, 1893; Andy McCarthy, "New York Public Library's 'Ghosts' File," *New York Public Library Blog,* December 28, 2017, www.nypl.org/blog/2017/12/28/ghosts -file.

31 *secret marriage ceremony:* "Six Capsules"; "New York Public Library's 'Ghosts' File."

31 *Old Nig arrived at the Tombs in 1883:* "Tombs Cat Is Dead"; "Death Sets 'Old Nig' Free," *New York Times,* June 1, 1901.

31 *only Old Nig was spared:* "The Cat Lived at the Tombs 18 Years," *Salem (OR) Statesman Journal,* July 3, 1901.

32 *his skin would be stuffed:* "Tombs Cat Is Dead."

32 *Completed in 1838:* John Josiah Munro, *The New York Tombs, Inside and Out! Scenes and Reminiscences Coming Down to the Present* (Brooklyn: author, 1909), 31.

32 *festering stench and perpetual dampness:* "Tombs Prison Full of Evils," *New York World,* June 28, 1895.

32 *"here entombed to fester and offend":* "City Intelligence," *New York Herald,* November 4, 1846.

33 *sixty-foot-deep Collect Pond:* Sergey Kandinsky, *Hidden Waters of New York City: A History and Guide to 101 Forgotten Lakes, Ponds, Creeks, and Streams in the Five Boroughs* (New York: Countryman, 2016), 1; New York City Department of Parks and Recreation, "Collect Pond Park," accessed October 5, 2018, www.nycgovparks.org/parks/collect-pond-park/history. In 1999, the New York City parks department created a Historical Sign Program by partnering with college students across the city to research and write historical signs for every named park across the five boroughs. Much of the information about the history of the pond comes from the historical signs at Collect Pond Park, located on Leonard Street between Centre and Lafayette Streets. For more information about this program, see New York City Department of Parks and Recreation, "Historical Signs," www.nycgovparks.org/about/history/historical-signs.

33 *never a direct water source:* As reported on the historical signs at Collect
    Pond Park; Edward Hagaman Hall, *The Catskill Aqueduct and Earlier
    Water Supplies of the City of New York* (New York: Mayor's Catskill Aque-
    duct Celebration Committee, 1917), 31.

33 *"suds and filth are emptied into the pond":* As reported on the historical
    signs at Collect Pond Park.

33 *condemned, partially drained, and filled in:* As reported on the historical
    signs at Collect Pond Park; Kandinsky, *Hidden Waters of New York City*, 6.

33 *the city erected its Corporation Yards:* Charles Hemstreet, *Nooks and Cor-
    ners of Old New York* (New York: Charles Scribner's Sons, 1899), 42.

34 *In a span of less than ten years:* New York City Department of Parks and
    Recreation, "Collect Pond Park"; New York Correction History Society, "A
    Tale of the Tombs," accessed October 1, 2018, www.correctionhistory.org/
    html/chronicl/nycdoc/html/histry3a.html.

34 *"was built upon a raft":* "Mysterious Waters Found under the Tombs," *New
    York Times,* June 29, 1902.

34 *"warping the prison cells":* New York Correction History Society, "Tale of
    the Tombs."

34 *Originally intended for about two hundred inmates:* Ibid.

34 *"comfortable cells":* Lawrence M. Friedman, *Crime and Punishment in
    American History* (New York: Basic Books, 1993), 167.

34 *Two prisoners sharing the single cot:* Ibid.; New York Correction History
    Society, "Tale of the Tombs."

35 *Harris died:* "Carlyle W. Harris Is Dead"; "Six Capsules."

35 *"Harris, Carlyle Wentworth, eldest son":* H. M. Snevily, "The Six Capsules,"
    Pierson's Magazine, January 1916, 22.

35 *"Murdered by Twelve Men":* Ibid.

35 *"Carlyle W. Harris. Aged 23 years":* Ibid.

35 *declared that the Tombs was crowded and unhealthy:* "Tombs an Unfit
    Prison," *New York Times,* June 29, 1895.

35 *demolished and replaced:* "Mysterious Waters Found."

35 *still referred to as the Tombs:* Sewell Chan, "Disgraced and Penalized,
    Kerik Finds His Name Stripped Off Jail," *New York Times,* July 3, 2006;
    Max H. Seigel, "Tombs Closing," *New York Times,* November 16, 1974.

35 *stabilized and placed under the jurisdiction:* New York City Department of
    Parks and Recreation, "Collect Pond Park."

35 *strange series of stone walls:* Dave Hogarty, "Old Tombs Excavated at Col-
    lect Pond Park Construction," *Curbed New York,* August 9, 2012, https://
    ny.curbed.com/2012/8/9/10389290/old-tombs-excavated-at-collect-pond
    -park-construction.

36 *sailed from Holland to New Amsterdam:* William R. Bronk, "Jonas Bronck,"
    Westchester County Magazine, April 1911, 54–55.

36 *Bronck established his homestead:* Ibid.; "Jonas Bronk, the Pioneer," *New
    York Times,* September 17, 1897; Stephen Jenkins, *The Story of the Bronx
    from the Purchase Made by the Dutch from the Indians in 1639 to the Pres-
    ent Day* (New York: Knickerbocker, 1912), 27.

36 *Kieft granted the land:* Jenkins, *Story of the Bronx,* 28–29.

36 *royal patent for Bronck's Land:* Adaline W. Sterling, *The Book of Englewood* (Englewood, NJ: Mayor and Council of the City of Englewood, NJ, 1922), 14.

36 *Edsall conveyed the land:* Ibid., 29; James Riker, *Revised History of Harlem: Its Origins and Early Annals* (New York: New Harlem, 1904), 235.

37 *about 1,920 acres:* Riker, *Revised History of Harlem*, 235; Jenkins, *Story of the Bronx*, 64.

37 *operated a gristmill and sawmill:* Edwin G. Burrows and Mike Wallace, *Gotham: A History of New York City to 1898* (New York: Oxford University Press, 1999), 123.

37 *Gouverneur Morris sold the farm:* Jenkins, *Story of the Bronx*, 371.

37 *Cauldwell commissioned:* "New Home for Bronx Police," *New York Times*, May 9, 1904.

37 *The building was wired:* Costello, *Our Police Protectors*, 393.

37 *reportedly quite lovely:* Ibid., 390; "New Home for Bronx Police."

38 *a favorite was Shiner:* "Shiner, Police Horse, Dead," *New York Sun*, September 27, 1903.

38 *"The accommodations are wretched":* Costello, *Our Police Protectors*, 390.

38 *workers began demolishing the building:* "New Home for Bronx Police."

38 *the building was used in exterior shots:* Norval White and Elliot Willensky, *AIA Guide to New York City*, 5th ed. (New York: Oxford University Press, 2010), 832.

38 *he was arresting the cat:* "Who Stole Egan's Steak?," *New York Times*, June 30, 1904.

39 *handsome white cat named Pete:* "Bronx Family Loses Its Donkey Friend," *New York Times*, July 31, 1911; "Cat Misses Friends and Refuses to Eat," *New York Herald*, July 31, 1911.

40 *The Bridge Squad was a much smaller precinct:* New York Police Department, *Annual Report of the Police Commissioner City of New York for the Year Ending December 31, 1910* (New York: Lecouver, 1911), 21.

40 *small three-story brownstone: Proceedings of the Commissioners of the Sinking Fund of the City of New York, 1911* (New York: Lecouver, 1911), 641.

40 *Bridge Precinct D was abolished:* "The Bridge Precinct," *The Squad Room* (blog), November 3, 2003, http://brooklynnorth.blogspot.com/2003/11/.

40 *Pete was back at the Morrisania police station:* "100 Cats Guard New York Police."

40 *"The owner evidently took no chances":* Randall Comfort, "The William H. Morris Mansion," in *Valentine's Manual of Old New York*, no. 7, edited by Henry Collins Brown (New York: Valentine's Manual, 1923), 242.

41 *"the one-story saloons":* Edith Wharton, *The Age of Innocence* (New York: J. J. Little and Ives, 1902), 24–25.

41 *Mrs. Mingott's house is based on the real home:* Christopher Gray, "Streetscapes: Edith Wharton; In 'The Age of Innocence,' Fiction Was Not Truth," *New York Times*, August 27, 1995.

41 *thousands of goats in Goatville:* "Where the Goat Is a King," *New York Times*, July 13, 1890.

41 *formed the Anti-Goat Club:* "The Goats Must Go," *Buffalo Evening News*, December 8, 1884.

42 *"the dangerous beast"*: "Shot a Stuffed Fox," *New York Times*, August 9, 1909.

42 *"looking piercingly at the red fox on the floor"*: Ibid.

42 *military veteran who had been awarded*: Costello, *Our Police Protectors*, 380.

43 *"This is a precinct that is being built up"*: Ibid., 381.

43 *negotiations had begun*: New York Landmarks Preservation Commission, *28th Police Precinct Station House*, February 23, 1999, 4, http:// neighborhoodpreservationcenter.org/db/bb_files/1999-28thPrecinct StationHouse.pdf.

43 *"the best . . . in the city"*: "New Police Precinct," *New York Times*, May 6, 1893.

43 *all the police precincts in the city were renumbered*: New York Landmarks Preservation Commission, *28th Police Precinct Station House*, 5.

44 *under a broad outlet for a brook*: As depicted on the John Randel Jr. atlas of ninety-two watercolor farm maps created between 1818 and 1820. Museum of the City of New York, "Before the Grid: Randel Composite Map," accessed October 16, 2018, http://thegreatestgrid.mcny.org/greatest -grid/randel-composite-map.

44 *large parcel of land owned by Johannes Benson*: John W. Pirrson, *The Dutch Grants, Harlem Patents and Tidal Creeks* (New York: L. K. Strouse, 1889), 1.

44 *conveyed to Benjamin Benson and his wife*: Ibid., 102–103.

44 *passengers aboard the SS Arctic perished*: Ibid., 103; William Flayhart, *Perils of the Atlantic: Steamship Disasters, 1850 to the Present* (New York: Norton, 2003), 28.

44 *police station designed by city architect Edward Pearce Casey*: "Concrete Police Station," *New York Times*, January 14, 1909.

45 *The grandiose, five-story building*: "Eldridge Street Police Station Is Abandoned," *New York Evening World*, December 6, 1911.

45 *"grew bigger and fatter"*: "Buster's Unhappy New Year," *New York Times*, January 2, 1912.

45 *"well-intentioned but almost fatal vigor"*: Ibid.

46 *"Are you a Topsy man or a Buster man?"*: "Police Take Sides in Feline Warfare," *New York Herald*, January 2, 1912.

46 *considered one of the oldest police stations*: "The Old Delancey Street Station," *New York Times*, April 29, 1894.

46 *the city purchased this lot*: Bureau of Municipal Investigation and Statistics, Department of Finance, *Real Estate Owned by the City of New York under the Jurisdiction of the Police Department* (New York: author, January 1, 1908), 7.

46 *home to Clinton Engine No. 41*: Augustine E. Costello, *Our Firemen: The History of the New York Fire Departments from 1609 to 1887* (New York: author, 1887), 617; *Documents of the Board of Aldermen of the City of New York*, vol. 6 (New York: Bryant and Bogg, 1839–1840), 198.

46 *Fire and Building Department called for a new two-story brick building*: Costello, *Our Firemen*, 97.

47 *occupied by Public Primary School No. 7:* Edwin Williams, *New York as It Is, in 1837* (New York: J. Disturnell, 1837), 56.

47 *The pole had a lantern on the end:* Costello, *Our Police Protectors,* 76.

47 *Board of Alderman adopted an ordinance:* Ibid., 102.

47 *"a primitive and unimproved building":* "Old Delancey Street Station."

47 *This theater made the headlines:* "Scandal Put in Films," *New York Tribune,* August 17, 1912.

47 *the city sold the building:* City of New York, *The City Record: Official Journal of the City of New York,* vol. 45, part 5 (New York: author, June 1917), 4286.

47 *sold the old building to Jacob Branfman:* "Former Police Building in Delancey Street Sold," *New York Tribune,* July 24, 1919.

48 *located on a double-wide lot:* Bureau of Municipal Investigation and Statistics, *Real Estate Owned by the City of New York,* 8.

48 *originally housed in the old Essex Market:* Costello, *Our Police Protectors,* 107.

48 *This market dates back to 1818:* Thomas F. De Voe, *The Market Book: Containing a Historical Account of the Public Markets in the Cities of New York, Boston, Philadelphia and Brooklyn* (New York: author, 1862), 479.

48 *market was ordered to be taken down:* Ibid., 485.

48 *the city replaced the old market:* Ibid., 486.

49 *housed a market and school:* New York City Board of Aldermen, *Proceedings of the Board of Aldermen of the City of New York,* vol. 218 (New York: Martin B. Brown, 1895), 462.

49 *"Where now some veterans":* "Essex Market School May Now Be Built," *New York Journal,* September 24, 1896.

49 *the city leased the police station to Moritz Tolk:* Lynn Edmonds, "Behind Bars: How a Police Station House Became a Speakeasy," *Bedford + Bowery,* January 1, 2015, http://bedfordandbowery.com/2015/01/behind-bars-how-a-police-station-house-became-a-speakeasy/.

49 *Sheinart converted the upper floors:* Joyce Mendelsohn, *The Lower East Side Remembered and Revisited* (New York: Columbia University Press, 2009), 159.

50 *suggested the establishment of a public park:* American Scenic and Historic Preservation Society, *Twenty-Second Annual Report of the American Scenic and Historic Preservation Society, 1917* (Albany, NY: J. B. Lyon, 1917), 249.

50 *New York City Department of Parks took over the 20,649 acres:* Ibid.; Board of Estimate and Apportionment of the City of New York, *Minutes of the Board of Estimate and Apportionment of the City of New York,* vol. 1 (New York: M. B. Brown, 1916), 398.

50 *The hen was set loose:* "Lady Alice, Police Mascot," *New York Times,* December 9, 1917.

51 *"was a very fine one":* "A New Home for the Suburban Riding and Driving Club," *New York Sun,* April 2, 1897.

51 *Waldo created two additional police precincts:* "Two New Precincts in Harlem Will Be Opened on Monday," *New York Evening World,* June 29, 1912.

51 *leased a new two-story brick store:* "Temporary Station Houses," *New York Times*, June 23, 1912.

52 *Woods promised:* "Old Arrowhead Inn Rural Police Rest," *New York Times*, August 12, 1914.

52 *Every married man went home:* "Police Farm Solves Food Problem," *New York Evening Telegram*, August 31, 1915.

52 *"greatly reduced their girth":* "New Home for the Suburban Riding and Driving Club"; "Policemen in Clover," *New York Sun*, October 11, 1914.

53 *Robert Chesebrough Rathbone:* "Robert C. Rathbone Dies in 90th Year," *New York Times*, February 11, 1915.

53 *the property was leased:* "New Home for the Suburban Riding and Driving Club."

53 *Rathbone sold all his property:* "Syndicate Buys Tract on Heights," *New York Times*, December 1, 1904.

53 *leased the former Rathbone property:* "Ben Riley Estates Seeks Time to Pay," *New York Times*, December 17, 1940.

53 *served more than four million frogs' legs:* H. Allen Smith, "Frog Leg Expert Makes Ready to Start Season," *San Bernardino County Sun*, April 30, 1934.

54 *The winners received a $500 cup:* "Four-in-Hand Road Race," *New York Times*, October 4, 1908.

54 *Howlett's Fort Washington Road Coach won:* "Vanderbilt Loses Four-in-Hand Race," *New York Times*, November 15, 1908.

54 *decided to build a new inn:* "To Build New Arrowhead Inn," *New York Sun*, September 3, 1913.

55 *flames coming from the second story:* "Policemen Save Comrades at Fire in Station House," *New York Evening World*, January 15, 1916.

55 *sold his block of land:* "Arrowhead Inn Will Move to Yonkers," *Variety*, October 4, 1923.

55 *the Arrowhead Inn was demolished:* On January 25, 1924, the Seagrit Bros. Wrecking Co. placed an ad in the *New York Evening Telegram* inviting the public to attend the demolition of the Arrowhead Inn in order to salvage plumbing fixtures, doors, windows, and other building materials.

56 *the hilly region:* Reginald Pelham Bolton, *Washington Heights Manual: Its Eventful Past* (New York: Dyckman Institute, 1924), 84.

56 *Joost van Oblienis:* "The Van Oblienis Farm," in *Twentieth Annual Report of the American Scenic and Historic Preservation Society* (Albany, NY: J. B. Lyon, 1915), 393–400.

57 *"to impress both officer and prisoner":* "New Police Stronghold Could Resist a Siege," *New York Times*, January 27, 1907.

57 *a grandiose entrance hall:* New York City Landmarks Preservation Commission, *Former Police Headquarters Building*, September 26, 1978, 2, http://s-media.nyc.gov/agencies/lpc/lp/0999.pdf; "300 Mulberry St. Passes into History," *New York Times*, November 28, 1909; "Our Illustrations," *Inland Architect and News Record* 45 (February 1905): 32; Michael Fiaschetti, "New York's Scotland Yard: Old NYPD Headquarters 240 Centre Street," Infamous New York, accessed October 18, 2018, https://infamousnewyork.com/tag/central-office/.

57 *"where fat policemen [could] reduce their weight"*: Ibid.
57 *"out among the goats"*: "Police Cat Nabs Prisoner on Beat," *New York Times*, July 2, 1934.
57 *"walked like a detective of the old school"*: Ibid.
58 *"And that's why we called him Arson"*: Ibid.
58 *"turning over in his mind"*: Ibid.
58 *"brings his prisoner right up to the desk"*: Ibid.
59 *the first principal office:* "Move Police Headquarters," *New York Times*, November 25, 1909; Costello, *Our Police Protectors*, 152.
59 *the location of the Mulberry Street headquarters:* "Police Headquarters in Long Acre Square," *New York Times*, September 14, 1902.
59 *Partridge suggested moving:* Ibid.
59 *Another proposal:* "Move Police Headquarters."
59 *he recommended demolishing:* New York City Estimate and Apportionment Board, *Journal of Proceedings* 2, pt. 1 (1902): 2143–2152.
60 *approved a new police headquarters:* "Move Police Headquarters."
60 *approved the old Centre Market site:* "Move Police Headquarters."
60 *message was received:* "300 Mulberry St. Passes into History."
60 *Whalen was already complaining:* "Whalen Asks $8,00,000 New Headquarters," *Brooklyn Daily Eagle*, January 27, 1930.
60 *Emil paid the city $4.2 million:* Paul Goldberger, "Architecture View: Three New York City Success Stories," *New York Times*, July 22, 1990.
60 *asking price of $31 million:* "On the Flatfoot Beat," *A New Yorker State of Mind* (blog), accessed October 19, 2018, https://newyorkerstateofmind .com/2018/07/.
61 *market dates back to 1812:* De Voe, *Market Book*, 461.
61 *Business was good:* Ibid., 461, 585.
61 *a large drill room upstairs:* New York State Military Museum, "New York City Grand and Centre Streets, Centre Market, Armory," updated October 17, 2012, https://dmna.ny.gov/historic/armories/NewYorkCityGrand CentreStreets.html.

3. FIRE CATS

Page
62 *permitted firemen to keep one dog or one cat:* "Adventures of Fire House Dogs and Cats," *New York Sun*, March 17, 1912.
62 *"A gentler phase"*: Alfred Michael Downes, *Fire Fighters and Their Pets* (New York: Harper Brothers, 1907), xii.
62 *about 90 dogs and 120 cats:* "The Unofficial Members of the Fire Department," *New York Press*, July 19, 1903.
63 *"It is a curious feature"*: Ibid.
64 *"the greatest of the novelties"*: "Varied Attractions for Poultry Show," *Brooklyn Daily Eagle*, November 28, 1915.
65 *a price starting at $600:* "Forty-Second Street Surveys 100 Years," *New York Times*, September 27, 1925.
65 *"Over mugs of ale"*: Ibid.

65 *The old Hermitage Farm had been in Norton's family:* I. N. Phelps Stokes, *The Iconography of Manhattan Island, 1498–1909* (New York: Robert H. Dodd, 1915), 125–126.

65 *diagonal tract:* John Bute Holmes, "Map of the Hermitage Farm and the Norton Estate," May 1872, available through the Museum of the City of New York, http://collections.mcny.org/.

65 *world's first street railway:* William Sloane Kennedy, *Wonders and Curiosities of the Railway . . . or Stories of the Locomotive in Every Land* (Chicago: S. C. Griggs, 1884), 169–170.

65 *filled in to expand Twelfth Avenue:* An act to establish a permanent exterior street along the Hudson River was passed on April 12, 1837. The act established a Thirteenth Avenue from Hammond Street (present-day West Eleventh Street) to 135th Street and extended Eleventh and Twelfth Avenues. See New York State, *Laws of the State of New York, Passed at the Sixtieth Session of the Legislature* (Albany, NY: E. Croswell, 1837), 166.

66 *a horse-drawn streetcar line:* "Our City Railroads," *New York Times,* December 26, 1865.

66 *approximately 565 horses were stabled:* "A Car Stable Destroyed," *New York Times,* June 13, 1886.

66 *five that were upstairs:* "The Ruined Car Stables," *New York Times,* June 14, 1886.

67 *"Rescued cats were a drug in the market":* Ibid.

68 *"a forlorn-looking cat":* Ibid.

68 *"were resuming":* Ibid.

68 *one of thirty-five steam engine companies:* "The Fire Department: Completion of the Metropolitan Fire Brigade of New York," *New York Times,* November 3, 1865; "The Metropolitan Fire Department Establishment of Headquarters Correspondence with the Comptroller," *New York Times,* June 25, 1865.

68 *The company's first station house:* Augustine E. Costello, *Our Firemen: The History of the New York Fire Departments from 1609 to 1887* (New York: author, 1887), 817.

68 *The Exempt Engine Company:* Ibid., 193.

68 *Engine Company No. 1 was reorganized:* Mike Boucher, "Fire Company Locations of New York City," NYFD.com, accessed October 20, 2018, http://nyfd.com/cityhist.pdf.

68 *The city had purchased this structure:* Bureau of Municipal Investigation and Statistics, Department of Finance, *Real Estate Owned by the City of New York under the Jurisdiction of the Fire Department* (New York: author, January 1, 1908), 28.

68 *occupied by Frederick William Nitschke's piano factory:* Antique Piano Shop, "Nitschke," accessed October 20, 2018, https://antiquepianoshop.com/online-museum/nitschke/.

68 *later was the headquarters for Fire Patrol No. 3:* Fire Patrol Committee, *Report of the Fire Patrol Committee, May 16, 1870* (New York: NY Economical Printing, 1870), 4.

69 *Chief McCabe:* J. Frank. Kernan, *Reminiscences of the Old Fire Laddies and Volunteer Fire Departments of New York and Brooklyn* (New York: M. Crane, 1885), 506.

69 *After talking with some friends:* "John McCabe a Suicide," *New York Sun,* April 26, 1895.

69 *"He had been intrusted":* "Firemen's $6,000 Bribe," *New York Evening World,* April 27, 1895.

69 *a mother cat and two of her four little kittens:* "No. 1's House Afire," *New York Herald,* July 16, 1895.

70 *the rebuilt car barns:* "Car Barns in 42d St. Make Brilliant Blaze," *New York Times,* March 5, 1906.

70 *"the last of the car barns":* "Car Barn Property on 12th Av. Leased," *New York Sun,* June 3, 1941.

70 *"a very convenient country seat":* James A. Stewart placed a three-inch ad in the real estate section of the *Evening Post* on multiple days in April 1809, including April 3, 4, 10, and 17.

70 *Sales of the lots:* Christopher Gray, "Where the Horses Slept and the Cars Idled," *New York Times,* December 5, 2008.

71 *"box" with her trainers:* "Some Well-Known Fire Dogs," *New York Times Illustrated Magazine,* October 17, 1897.

71 *The fire started:* "Destructive Fire," *New York Evening Post,* March 15, 1824.

72 *formation of Live Oak Company No. 44:* Costello, *Our Firemen,* 619.

72 *"We Extinguish One Flame":* George W. Sheldon, *The Story of the Volunteer Fire Department of the City of New York* (New York: Harper and Brothers, 1882), 533–534.

72 *the city purchased a large lot:* Bureau of Municipal Investigation and Statistics, *Real Estate Owned by the City of New York,* 14.

72 *Metropolitan Steam Engine Company No. 11:* "The Fire Department," *New York Times,* October 3, 1865.

73 *following members:* City of New York, *The City Record: Official Journal of the City of New York* 26, pt. 1 (New York: author, March 1, 1898), 40.

73 *Baruch Houses:* "Big Housing Plan Disclosed by City," *New York Times,* July 11, 1951; "$31,410,000 Housing Project to Be Erected Here," *New York Times,* April 7, 1952.

73 *six blocks of buildings:* "159 Slum Acres to be Condemned," *New York Times,* January 7, 1951; "Baruch at 79, Looks Ahead to 100th Year; City House to Bear His Father's Name," *New York Times,* August 19, 1949; "Old Folk Quit Tenements Sadly to Make Way for Baruch Housing," *New York Times,* February 22, 1952.

73 *may own either one domesticated dog or one domesticated cat:* City of New York, "New York City Housing Authority Pet Policy Non-Compliance Complaint," accessed October 22, 2018, http://www1.nyc.gov/nyc -resources/service/2144/nycha-pet-policy-non-compliance-complaint.

74 *"white-fleeced feline fire fighter":* "This Dog Dresses in Army Blue, and This Cat Goes to Fires," *New York Press,* March 29, 1896.

74 *"boudoir and reception room":* Ibid.

75 *"Tootsy saw Babe":* Ibid.

75 *"as though she were in quarters"*: Ibid.
75 *"Tootsy was dying to get into Broadway"*: Ibid.
75 *"the gong began its song of danger"*: Ibid.
76 *"When Tootsy dies"*: "A Feline Fireman," *Vernon (AL) Courier*, June 18, 1896.
76 *"all of his old comrades"*: "Thirty Firemen Overcome by Gas," *New York Evening World*, March 26, 1904.
76 *The Metropolitan Steam Engine Company No. 27*: Costello, *Our Firemen*, 822.
77 *North River was organized*: Ibid., 607, 674.
77 *the city had purchased*: Bureau of Municipal Investigation and Statistics, *Real Estate Owned by the City of New York*, 10.
77 *Napoleon LeBrun & Son*: New York City Landmarks Preservation Commission, *Tribeca West Historic District Designation Report*, May 1991, 293, http://architecturaltrust.org/~architec/wp-content/uploads/2013/06/Report_LPC_Tribeca_West.pdf.
77 *"were entered in sorrow"*: "Chops and Peter Dead," *New York Times*, August 26, 1896.
78 *"was a Catholic cat"*: Ibid.
78 *"until someone appeared," "death spasms"*: Ibid.
79 *"He turned a somersault"*: Ibid.
79 *"It will certainly find there"*: Ibid.
79 *mostly open pastures*: Fifth Avenue Bank of New York, *Fifth Avenue* (Boston: Walton, 1915), 8.
79 *Isaac Varian was a butcher*: Sam Briggs, *The Varian Family* (Cleveland: T. C. Schenk, 1881), 20–21.
80 *accumulated a considerable amount of property*: Stokes, *Iconography of Manhattan Island*, 156; Fifth Avenue Bank of New York, *Fifth Avenue*, 19.
80 *The Varian homestead*: Briggs, *Varian Family*, 61–62.
80 *Gross sold his house*: Bureau of Municipal Investigation and Statistics, *Real Estate Owned by the City of New York*, 29.
80 *Metamora Hose Company No. 29*: Costello, *Our Firemen*, 654.
80 *It occupied this building*: "Metropolitan Fire Department," *New York Times*, October 7, 1865.
80 *"a delicate Italian Renaissance town house"*: Norval White and Elliot Willensky, *AIA Guide to New York City*, 5th ed. (New York: Oxford University Press, 2010), 235.
82 *he could make the descent*: "Horses, Dogs and Cats Make Good Firemen," *Brooklyn Daily Eagle*, July 20, 1913.
82 *Engine Company No. 152 didn't switch*: New York City Fire Department Squad 252, "FDNY Squad Company 252 History," accessed October 23, 2018, http://archive.is/If5Jh.
82 *first went into service*: Ibid.
82 *world's second largest*: Robert D. McFadden, "Rockets' Red Glare Marked Birth of Merged City in 1898," *New York Times*, January 1, 1973.
83 *Peter's old firehouse*: New York City Landmarks Preservation Commission, *Engine Company 252*, October 19, 1995, 6, www.neighborhoodpreservationcenter.org/db/bb_files/95-ENGINE-CO.-252.pdf; In re Decatur St. in City

of New York, Walker v. Schauf et al., 89 N.E. 829 (Ct. App. N.Y. Nov. 9, 1909).

83 *purchased a standard lot:* Bureau of Municipal Investigation and Statistics, *Real Estate Owned by the City of New York,* 29; "Sewing School Exercises," *Brooklyn Daily Eagle,* June 10, 1890.

83 *"one of the finest firehouses":* New York City Landmarks Preservation Commission, *Engine Company 252,* 1.

83 *masonry minority:* E. Belcher Hyde, *Atlas of the Borough of Brooklyn: City of New York, Sections 1–4, Wards 1–28* (Brooklyn, NY: E. Belcher Hyde, 1916), available through the New York Public Library, https://digital collections.nypl.org/.

84 *"for the more effectual extinguishment of fires":* This section is based on: Brooklyn Fire Department, *Our Firemen: The Official History of the Brooklyn Fire Department, from the First Volunteer to the Latest Appointee* (Brooklyn:1892), 24–26.

84 *completed in 1895:* Christopher Gray, "Streetscapes: Engine Company 31 Firehouse; Getting to the Bottom of a Restoration," *New York Times,* September 23, 1990.

85 *"The Finest Firehouse in the World":* Richard Peck, "Old Firehouses Clang in the Past," *New York Times,* March 2, 1975.

85 *"elaborate and pretentious":* Montgomery Schuyler, "The Work of N. LeBrun & Sons," *Architectural Record* 27 (May 1910): 375.

85 *large enough for seventeen horses:* Peck, "Old Firehouses Clang in the Past."

86 *"she had returned from there":* "One-Eye Horace Is Sought by Cops," *Stevens Point (WI) Journal,* October 13, 1924.

86 *she continued her hunger strike:* "Smoke, Famous Firemen's Cat, Starves Himself to Death," *New York Times,* August 28, 1924.

86 *she was a sympathizer:* "Cat Dies as Result of Hunger Strike," *Kingsport (TN) Times,* September 2, 1924.

87 *$83,000 to build a replacement:* Gray, "Streetscapes: Engine Company 31 Firehouse."

89 *a three-story brick building:* Nancy L. Todd, *New York's Historic Armories* (Albany: SUNY Press, 2006), 39.

89 *tournaments known as trials of skill:* Emmons Clark, *History of the Seventh Regiment of New York, 1806–1889* (New York: Seventh Regiment, 1890), 65.

89 *replaced in 1844 by the Downtown Arsenal:* Todd, *New York's Historic Armories,* 40.

89 *featured narrow windows:* Ibid., 50.

89 *"From an examination made by the Engineer":* Commissioners of the Sinking Fund of the City of New York, *Proceedings of the Commissioners of the Sinking Fund of the City of New York, 1893–1894* (New York: Martin and Brown, 1904), 466.

89 *"roll and heave like waves":* Gray, "Streetscapes: Engine Company 31 Firehouse."

4. ARTIST AND EDITORIAL CATS

Page

90 *most photographed cat:* "The Original Grumpy Cat, in Full Color," *Bruton Stroube* (blog), March 2, 2016, http://brutonstroube.com/blog/the-original -grumpy-cat-in-full-color/.

90 *"Buzzer was certainly an important figure":* Arnold Genthe, *As I Remember* (New York: Reynal and Hitchcock, 1936), 277–278.

91 *spent many years in New York City:* Bronx County Historical Society, "Edgar Allan Poe in New York City," October 1, 2015, http://bronxhistorical society.org/poe-cottage/poe-edgar-allan-poe/.

91 *"one of the most remarkable":* Edgar Allan Poe, "Instinct versus Reason— A Black Cat," in *Collected Works of Edgar Allan Poe*, vol. 2, *Tales and Sketches 1831–1842*, ed. Thomas Ollive Mabbott (Cambridge, MA: Belknap Press of Harvard University Press, 1978), 478.

91 *reportedly died of starvation:* Burton R. Pollin and Robert E. Benedetto, "If Only Poe Had Succeeded When He Said Nevermore to Drink," *New York Times*, September 23, 1996.

92 *"A single member":* Helen Maria Winslow, *Concerning Cats: My Own and Some Others* (Boston: Lothrop, Lee and Shepard, 1900), 59.

92 *may date to a story:* William ApMadoc, "Music," *Cambrian* 25 (September 1905): 396.

93 *because he was angry:* Andrew Glass, "Pendleton Act Inaugurates U.S. Civil Service System, Jan. 16, 1883," *Politico*, January 16, 2018, www.politico .com/story/2018/01/16/pendleton-act-inaugurates-us-civil-service-system -jan-16-1883-340488.

93 *"Oh, say that the office cat ate it up":* Frank M. O'Brien, *The Story of the Sun* (New York: George H. Doran, 1918), 287.

93 *"We are frequently obliged":* Charles A. Dana, *Dana and the Sun* (New York: Dodd, Mead, 1938), 183–184.

94 *"the most astonishing confession":* "It Was the Cat!," *New York Times*, January 2, 1885.

94 *"The universal interest":* Charles A. Dana, "Our Office Cat," *New York Sun*, January 12, 1885.

95 *office cat must have chewed up:* Ibid.

96 *"soon tranquilized the emotions":* "A Great Scene in the Sun Office," *New York Sun*, September 24, 1885.

96 *"weaned on reports":* Winslow, *Concerning Cats*, 60.

96 *"a creditable specimen":* Ibid.

96 *"I can only vouch for its veracity":* Ibid., 59.

97 *from the family of Moses Yale Beach:* Frank M. O'Brien, "The Story of The Sun 1833–1918," *New York Sun*, April 14, 1918.

97 *moved to 150 Nassau Street:* Frank M. O'Brien, *The Story of the Sun* (New York: George H. Doran, 1918), 433.

97 *"What J. G. Brown has done":* As quoted in Mary Sayre Haverstock, Jeannette Mahoney Vance, and Brian L. Meggitt, eds., *Artists in Ohio,*

1787–1900: A Biographical Dictionary (Kent, OH: Kent State University Press, 2000), 234.

98 *"It takes some time":* W. Lewis Fraser, "An Artist Who Loves Cats and Dogs, and Paints Them," *St. Nicholas: An Illustrated Magazine for Young Folks* 18, pt. 2 (1891): 896.

99 *it was soon after he returned:* Ibid., 899.

99 *"one of those great, ugly houses":* Ibid., 892.

99 *first apartment building:* Christopher Gray, "Streetscapes: The 1880 Sherwood Studios, Once at 57th and Sixth; Building That Was 'the Uptown Headquarters of Art,'" *New York Times*, August 9, 1998.

99 *"plain and cold":* Fraser, "Artist Who Loves Cats and Dogs," 892.

100 *"Once in the studio":* Ibid.

100 *"were a trifling distracting":* Ibid., 898.

101 *"to find Christian homes":* Theodore Dreiser, "James H. Dolph," *New York Times Illustrated Weekly Magazine*, December 4, 1897, 15.

101 *"Yes, cats are easily spoiled":* Fraser, "Artist Who Loves Cats and Dogs," 898.

102 *"She looked at me":* Ibid., 901.

102 *planned to marry:* "Sudden: Was Dread Summons Made by John H. Dolph, the 'Landseer of America,'" *Cincinnati Enquirer*, September 29, 1903.

102 *sitting in a chair:* "Artist Dolph Died in a Chair," *New York Evening World*, September 29, 1903.

102 *donated to the University of Nebraska:* "New Art Gift Received," *Lincoln (NE) Journal Star*, July 14, 1923.

102 *James T. Hyde organized:* "Cats Purr for Prizes," *New York Times*, May 9, 1895; "Choice Mews Entered for the Big Show," *Washington Times*, March 26, 1895.

103 *Little Billie, Leo, and David:* "Cats Purr for Prizes."

103 *Taffy, The Laird, and Little Billee:* Winslow, *Concerning Cats*, 156.

103 *leading male characters:* George Du Maurier, *Trilby* (New York: International, 1899).

103 *"One may always see":* Winslow, *Concerning Cats*, 157.

104 *"monstrous, shiny black fellow":* Ibid.

104 *humble beginning:* This section is based on Andy Logan, *The Man Who Robbed the Robber Barons* (New York: Norton, 1965); Andy Logan, "Town Topics," *New Yorker*, August 14, 1965; Mark Caldwell, *A Short History of Rudeness: Manners, Morals, and Misbehavior in Modern America* (New York: Picador, 2000).

105 *"dedicated to art":* Caldwell, *Short History of Rudeness*, 16.

105 *William K. Vanderbilt paid $25,000:* "How Rich Men Were Bled by Town Topics," *Buffalo Courier*, January 23, 1906.

106 *the complainant in this case:* "Col. Mann Challenged," *New York Daily Tribune*, September 15, 1905.

106 *Mann's estate sold the property:* "Mann Estate Sells Garment Center Plot," *New York Times*, April 11, 1925.

106 *"Mr. Clemens, you know":* Robert D. Jerome and Herbert A. Wisbey Jr., *Mark Twin in Elmira*, 2nd ed. (Elmira, NY: Elmira College for Mark Twain Studies, 2013), 91.

106 *absolute passion:* Albert Bigelow Paine, *Mark Twain, a Biography: The Personal and Literary Life of Samuel Langhorne Clemens, Volumes I and II* (New York: Harper and Brothers, 1912), 68.

106 *"The difference between Papa and Mamma":* Ibid.

106 *He reportedly had up to eleven cats:* Jerome and Wisbey, *Mark Twain in Elmira,* 91.

107 *"It has been discovered":* Mark Dawidziak, *Mark Twain for Cat Lovers: True and Imaginary Adventures with Feline Friends* (Lanham, MD: Rowman and Littlefield, 2016), 114.

107 *Twain leased:* "Mark Twain Leases Home: Gets Lower Fifth Avenue Residence for Term of Years," *New York Times,* August 18, 1904.

108 *For hours a day:* "Mark Twain's Bed," *Washington Post,* March 26, 1905.

108 *"I think that perhaps the funniest thing":* Ibid.

108 *his instinctive wanderlust:* "A Talk with Mark Twain's Cat, the Owner Being Invisible," *New York Times,* April 9, 1905.

109 *"A CAT LOST":* Dawidziak, *Mark Twain for Cat Lovers,* 116.

109 *"anything to get a glimpse":* Mary Lawton, *A Lifetime with Mark Twain: The Memories of Katy Leary, for Thirty Years His Faithful and Devoted Servant* (New York: Harcourt, Brace, 1925), 292.

109 *"fearing a rush":* "Mark Twain's Cat Came Back," *York (PA) Daily,* April 4, 1905.

109 *"When they was doin' that":* Lawton, *Lifetime with Mark Twain,* 289.

109 *designed by noted architect James Renwick Jr.:* Howard A. Lamb, "Mark Twain's Former Home Still Remains a Landmark," *New York Times,* August 10, 1924.

110 *The home was constructed:* Ibid.; "Oppose Bank Offices in Mark Twain House," *New York Times,* July 7, 1929; Marilyn H. Pettit, "Brevoort Family Papers (1760–1879)," Brooklyn Historical Society, December 2005, http://brooklynhistory.org/library/wp/wp-content/uploads/2009/09/arms_1977_285_brevoort1.pdf.

110 *It passed from Elyessen:* James Riker, *Revised History of Harlem: Its Origins and Early Annals* (New York: New Harlem, 1904), 476–477.

110 *Henry agreed to build in the woods:* "The Lost Brevoort Mansion—5th Ave. and 9th St," *Daytonian in Manhattan* (blog), April 22, 2013, http://daytoninmanhattan.blogspot.com/2013/04/the-lost-brevoort-mansion-5th-ave-and.html.

110 *the home was owned:* Lamb, "Mark Twain's Former Home."

111 *"erect something on the site":* "Oppose Bank Offices."

111 *$103,911 for unpaid taxes and other debts:* "Mark Twain House Up for Sale Today," *New York Times,* July 10, 1933.

111 *"tall ultramodern apartment building":* Lee E. Cooper, "Apartment to Rise on Brevoort Site," *New York Times,* January 11, 1952.

111 *several efforts were made:* "Law Student Seeks to Save Twain House," *New York Times,* January 15, 1954; "Last Tenant Leaves Mark Twain House but Efforts to Preserve It Are Pushed," *New York Times,* March 2, 1954.

111 *Brevoort had no intention:* Lamb, "Mark Twain's Former Home."

112 *He supposedly protested the plan:* Alvin F. Harlow, *Old Bowery Days: The Chronicles of a Favorite Street* (New York: D. Appleton, 1931), 158.

112 *"stubborn old Knickerbocker":* Lamb, "Mark Twain's Former Home."

112 *Henry sold the grove:* Grace Church New York City, "Grace Church in New York: History," accessed October 4, 2018, https://gracechurchnyc.org/history/.

5. HOSPITALITY CATS

Page

113 *"My father wanted me to keep cats":* Don Allen, "'Wurra Wurra,' McSorley's Bartender Will Mix Nut Sundaes after July 1st in Saloon That Has Been Meeting Place for a Century," *New York Evening Telegram,* May 1, 1919.

114 *"When it came time to feed them":* Joseph Mitchell, "The Old House at Home," *New Yorker,* April 13, 1940.

114 *One of a series of five:* Mariea Caudill Dennison, "McSorley's: John Sloan's Visual Commentary on Male Bonding, Prohibition, and the Working Class," *American Studies,* Summer 2006, 25.

114 *"The hardy camaraderie":* Ibid., 30.

115 *"Minnie was made of strong stuff":* Joseph Driscoll, "Minnie, the Cat That Knew Caruso," *New York Herald Tribune,* July 23, 1934.

115 *"cheap cuts of meat," "near beer":* Ibid.

116 *"These rats were the biggest":* Ibid.

118 *"She has a face":* "Cat Whose Acquaintance of Many Notables Never Turned Her Head Is Dead in New York," *Greeley (CO) Daily Tribune,* November 9, 1934.

118 *"Just some soot":* "Dying Cat Brings Tears to Notables," *El Paso Herald-Post,* July 20, 1934.

118 *"When, full of years":* Eleanor Booth Simmons, "Cats and Their Care." *New York Sun,* December 31, 1937.

118 *It took Bleeck ten months:* Richard Manley, "*Life* Goes to Bleeck's," *Life,* November 26, 1945, 141.

118 *He died at the age of eighty-three:* "John Bleeck Dies: Restaurateur, 83," *New York Times,* April 24, 1963.

119 *twenty thousand to one hundred thousand speakeasies:* New-York Historical Society, "How Many Speakeasies Were Open in New York City during Prohibition?," accessed October 4, 2018, www.nyhistory.org/community/speakeasies.

119 *Mixed drinks took off:* Jennifer Lee, "A Speakeasy That's Not So Secret," *City Room* (blog), *New York Times,* July 14, 2009, https://cityroom.blogs.nytimes.com/2009/07/14/a-speakeasy-thats-not-so-secret/?_r=0.

119 *smuggled in from Nova Scotia:* Mob Museum, "Bootleggers and Bathtub Gin," in *Prohibition: An Interactive History,* accessed October 24, 2018, http://prohibition.themobmuseum.org/the-history/the-prohibition -underworld/bootleggers-and-bathtub-gin/; "Prohibition Era: The History of Montauk's Rum Runners," *The Usual,* February 2, 2015, http://theusual montauk.com/prohibition-era-the-history-of-montauks-rum-runners/.

119 *McCoy established his reputation:* Frederic F. Van de Water, "William McCoy. The Original Rum Runner," *Got Rum?*, November 2013, 10–13, http://www.rumshop.net/newsletters/november2013.pdf.

120 *"A half-grown cat":* "Abe, the Cat Who Wouldn't Scat, Has a Fine Home Now," *Olean (NY) Evening News*, March 22, 1928.

121 *largest hotel west of Broadway:* "New Hotel Lincoln Formerly Opened," *New York Times*, February 14, 1928.

121 *The Hotel Lincoln opened:* Ibid.

121 *"You can get away with anything":* "Abe, the Cat Who Wouldn't Scat."

121 *He managed numerous hotels:* "Who's Who in Red Bank and Vicinity," *Red Bank Standard*, June 13, 1930.

121 *"Mr. Clyde is widely known":* John Willy, "James T. Clyde," *Hotel Monthly* 23, no. 272 (November 1915): 73.

122 *Clyde left the hotel:* William M. Myers, "All Around the Town," *Asbury Park Press*, December 27, 1946.

122 *offered each person $3,000:* "Holdouts Yield at Lincoln Hotel: Last Is Woman Guest since 1929," *New York Times*, August 8, 1956.

122 *short stint as the Royal Manhattan:* "Row NYC Hotel," Revolvy, accessed October 5, 2018, www.revolvy.com/page/Row-NYC-Hotel.

122 *they did not want to change:* Ibid.

122 *Rockpoint Group and the hotel operator Highgate Holdings:* Jane L. Levere, "New York Hotels Decide It's Time for a Makeover," *New York Times*, August 20, 2013.

123 *Eden never had much luck:* Hopper Striker Mott, *The New York of Yesterday: A Descriptive Narrative of Old Bloomingdale* (New York: G. P. Putnam's Sons, 1908), 2–3.

123 *The men foreclosed on the mortgage:* "The Evolution of Medcef Eden's Farm," in *The World's Work*, vol. 40, *May 1920–October 1920* (Garden City, NY: Doubleday, Page, 1920), 17.

123 *included two dwelling houses:* Mott, *New York of Yesterday*, 2–3.

123 *dragged on for twenty years:* "Evolution of Medcef Eden's Farm," 17.

123 *"Farm at Bloomingdale":* Mott, *New York of Yesterday*, 3.

123 *"the breadth of four rods":* Ibid., 4–5.

124 *Rusty, the Algonquin's "snooty cat":* Dorothy Kilgallen, "Voice of Broadway," *Olean (NY) Times Herald*, May 16, 1945.

124 *"Three days later":* Frank Case, *Do Not Disturb* (New York: Frederick A. Stokes, 1940), 123.

125 *"If he is on the eighth floor":* Ibid., 125.

125 *Rusty spent much of the day:* Simmons, "Cats and Their Care," *New York Sun*, August 2, 1946.

126 *"The news of his desperate illness":* L. L. Stevenson, "Manhattan Moods," *Buffalo Evening News*, February 2, 1946.

126 *Case had purchased:* "Buys Sag Harbor Place," *Brooklyn Daily Eagle*, June 14, 1919.

126 *many famous thespians:* "Hamptons Deeds & Don'ts," *Cottage & Gardens*, September 2013, www.cottages-gardens.com/Hamptons-Cottages-Gardens/September-2013/Hamptons-Deeds-Donts/.

126 *a shudder:* Dorothy Kilgallen, "Voice of Broadway: Tales of a Famous Inn," *Elmira (NY) Star-Gazette,* April 12, 1947.

126 *Martin found Rusty:* Ibid.

127 *Rusty was buried in the Case garden at their summer home:* Simmons, "Cats and Their Care."

127 *"Rusty was sick":* Ibid.

127 *all been named Matilda:* Algonquin Hotel, "The Legend behind the Algonquin Cat," accessed October 5, 2018, www.algonquinhotel.com/story/algonquin-cat/.

128 *He replaced Matilda III:* Raquel Laneri, "RIP Matilda, the Famous Algonquin Cat," *New York Post,* October 23, 2017, https://nypost.com/2017/10/23/rip-matilda-the-famous-algonquin-cat/.

128 *Hamlet came to the Algonquin:* Raquel Laneri, "This Will Soon Be the Most Famous Cat in NYC," *New York Post,* July 29, 2017, http://nypost.com/2017/07/29/this-will-soon-be-the-most-famous-cat-in-nyc/.

128 *The hotel installed an electric fence:* Eli Epstein, "No Money in a Dirty Kitchen: The Repercussions of NYC's Restaurant Grading System," *Atlantic,* July 23, 2012, www.theatlantic.com/health/archive/2012/07/no-money-in-a-dirty-kitchen-the-repercussions-of-nycs-restaurant-grading-system/260183/.

6. THEATRICAL AND SHOW CATS

Page

129 *on display in stacked wooden boxes:* "A Collection of Cats: The Feline Exhibition in the New Broadway Museum," *New York Times,* March 6, 1881.

130 *wide range of tricks:* "Most Wonderful Performing Cats in the World," *New York World,* May 24, 1896.

130 *"some of the greatest curiosities":* "The New York Cat Show," *Valley Falls (KS) New Era,* December 29, 1877.

131 *"The New York cat show":* "Current Comment," *Brooklyn Daily Eagle,* December 18, 1877.

131 *"Damn all cats anyway":* "Speaking about Cats!," *New York Times,* March 16, 1881.

131 *"The cat is a cuss":* "This Is a Cat," *Wayne County Herald* (Honesdale, PA), June 23, 1881.

131 *owned by the late George L. Fox:* "A Collection of Cats: The Feline Exhibition in the New Broadway Museum," *New York Times,* March 6, 1881.

132 *"was a black and white gentleman cat":* Ibid.

132 *"Manager Bunnell stood":* Ibid.

132 *Barnum's Grand Traveling Museum:* Barnum Museum, "Biographies," accessed November 13, 2018, https://archives.lib.uconn.edu/islandora/object/60002%3A3965.

132 *Barnum's dime museum:* Andrea Stulman Dennett, *Weird and Wonderful: The Dime Museum in America* (New York: NYU Press, 1997), 24–25; New-York Historical Society, "Barnum's Museum Token," accessed October 5, 2018, www.nyhistory.org/exhibit/barnums-museum-token.

133   *He purchased the collection:* Dennett, *Weird and Wonderful*, 40.

133   *he opened a combination museum:* T. Allston Brown, *A History of the New York Stage from the First Performance in 1732 to 1901*, vol. 2 (New York: Dodd, Mead, 1903), 593.

133   *This site was formerly occupied:* Alvin F. Harlow, *Old Bowery Days: The Chronicles of a Famous Street* (New York: D. Appleton, 1931), 118; John Thorn, "The New York Base Ball Club (a.k.a. Washington BBC, Gotham BBC), Part 3," *Our Game* (blog), accessed October 6, 2018, https://our game.mlblogs.com/the-new-york-base-ball-club-a-k-a-washington-bbc -gotham-bbc-part-3-d58563d099a0.

133   *he moved to 771 Broadway:* Theatre Historical Society, "Manhattan," 771, accessed October 23, 2018, https://historictheatres.org/wp-content/ uploads/2015/10/Michael-Miller-Index-Card-Collection-Full.pdf. Additional information about the building at 771 Broadway was obtained from numerous estate-sale notices and retail ads placed in the *New York Evening Post* and other newspapers from the 1850s through 1883.

134   *six rooms of curiosities:* Brown, *History of the New York Stage*, 593.

134   *Sailor's Snug Harbor Corporation:* "Building Intelligence," *Manufacturer and Builder* 15 (1883): 128.

134   *this building was destroyed:* "A Holocaust: The 'Richmond' and Bunnell's Burned," *Buffalo Times*, March 18, 1887.

134   *where he stayed until his death:* "Geo. B. Bunnell, Show Business Veteran, Dead," *Bridgeport (CT) Times*, May 3, 1911.

134   *named for Captain Robert Richard Randall:* Trustees of the Sailors' Snug Harbor in the City of New York, "Brief History," accessed October 6, 2018, https://thesailorssnugharbor.org/brief-history/.

134   *Born in New Jersey:* "Randall, Robert Richard," in *Appleton's Cyclopedia of American Biography*, ed. James Grant Wilson and John Fiske (New York: D. Appleton, 1910), 170; Trustees of the Sailors' Snug Harbor, "Brief History."

134   *Robert Richard Randall paid £5,000:* D. D. McColl, *Sketches of Old Marlboro* (Columbus, SC: Presses of The State, 1916), 14–15.

134   *"retiring old bachelor":* Ibid., 16.

134   *"an asylum":* "Randall, Robert Richard," 171.

135   *better to subdivide the land:* McColl, *Sketches of Old Marlboro*, 16; Trustees of the Sailors' Snug Harbor, "Brief History."

135   *the institution expanded:* Snug Harbor Cultural Center & Botanical Garden, "History," accessed October 6, 2018, http://snug-harbor.org/about-us/ history/.

135   *"either an exceptional cat":* "Picked Up in New York," *Detroit Free Press*, August 14, 1887.

136   *Jim's favorite person:* "Jim the Mascot," *New York Times*, February 19, 1888.

136   *"and otherwise distinguish himself":* Ibid.

136   *a quiet brindle cat:* Harmon Lee Ensign, "Union Square Jim," in *Lady Lee and Other Animal Stories* (Chicago: A. C. McClurg, 1902), 65–91.

137   *One of Jim's biggest fans:* "Jim the Mascot."

137   *"with the relish of an epicure":* Ibid.

137 *"Poor Jim!"*: Ensign, "Union Square Jim," 79.
138 *They even tried to buy Jim:* "Jim the Mascot"; "Blonde Jim's Debut," *New York Times*, May 27, 1888.
138 *The flames were discovered:* "Burning of a Playhouse," *New York Times*, February 29, 1888.
138 *"Has anyone seen Jim?"*: Ensign, "Union Square Jim," 83.
139 *"general jollification"*: "Burning of a Playhouse."
139 *"Blonde Jim"*: "Blonde Jim's Debut."
139 *"He purred"*: Ibid.
139 *"a delirium of delight"*: Ibid.
140 *Jim died from an incurable illness:* "Notable Cats," *Allentown (PA) Morning Call*, April 26, 1890.
140 *Cornelius Tiebout, a New York merchant:* "Cornelius Tiebout and His Home 'Roxborough,'" *New-York State Historical Society Quarterly Bulletins* 16 (January 1933): 112.
140 *Shook renamed the hotel:* I. N. Phelps Stokes, *The Iconography of Manhattan Island, 1498–1909* (New York: Robert H. Dodd, 1915), 703.
140 *The new theater opened:* "Burning of a Playhouse."
141 *the Union Square Theatre Stock Company:* Arthur Hornblow, *A History of the Theatre in America from Its Beginnings to the Present Time* (Philadelphia: J. B. Lippincott, 1919), 387.
141 *The revamped theater:* Christopher Gray, "Streetscapes: The Union Square Theater, the Ghost behind a Huge Sign," *New York Times*, January 29, 1989.
141 *"the most dubious activities"*: Gray, "Streetscapes: The Union Square Theater."
141 *sold at auction:* "Will Sell Holdings in Union Square," *New York Times*, May 15, 1920.
141 *sealed off and divided:* Ibid.
142 *"Mr. Brian Hughes died"*: "The Practical Jokes That Made Everybody Laugh," *Philadelphia Inquirer Magazine*, January 4, 1925.
142 *One of Hughes's biggest jokes:* "Cats with Decorations," *New York Times*, March 6, 1896; "Brian G. Hughes, Practical Joker," *New York Sun*, October 15, 1911; "How Brian G. Hughes Won Fame as Joker: Cat and Car Horse Helped," *Brooklyn Daily Eagle*, December 14, 1924.
142 *"aristocratic angle"*: Sarah Hartwell, "Nicodemus—New York's Fake Champion Cat of the 1890s," Messybeast Cats, 2015, http://messybeast.com/nicodemus.htm.
142 *"brindled Dublin tomcat"*: "Offer Thousands for a 10-Cent Cat," *Chicago Tribune*, May 20, 1895.
143 *Nicodemus, by Bowery, out of Dust-Pan:* "Practical Jokes That Made Everybody Laugh."
143 *"It seems to me"*: "Offer Thousands for a 10-Cent Cat."
144 *"The class calls for he cats"*: "Sporting Gossip of New York," *Philadelphia Times*, March 7, 1886.
144 *Nairb G. Sehguh:* "Joke Cats and Other Cats," *New York Sun*, January 11, 1899.

145 *he purchased an old streetcar mare:* "How Brian G. Hughes Won Fame";
      "Practical Jokes That Made Everybody Laugh."
145 *sent the horse to his farm:* "Hughes's Joke," *Cincinnati Enquirer*, November
      24, 1900.
145 *"Puldeka Orphan":* "Brian G. Hughes, Practical Joker."
145 *"Pulled a car often":* Ibid.
145 *born in Ireland:* All biographical information about Brian G. Hughes was
      obtained through official birth, death, and census reports and city directo-
      ries retrieved from Ancestry.com.
146 *the site of the former African Free School #2:* Ariel Kates, Greenwich
      Village Society for Historic Preservation, "African Free School, First in
      America for Black Students, Found a Home in Greenwich Village," *Off the
      Grid* (blog), November 2, 2017, http://gvshp.org/blog/2017/11/02/african
      -free-school-first-in-america-for-blacks-found-a-home-in-greenwich
      -village/.
146 *succumbed to a long illness:* "Wife of Brian G. Hughes Dead," *Middletown
      (NY) Times-Press*, August 2, 1915.
146 *finally putting an end to the pranks:* "Hughes Who Hoaxed N.Y. Now a
      Reformer Joker Turned Serious by War," *New York Evening World Daily
      Magazine*, August 28, 1918.
146 *died at his home:* "Brian G. Hughes Services," obituary, *New York Times*,
      December 12, 1924.
146 *his son shot himself:* "Brian G. Hughes, 42, Ends Life by Bullet," *New York
      Times*, January 13, 1928.
147 *"Tommy C. Lamb":* Joe Laurie Jr., *Vaudeville from the Honky-Tonks to the
      Palace* (New York: Henry Holt, 1953), 308.
147 *the Feline Bar Fly:* "Feline 'Bar Fly' of Lambs Club to Be Guest of Gallery
      Boys," *New York Times*, March 21, 1936.
147 *"evicted him with a few accurate and destructive lefts":* Ibid.
147 *Two hours later:* O. O. McIntyre, "New York Day by Day," *Olean (NY)
      Times-Herald*, January 2, 1936.
148 *a direct descendant:* "Feline 'Bar Fly' of Lambs Club."
148 *"Great Lover of the Forties":* Simmons, "Cats and Their Care," *New York
      Sun*, December 31, 1937.
148 *"New York's Toughest Tomcat":* Henry W. Clune, "Seen and Heard," *Roches-
      ter (NY) Democrat and Chronicle*, April 18, 1936.
149 *"Lambs Club's Tough Tomcat":* "Lambs Club's Tough Tomcat to Take Girl-
      friend to Party," *New York Post*, March 21, 1936.
149 *"black and white cutie":* Ibid.
149 *everyone wore evening clothes:* Laurie, *Vaudeville*, 309.
150 *"Thomas Casanova Lamb crept":* "Cat 'Bouncer' at N.Y. Bar Awarded
      Devotion Prize," *Salt Lake Tribune*, April 26, 1936; "Heroic Pets Win Med-
      als for Deeds," *New York Times*, April 26, 1936.
150 *"alleged super-intelligence and devotion":* "Heroic Pets Win Medals."
150 *had to shoot around him:* Laurie, *Vaudeville from the Honky-Tonks to the
      Palace*, 309.

150 *The Lambs club was formed:* The Lambs, "History of the Lambs," accessed October 8, 2018, https://the-lambs.org/history/; The Lambs, "Past Clubhouse Locations," accessed October 8, 2018, https://the-lambs.org/clubhouse/past-clubhouse-locations/.

151 *"their bleatings":* "The Fold Is a Nuisance," *New York Times,* August 10, 1890.

151 *quite a ruckus:* "After the Lambs' Club," *New York Sun,* May 18, 1896.

151 *Sir Oliver, a parrot mascot:* "Queer Mascots of Many Clubs," *New York Times,* November 2, 1902.

7. CIVIL SERVANT CATS

Page

153 *"Last August I sailed":* "An Irish Cat for Mayor Gilroy," *New York Tribune,* February 14, 1894.

153 *Mayor Gilroy sent Bridget to his home:* "Mayor Gilroy Gets an Irish Cat," *New York World,* February 14, 1894.

154 *"the cat came back":* Harry S. Miller, *The Cat Came Back* (Chicago: Will Rossiter, 1893).

154 *"a looter of the city feed bag":* "City's Mascot Celebrates," *New York Times,* June 26, 1906.

155 *"what the ancient cat does not know":* Ibid.

155 *Guggenheimer spent fifty cents:* "City Hall Loses Old Tom," *New York Times,* July 23, 1908.

155 *"a homelike look":* "City Hall Is His Castle," *New York Times,* April 25, 1897.

155 *"worthy a resolution":* "City's Mascot Celebrates."

157 *"Marty Keese, as the aged janitor":* "Marty Keese Dead on 72nd Birthday," *New York Times,* June 28, 1909.

157 *in a little brick house:* "Marty Keese Dead at 72," *New York Sun,* June 28, 1909; "The City Marty Keese Knew," *New York Sun,* July 28, 1907.

158 *"she'd need a stepladder":* "Tweed's Captor Tells of Days When New York Needed 'A Step-Ladder to Climb into H——,'" *Washington Post,* October 13, 1907.

159 *Tweed was tried and convicted:* Ibid.

159 *"I was always sorry":* "Marty Keese Dead on 72nd Birthday."

159 *"the little buildings":* "City Marty Keese Knew."

159 *"I was proud":* "Marty Keese Dead at 72."

160 *"helped himself or herself":* "Federal Cats Celebrate George Cook's Birthday," *New York Times,* November 6, 1904.

160 *budget of about five dollars:* "Uncle Sam's Dead and Dumb Cat Is Not Now Official Rat-Catcher," *New York World,* March 8, 1898.

161 *"That darned low critter":* "Federal Cats Celebrate."

161 *"He just stuffed them bags":* Ibid.

162 *"Never was a greater variety":* "Some Cats Must Depart," *Indianapolis News,* December 10, 1906.

162 *"a two-platoon system":* "Federal Cats Celebrate."

163 *"King of the Cats":* "Two Hundred Cats in Government Employ," *Buffalo Sunday Morning News,* October 2, 1910.

164 *a black-and-white cat named Mollie:* "200 Cats Employed by Uncle Sam in New York," *New York Press*, September 11, 1910.

164 *"armed with bags of food":* "Lady Bountiful Lures U.S. Post Office Cats to the City Hall Park," *Brooklyn Daily Eagle*, October 5, 1924.

164 *an intricate pneumatic-tube system:* Robin Pogrebin, "Underground Mail Road: Modern Plans for All-but-Forgotten Delivery System," *New York Times*, May 7, 2001; Kenneth E. Stuart, "Pneumatic Mail Tubes and Operation of Automatic Railroads," *Engineers and Engineering* 39, no. 10 (1922): 337–343; Office of the Postmaster, "New York, N.Y., Underground Post Office," in *Hearing before a Subcommittee of the Committee on Post Office and Civil Service United States Senate, Eighteenth Congress, Second Session* (Washington, DC: United States Printing Office, 1948), 24.

164 *around ninety-five thousand letters:* Megan Garber, "That Time People Sent a Cat through the Mail Using Pneumatic Tubes," *Atlantic*, August 13, 2013, www.theatlantic.com/technology/archive/2013/ 08/that-time-people -sent-a-cat-through-the-mail-using-pneumatic-tubes/278629/.

165 *"How [the cat] could live":* As reported in Tim Rowland, *Strange and Obscure Stories of New York City: Little-Known Tales about Gotham's People and Places* (New York: Skyhorse, 2016), 45.

165 *a thin glass globe:* Stuart, "Pneumatic Mail Tubes."

166 *"promptly at 1 o'clock every morning":* "Oldest Cat in Brooklyn Back— Driver with Aspirations," *New-York Tribune*, February 19, 1905.

167 *"a certain quaint dignity":* "Famous Brooklyn Cat Dead," *New York Times*, April 7, 1905.

168 *the policemen turned in an alarm:* "Blind Cat Saves Borough Hall," *New York Evening Telegram*, May 20, 1904.

168 *the judge returned to his office:* Ibid.; "Justice Jenks Fought Fire," *New York Times*, May 21, 1904.

168 *hangout for "benchers":* "An Epidemic of Spring Fever Lays Low the 'Benchers' in the Public Parks," *Brooklyn Standard Union*, April 2, 1905.

168 *"Jerry Fox was decent":* "Town Talk and Doings," *Brooklyn Standard Union*, August 17, 1899.

169 *"Had each of the several hundred":* "Famous Brooklyn Cat Dead."

169 *"He was a student":* Ibid.

169 *"I had known him":* Ibid.

169 *"In an earlier day":* Ibid.

169 *part of Philip Livingston's farm:* "Old Brooklyn Farm Lands," *Brooklyn Daily Eagle*, July 19, 1896; Henry R. Stiles, *A History of the City of Brooklyn, Including the Old Town and Village of Brooklyn, the Town of Bushwick, and the Village and City of Williamsburgh* (Brooklyn, NY: City of Brooklyn, 1867), 162.

169 *built its third church:* "A Fine Church Edifice," *Brooklyn Daily Eagle*, December 4, 1887.

169 *"reared its head":* Ibid.

169 *139 feet in diameter and 75 feet high:* "Gettysburg: Stirring Battle Scene in the Cyclorama," *Brooklyn Daily Eagle*, October 2, 1886.

170 *the honor goes to George Murphy:* "Why Mr. Leich Wants to Create a 'Murphy Park,'" *Brooklyn Daily Eagle*, May 29, 1894.

170 *"loafers, bums, tramps, and thieves":* "Murphy Park as It Is To-day," *Brooklyn Daily Eagle*, July 3, 1902.

170 *"The scoundrels":* Ibid.

170 *to turn the lots:* "Result of Pounds' Refusal to Provide Auto Parking Space," *Brooklyn Daily Eagle*, October 21, 1916.

170 *the lots were put into use:* "Brooklyn Colleges to Train for Army," *Brooklyn Daily Eagle*, September 7, 1918.

170 *a practice golf-putting course:* "Doesn't Want Judicial Putters Hidden from Public," *Brooklyn Daily Eagle*, August 14, 1921.

170 *Riegelmann broke ground:* "Start Brooklyn's New City Building," *New York Times*, August 14, 1924.

171 *"honest Democratic parentage":* "Cat, Perching beside Aldermanic Orator, Brings Ignoble Halt to Tirade on Mayor," *New York Times*, March 2, 1934.

171 *"a bold, swashbuckling lad":* "Tammany, City Hall Cat Dies," *New York Sun*, April 11, 1939.

171 *"Library Lion" pose:* "Tammany, City Hall Cat, Tastes Publicity, but Retires after Forced Posing for Pictures," *New York Times*, June 15, 1938.

172 *"What with all the hullabaloo":* Ibid.

172 *"a self-declared monarch":* "Cat, Perching beside Aldermanic Orator."

174 *"the wisest and bravest":* "City Hall in 'Siege' to Save Its Pet Cat: Curran Defends 'Boss' Tammany against Liquidation," *New York Times*, June 14, 1938.

174 *"The carnage":* Ibid.

174 *Halton could not find Tammany:* "City Hall Cat Falls Ill, Rushed to Hospital," *New York Times*, April 11, 1939; "Death Ends Reign of Tammany, City Hall's Official Ratcatcher," *Brooklyn Daily Eagle*, April 11, 1939.

174 *"quiet and trustful":* "City Hall Cat Falls Ill."

174 *"Tammany—In Fond Memory":* Ibid.

174 *"Some say Tammany":* Ibid.

175 *an eleven-month-old female calico cat:* "Fusion Succeeds Tammany as City Hall Cat: Name Reflects Both Politics and Ancestry," *New York Times*, May 4, 1939.

176 *"the apple of Tom's eye":* "Snooky, the City Hall Cat Plays Hooky: Devoted Custodian Is Left in a Dither," *New York Times*, November 3, 1944.

176 *Snooky would resort to killing:* "Cat Hit by Fish 'Freeze,' May Resort to Savagery," *New York Times*, February 20, 1943.

176 *"The dehydrated sawdust":* "World Brightens for Snooky, City Hall Cat, as Slippers, Heart-Wrung, Sends Can of Fish," *New York Times*, February 25, 1943.

177 *"I bet someone stole Snooky":* Ibid.

177 *"Glad to see you back":* "Prodigal Snooky, Pet City Hall Cat, Found by Police," *Brooklyn Daily Eagle*, November 26, 1944.

177 *"When Snooky first arrived":* "Snooky, City Hall Cat, Has Anniversary Dinner," *Binghamton (NY) Press*, June 17, 1944.

177 *AWOL one last time:* "Snooky of City Hall Goes AWOL on VJ Jaunt Again," *Brooklyn Daily Eagle*, September 6, 1945.
177 *This new cat was presented:* "Meow! Another Irish Tenant for City Hall," *New York Daily News*, January 30, 1946.

8. GOOD-LUCK CATS

Page
178 *a handsome young aviator:* Gavin Mortimer, "The Darling Mr. Moisant," *Air & Space Smithsonian*, December 30, 2010, www.airspacemag.com/history-of-flight/the-daring-mr-moisant-78148130/?page=1.
178 *at least fourteen documented flights:* L. A. Vocelle, "Cats in 20th Century History (Part 2–Kiddo, Fifi, Whoopsy and Patsy)," *The Great Cat* (blog), July 12, 2014, www.thegreatcat.org/cats-20th-century-history-part-2-kiddo-fifi-whoopsy-patsy/; "Moisant Flies 20 Miles in Blinding Fog: Wins $850 Prize," *New York World*, October 24, 1010.
178 *close to one million spectators:* "Moisant Wins Statue Race," *New York Times*, October 31, 1910.
179 *caught in a gust of wind:* "How Moisant Fell," *New York Times*, January 1, 1911.
180 *"Then all of a sudden":* "Worker Shot Skyward from Under River Bed," *New York Times*, March 28, 1905.
180 *The committee suggested a route:* "Tunnel Plan Presented," *Brooklyn Daily Eagle*, May 2, 1900.
180 *the contract:* James Blaine Walker, "The First Subway Complete and Placed in Operation," in *Fifty Years of Rapid Transit: 1864 to 1917* (New York: Law Printing, 1918), 179.
180 *The contract was signed:* "Tunnel Contract Signed," *Brooklyn Daily Eagle*, September 11, 1902.
180 *the War Department:* Board of Rapid Transit Railroad Commissioners, *Report of the Board of Rapid Transit Railroad Commissioners for and in the City of New York* (New York: author, 1903), 298–299.
181 *Three other laborers:* "Worker Shot Skyward."
181 *"small, pale, wiry Irishman":* "Blown through River Bed and Escapes Unhurt," *Buffalo Courier*, March 28, 1905.
181 *had not had much luck:* All of the biographical information about Richard Creegan was obtained through official birth, death, census, and other records retrieved from Ancestry.com.
182 *"like a pea":* "Worker Shot Skyward."
182 *Bright Eyes first made his appearance:* "Mascot Deep Down with Tunnel Men," *Brooklyn Standard Union*, May 14, 1905.
183 *"but, law sakes!":* Ibid.
184 *One of those guests:* "Rush Work on Tunnels, with Subway Section Nearly Complete," *New York Herald*, June 10, 1907.
184 *Nellie had arrived:* Ibid.
184 *"Here comes Subway Nellie":* "Subway Nellie the Pet of Workmen in Tunnel," *Brooklyn Daily Eagle*, June 30, 1907.

184 *the chief motorman G. W. Morrison:* "Train Goes through the Battery Tunnel," *New York Times,* November 28, 1907; "Subway to Brooklyn Opened," *New York Sun,* January 9, 1908.

185 *a large orange tabby cat:* "A Wellman Exhibition," *New York Times,* October 23, 1910. An advertisement for Gimbels appearing in the same issue noted that the exhibit was located on the fourth floor.

185 *Navigator Simon decided:* "The Airship 'America' of 1910: The First Attempt to Fly the Atlantic," Airships.net, accessed October 11, 2018, www.airships.net/first-attempt-fly-atlantic-wellman-vaniman-airship-america/.

186 *rescued by the night watchman:* David L. Bristow, *Flight to the Top of the World: The Adventures of Walter Wellman* (Lincoln: University of Nebraska Press, 2018), 228–229.

186 *The men called the male cat Kiddo:* Navigator Simon referred to the cat as a female in his log book, but the cat was an orange tabby, which are typically male. Additionally, all the newspapers referred to the cat as a male.

186 *"Roy, come and get this goddamn cat!":* Rebecca Maksel, "Animals Aloft," *Air & Space Smithsonian,* November 20, 2008, www.airspacemag.com/history-of-flight/animals-aloft-94381943/.

187 *"Cat seemed unhappy":* "Wellman Tells of His Record Airship Voyage," *New York Times,* October 20, 1910.

187 *"We are in distress":* "John R. Irwin, Wireless Operator of the Airship 'America,'" *Telegraph and Telephone Age,* January 1–December 16, 1910, 744.

188 *"cats have nine lives!":* Walter Wellman, *The Aerial Age: A Thousand Miles by Airship over the Atlantic Ocean* (New York: A. R. Keller, 1911), 333.

188 *"We sacrificed our airship":* Ibid., 367.

188 *made some test trips:* Bristow, *Flight to the Top of the World,* 275.

188 *The gas bag was torn:* "Vaniman Killed with Four Men Aloft in Airship," *New York Times,* July 3, 1912.

188 *All the proceeds:* "Dead Airship Crew Left Needy Families," *New York Times,* July 4, 1912.

189 *the history of this particular store:* Anthony Fitzherbert, "The Public Be Pleased: William Gibbs McAdoo and the Hudson Tubes," nycsubway.org, accessed October 11, 2018, www.nycsubway.org/wiki/The_Public_Be_Pleased:_William_Gibbs_McAdoo_and_the_Hudson_Tubes.

189 *The proposed site:* "New M'Adoo Station," *New York Tribune,* November 21, 1905.

189 *Many smaller old buildings:* "Broadway Property for Subway Terminal," *New York Times,* November 21, 1905.

189 *Adams also had grand plans:* "'Al' Adams to Build a 42-Story Hotel," *New York Times,* August 30, 1905.

189 *signed a twenty-one-year lease:* "Gimbel Brothers," in *Poor's Manual of Industrials, 1917* (New York: Poor's Manual, 1917), 268.

189 *"be the terminal of the McAdoo tunnel system":* "Gimbels Tell Plan for Big Store Here," *New York Times,* January 30, 1909.

190 *"The love of a man for a dog":* Harold C. Burr, "Rangers Have the Best of the Mascoting—and Young Mr. Cecil Dillon," *Brooklyn Daily Eagle,* February 6, 1931.

190 *"The Rangers will never win"*: "A Legacy of Curses," *New York Daily News*, June 16, 1994.

191 *The corporation comprised:* "Rickard to Build Garden on 8th Av," *New York Times*, June 18, 1924.

191 *"the largest indoor arena"*: "Plan Uptown Arena Twice Garden's Size," *New York Times*, June 28, 1923.

191 *making plans with Bing & Bing:* "Boro Men Invest Millions in Site for Manhattan Arena," *Brooklyn Daily Eagle*, August 7, 1924.

191 *purchased the old trolley barn:* "New Garden for Car Barn Site to Cost $3,000,000," *Brooklyn Daily Eagle*, June 29, 1924.

191 *workmen began:* "Work on New Garden Started by Rickard," *New York Evening Post*, January 10, 1925.

191 *planned to name his new team:* Michael Strainkamp, "A Brief History: New York Rangers," NHL.com, August 21, 2010, www.nhl.com/ice/m _news.htm?id=535779.

192 *"Don't you think"*: Harold C. Burr, "Here's One Black Cat Which Brought Rangers Nothing but Good Luck," *Brooklyn Daily Eagle*, January 13, 1931.

192 *ten teams played forty-forty games each:* New York Rangers, "1927–28 New York Rangers," accessed October 11, 2018, http://rangers.ice.nhl.com/club/ page.htm?id=53989.

192 *The press attributed:* "Of Course Cat's No Magic, but Here's Tip for Robbie," *Brooklyn Daily Eagle*, March 19, 1927.

193 *He credited the win:* George Currie, "Bob McAllister's Black Cat Source of Trouble for A.A.U. Officials," *Brooklyn Daily Eagle*, March 25, 1927.

193 *"More than one aspirant"*: Burr, "Here's One Black Cat."

193 *"That's why we lost"*: Ibid.

193 *"She wouldn't let anyone feed her"*: Ibid.

194 *"You'd better get a new mascot"*: Harold C. Burr, "Arrival of Ranger III, New Hockey Mascot, Gives Patrick Hope," *Brooklyn Daily Eagle*, February 3, 1931.

194 *"Ranger III is a carbon copy"*: Ibid.

194 *"If you do"*: Burr, "Rangers Have the Best."

194 *the players also blamed:* Harold C. Burr, "Garden Cat Prefers Rain to Mascoting for Ranger Sextet," *Brooklyn Daily Eagle*, February 18, 1931.

195 *a three-hundred-acre estate:* "Old Houses: John Hopper's Homestead, Corner of Broadway and Fiftieth-Street," *New York Times*, October 31, 1872; Hopper Striker Mott, *The New York of Yesterday: A Descriptive Narrative of Old Bloomingdale* (New York: G. P. Putnam's Sons, 1908), 8; H. Croswell Tuttle, *Abstracts of Farm Titles in the City of New York* (New York: Spectator, 1881), 279.

195 *Originally established:* Mott, *New York of Yesterday*, 8; Tuttle, *Abstracts of Farm Titles*, 201.

196 *his last will and testament:* Tuttle, *Abstracts of Farm Titles*, 203; "Old Houses: John Hopper's Homestead."

196 *a wild, savage-looking cat:* "Old Houses: John Hopper's Homestead."

196 *a small family graveyard:* Tuttle, *Abstracts of Farm Titles*, 268; Mary French, "Hopper Family Burial Ground," *New York City Cemetery Project*

(blog), December 30, 2010, https://nycemetery.wordpress.com/2010/12/
30/hopper-family-burial-ground/.

196 *The stables were destroyed:* "A Car Depot Swept Away," *New York Times,*
November 26, 1879.

197 *"Mr. Robinson, here is something":* Thomas Holmes, "Victory, the Cat,
and Elliott, the Southpaw, Shut Out the Phillies," *Brooklyn Daily Eagle,*
April 30, 1927.

199 *The Robins finished:* Baseball Almanac, "1927 Brooklyn Robins Schedule,"
accessed October 12, 2018, www.baseball-almanac.com/teamstats/
schedule.php?y=1927&t=BR7.

199 *Byrne set up a grandstand:* Glenn Stoute, *The Dodgers: 120 Years of
Dodgers Baseball* (Boston: Houghton Mifflin, 2004), 18; Ellen M. Snyder-
Grenier, *Brooklyn! An Illustrated History* (Philadelphia: Temple University
Press, 1996), 232.

199 *Trolley Dodgers:* Stoute, *The Dodgers,* 28.

200 *disreputable, ramshackle:* Bob McGee, *The Greatest Ballpark Ever* (New
Brunswick, NJ: Rivergate, 2005), 40.

200 *using proceeds:* Frederick Boyd Sevenson, "Ebbets, for 38 Years in Baseball, Tells of the Great American Game," *Brooklyn Daily Eagle,* October 3,
1920.

200 *$22 million, twenty-story, 1,377-unit housing project:* "End of a Ball Park,"
New York Times, February 24, 1960.

9. LUCKY CATS

Page

201 *"just about burned to death":* "The Love of the Mother," *(Portland) Oregon
Daily Journal,* March 6, 1917.

202 *Four of the lucky kittens:* "Orphan Kittens Adopted," *New York Times,* January 20, 1917.

202 *"an ideal hero," "most popular idol":* "Two Millions Pay Tribute to Dewey,"
New York Times, October 1, 1899.

203 *The city accepted the offer:* Christopher Gray, "Streetscapes: Monumental
Parallels—The Arch and the Bandshell," *New York Times,* May 10, 1992.

204 *the stray feline took refuge:* "Born in Dewey Arch," *New York Herald,*
December 11, 1899.

204 *gave birth to seven kittens:* "Many Bogus Dewey Arch Kittens Sold," *Buffalo
Review,* December 20, 1899.

204 *"the happiest cat":* "The Dewey Arch Cat," *Brooklyn Daily Eagle,* December
24, 1899.

205 *"Are these really the kittens":* "Many Bogus Dewey Arch Kittens Sold."

205 *many gaping holes:* "Lodgers in the Dewey Arch," *New York Times,* July 15,
1900.

205 *"variable eyesore":* "The Dewey Arch," *New York Evening Post,* August 27,
1900.

205 *Church announced:* "Dewey Arch Soon to Go," *New York Times,* November 14, 1900.

206 *"a colossal pepper box"*: "South Wants Dewey Arch," *New York Times*, November 25, 1900.

206 *the exposition closed:* Gray, "Streetscapes: Monumental Parallels."

206 *1,021 of the 1,358 passengers:* Valerie Wingfield, "The General Slocum Disaster of June 15, 1904," *New York Public Library Blog*, June 13, 2011, www.nypl.org/blog/2011/06/13/great-slocum-disaster-june-15-1904.

206 *Many of the dead:* "New Names on the List of the Dead," *New York Times*, June 18, 1904.

207 *originally part:* New York City Landmarks Preservation Commission, *East Village / Lower East Side Historic Designation Report*, October 9, 2012, 9, www.nyc.gov/html/lpc/downloads/pdf/reports/2491.pdf.

207 *"and a good bearing orchard"*: I. N. Phelps Stokes, *The Iconography of Manhattan Island, 1498–1909* (New York: Robert H. Dodd, 1915), 122.

207 *the farm was divided:* Hopper Striker Mott, "The Road to the Bouwerij," *Americana*, vol. 8 (New York: National Americana Society, 1913), 589.

207 *220 lots.* Ibid., 591–592.

208 *one of the city's most prestigious:* New York City Landmarks Preservation Commission, *East Village / Lower East Side Historic Designation Report*, 6.

208 *the dumbbell shape:* Alan S. Oser, "Making Tenements Modern," *New York Times*, April 4, 1999.

208 *several inches near the ground:* "Two Years in Hole, Cat Freed To-Day," *New York Evening Telegram*, July 22, 1904.

209 *"Every time I looked down"*: Ibid.

210 *a former cowboy:* "Tabby's Two Years in a Three-Inch Prison," *New York Times*, July 23, 1904.

210 *"rather would have parted"*: "A Minstrel Tunes His Lyre," *New York Sun*, July 25, 1908.

211 *"there lies our Gittel"*: Ibid.

211 *eighteen hundred families:* "Levitt Attacks Evictions by City," *New York Times*, August 3, 1961.

212 *"To the Coroner"*: "Legacy of Two Kittens Accepted by Roosevelt," *New York Times*, December 22, 1906.

212 *the daughter of a rancher:* "Roosevelt Obeys Wishes of the Woman Who Loved Him to the Last," *Berea (KY) Citizen*, December 27, 1906.

213 *sent the boy a shotgun:* "Legacy of Two Kittens."

213 *main interest in life:* "Roosevelt Won't Take Legacy of Woman's Suicide," *New York Evening World*, December 22, 1906; "Roosevelt Had Her Buried," *New York Sun*, December 22, 1906; "Woman Trying Suicide, Leaves Roosevelt All," *New York Times*, December 10, 1906.

213 *"dear little kitten"*: "Appeals to Court to Save Pet Angora," *New York World*, January 3, 1906.

213 *"good angel"*: "President's Tooth in Ring," *Boston Globe*, September 7, 1907.

213 *the idea to ingest:* "Woman Not Driven to Death," *New York Press*, December 23, 1898.

214 *"woman in blue"*: "Woman Trying Suicide."

216 *an eighteen-carat gold ring:* "Roosevelt Tooth for Sale?," *New York Times*, September 7, 1907.

216 *constructed in 1848:* Christopher Gray, "Streetscapes: Where Theodore Roosevelt Was Born (Sort Of)," *New York Times,* December 18, 2005.

216 *a large fenced-in yard:* David McCullough, *Mornings on Horseback* (New York: Simon and Schuster, 1982), 20.

216 *The four-story-with-basement brownstone mansion:* William Smith Pelletreau, *Early New York Houses: With Historical and Genealogical Notes* (New York: Francis P. Harper, 1900), 68.

216 *"The extraordinary spectacle":* "An Eccentric Man Gone: Death of Peter Goelet," *New York Times,* November 22, 1879.

217 *then valued at $850,000:* "Two Landmarks Doomed," *New York Times,* April 2, 1897.

217 *started accidentally:* "Walls May Fall on Skyscrapers," *Washington Herald,* January 11, 1912; "Fail to Reach Bodies and Billion Dollar Fortune, Equitable Ruins Menace Offices and Halt Business," *New York Herald,* January 11, 1912; "The Equitable Building Fire," *Quarterly of the National Fire Protection Association* 5, no. 1 (July 1911): 413.

217 *a large shaft:* "Equitable Building Fire," 413.

218 *considered the first skyscraper:* New York City Landmarks Preservation Commission, *Equitable Building,* June 25, 1996, 2, http://s-media.nyc.gov/agencies/lpc/lp/1935.pdf.

218 *the architectural treatment:* Moses King, "The Equitable Life-Assurance Society," in *King's Handbook of New York City* (Boston: author, 1892), 622–624.

219 *plans were filed:* "909-Foot Skyscraper to Tower above All," *New York Times,* June 30, 1908.

219 *Committee of Congestion of Population in New York:* "Skyscrapers Bad for City," *New York Times,* July 3, 1908.

219 *the first fire alarm:* Details of the Equitable Building fire are based on numerous sources: New York Board of Fire Underwriters, *Report on the Fire in the Equitable Building* (New York: author, February 29, 1912); "4 Dead, 2 Missing, as Fire Destroys Equitable Building: Battalion Chief Walsh Lost in Ruins, $924,000,000 Buried," *New York Herald,* January 10, 1912; "Big Blaze Started in Rubbish Heap," *New York Times,* January 10, 1912; "Menace in the Ruins of the Equitable," *New York Times,* January 11, 1912.

219 *first time in the history:* "100 Years Ago—The Equitable Building Fire," *MCNY Blog,* Museum of the City of New York, accessed October 14, 2018, https://blog.mcny.org/2012/01/10/100-years-ago-the-equitable-building-fire-2/.

222 *"sad wreck of a cat":* "Ups and Downs of a Cat," *New York Evening Post,* March 9, 1912.

222 *"shed real tears":* "The Story of Faithful and Bacillus," *Christian Advocate* 87 (January–June 1912): 787.

222 *The collar was inscribed:* Ibid.

223 *"I was certainly surprised":* "Guinea Pig Alive in Equitable Ruins," *New York Times,* January 26, 1912.

223 *gave his guinea pig to Henry W. Ward:* "Ups and Downs of a Cat."

223 *proposed turning the site:* "Want Equitable Site for Broadway Park," *New York Times,* November 28, 1912.

224 *du Pont and his associates:* Ibid.

224 *"the nearest to an absolutely fireproof building":* "Equitable Plans Approved," *New York Times,* June 17, 1913.

224 *"It was, in its time":* Christopher Gray, "1915 Equitable Building Becomes a 1996 Landmark," *New York Times,* September 8, 1996.

224 *Silverstein purchased the property:* Ibid.

224 *The following is a summary:* This section is based on the following news articles: Victor H. Lawn, "Equitable Building Where Once Was a Tulip Garden," *New York Evening World,* February 24, 1926; "Equitable Site Long a Place of Gardens," *New York Times,* November 29, 1912; "Early New York Resorts That Bore the Name Vauxhall," *New York Herald,* March 29, 1918.

224 *"Beyond the great pile":* Lawn, "Equitable Building."

225 *"From the little lane called Broadway":* "Acre on Broadway with a Romantic History," *New York Sun,* September 8, 1912.

225 *"a remarkable lot and large house":* "Early New York Resorts."

226 *hosted a dinner:* "Police Hero Dined," *New York Sun,* June 7, 1909.

227 *The cat was the mouser:* "Traffic at Halt as Feline Mother Treks with Brood," *New York Daily News,* July 29, 1925.

227 *"A guy just phoned":* John Faber, *Great News Photos and the Stories behind Them* (New York: Dover, 1978), 38.

228 *"His kindness to this cat":* "Kindness to Feline Mother Wins Reward," *New York Daily News,* October 30, 1925.

229 *a unit of forty-one officers:* D. T. Valentine, *Manual of the Corporation of the City of New York* (New York: Edmund Jones, 1864), 118.

229 *the city's first police unit:* Joseph A. Amato, *On Foot: A History of Walking* (New York: NYU Press, 2004), 244.

229 *this intervention was not enough:* "Freeing the Business Streets," *New York Times,* April 10, 1904.

229 *Piper traveled to London:* Royal Commission on London Traffic, *Appendices to the Report of the Royal Commission on London Traffic* (London: Wyman and Sons, 1906), 68.

229 *Chamber of Commerce adopted a resolution:* "Chamber of Commerce for Traffic Control," *New York Times,* April 8, 1904.

229 *a plan was put in place:* "Mounted Police Will Handle Busy Traffic," *New York Times,* July 30, 1904.

229 *the new Traffic Squad:* Police Department of the City of New York, *Report of the Police Department of the City of New York for the Year Ending December 31, 1905* (New York: Martin B. Brown, 1906), 43.

229 *Manhattan also installed:* Ibid., 48.

229 *Iron traffic signs:* Ibid.

229 *Simpson introduced a bill:* "Larger Traffic Squad Is Favored," *Greater New York: Bulletin of the Merchants' Association of New York,* March 23, 1914, 14.

229 *got some much-needed help:* "Beautiful Bronze Towers for Fifth Avenue Traffic," *New York Times,* November 5, 1922.

230 *the city was able to save:* Henry Petroski, *The Road Taken: The History and Future of America's Infrastructure* (New York: Bloomsbury, 2016), 78.

INDEX

Page references in italics refer to photos.

ABOUT THE AUTHOR

Peggy Gavan is a journalist, editor, and New Yorker who has a passion for cats and New York City history. She is the author of several nonfiction books for children and the creator of The Hatching Cat: True and Unusual Animal Tales of Old New York (www.hatching catnyc.com), a website that has been profiled in several publications, including *Newsweek* and the *New York Times*. She lives in the Hudson Valley with her husband and their two cats.